Anti-Cultic Theology in Christian Biblical Interpretation

Studies in Biblical Literature

Hemchand Gossai
General Editor

Vol. 97

PETER LANG
New York • Washington, D.C./Baltimore • Bern
Frankfurt am Main • Berlin • Brussels • Vienna • Oxford

Valerie A. Stein

Anti-Cultic Theology in Christian Biblical Interpretation

A Study of Isaiah 66:1–4 and Its Reception

PETER LANG

New York • Washington, D.C./Baltimore • Bern
Frankfurt am Main • Berlin • Brussels • Vienna • Oxford

Library of Congress Cataloging-in-Publication Data

Stein, Valerie A.
Anti-cultic theology in Christian biblical interpretation:
a study of Isaiah 66:1–4 and its reception / Valerie A. Stein.
p. cm. — (Studies in biblical literature; v. 97)
Includes bibliographical references and indexes.
1. Bible. O.T. Isaiah LXVI, 1–4—Criticism, interpretation, etc. I. Title.
BS1520.5.S74   224'106—dc22   2006026032
ISBN-13: 978-0-8204-8618-5
ISBN-10: 0-8204-8618-3
ISSN 1089-0645

Bibliographic information published by **Die Deutsche Bibliothek**.
Die Deutsche Bibliothek lists this publication in the "Deutsche
Nationalbibliografie"; detailed bibliographic data is available
on the Internet at http://dnb.ddb.de/.

The paper in this book meets the guidelines for permanence and durability
of the Committee on Production Guidelines for Book Longevity
of the Council of Library Resources.

In memory of my grandmother
Lieselotte Rothermel
1918-2002

and
for Tom

Contents

Editor's Preface

More than ever the horizons in biblical literature are being expanded beyond that which is immediately imagined; important new methodological, theological, and hermeneutical directions are being explored, often resulting in significant contributions to the world of biblical scholarship. It is an exciting time for the academy as engagement in biblical studies continues to be heightened.

This series seeks to make available to scholars and institutions, scholarship of a high order, and which will make a significant contribution to ongoing biblical discourse. This series includes established and innovative directions, covering general and particular areas in biblical study. For every volume considered for this series, we explore the question as to whether the study will push the horizons of biblical scholarship. The answer must be *yes* for the inclusion.

In this volume Valerie Stein examines the three significant groups that have historically shaped the interpretation of Isaiah 66:1–4. The inheritance of these interpretations without serious and sustained examination has often led to a misuse and misappropriation of the text as a basis for anti-cultic arguments and supersessionist theological claims. The author not only examines these interpretations, but contextualizes them and proposes a manner for future use of this text, coupled with implications. Both the Academy and the Church will find this study a basis for a new and important understanding of Isaiah 66:1–4 that lends itself to a more constructive appropriation.

The horizon has been expanded.

Hemchand Gossai
Series Editor

Acknowledgments

This book is a revision of my doctoral dissertation, submitted in 2004 to Harvard University. I am grateful to my thesis committee: Drs. Paul D. Hanson, Jon D. Levenson, and François Bovon. They were more than generous with their time, knowledge, and encouragement, and their guidance is greatly appreciated.

For making the revision and publication of the dissertation possible my gratitude goes to the Wabash Center for Teaching and Learning in Theology and Religion for the Wabash Center Summer Fellowship and to the University of Evansville for the Alumni Research and Scholarly Activity Fellowship.

I would like to thank two of my colleagues at the University of Evansville: Dr. Annette Parks aided me in the translation of some of the Latin material. Dr. Dianne Oliver gave of her time and expertise to provide technical assistance and was always available to offer comments, suggestions, and most importantly, friendship.

Two student workers at the University of Evansville, Kirsten Lewis and Traci Hoehn, cheerfully assisted in a variety of tedious tasks.

I have had the fortune of many exceptional teachers throughout the years. I am especially indebted to Dr. Carl Skrade, who first introduced me to critical analysis of the biblical text and of my own religious worldview when I was an undergraduate at Capital University. He continues to inspire me and to shape how I think about and engage the Bible and religion.

Above all I would like to acknowledge and thank my husband, Dr. Thomas Stratton. He gave up many of his precious days off from medical school to assist with various stages of this project. I am most grateful for his unwavering love, support, and encouragement.

Introduction

Although both Jews and Christians consider the Hebrew Bible to be sacred scripture, they often differ on the interpretation of this text. In fact, history provides all too many instances in which Christians have interpreted Hebrew Bible passages in such a way as to criticize or condemn Jewish religious practices and beliefs. The very book that could serve as common ground for the two religions thus has a tradition of interpretation in Christian theology that has instead served to poison relations between Jews and Christians. Specifically, many Christians have used the biblical text theologically to proclaim God's rejection of the Jerusalem temple and cult and thereby the rejection of the Jewish religion. The arguments tend to fall into one of two categories: (1) Proper interpretation of the Law is not literal but spiritual or allegorical, and thus Jews have gotten it wrong all along (i.e., God never wanted sacrifice). (2) The Law has been superseded by Christ and is thus null and void, and now the Church is the new Israel (theology of substitution). This anti-cultic Christian exegesis has continued even in some modern biblical scholarship albeit in different forms, such as a preference for Deuteronomy or the prophets over and against the Priestly material.

There has been much done in the decades since the Holocaust striving to purge anti-Judaism from Christian theology and self-understanding. Many mainline Christian groups have formally taken stances to try to heal the wounds of the past caused by Christian supersessionist theology. For example, the Roman Catholic declaration *Nostra Aetate*, passed at the Second Vatican council, affirms Christianity's roots in Judaism while also declaring that God *still* cherishes the Jews and continues in covenant with them *as Jews*. The document encourages dialogue and mutual understanding and respect. In the *Declaration of the Evangelical Lutheran Church in America to the Jewish Community* (1994) the E.L.C.A. repudiated the anti-Jewish writings of Martin Luther and repented for the history of Jewish hatred within the tradition. The statement calls on the community to work for the end to anti-Semitism in the E.L.C.A. and in society at large.[1] On the other hand, tensions increased between Jews and Christians when in 1979 Bailey Smith, head of the Southern Baptist Convention, declared "God doesn't hear the prayers of Jews." Controversy ensued again in 1999 when the International Missions Board of the SBC issued a prayer guide on the eve of Rosh Hashanah to urge Christians to pray for Jews to accept Jesus. The storm that erupted in 2004 over Mel Gibson's film *The Passion of the Christ* further demonstrated that despite strides that have been made in some areas, Jewish-Christian relations are often still tense.

In the scholarly community Franz Mussner's *Tractate on the Jews: The Significance of Judaism for Christian Faith* stands out as a theological and exegetical example of Christian attempts to build bridges between the two religious traditions. He offers a tractate *for* the Jews, stressing the continuity between Judaism and Christianity, to counter the *Adversus Judaeos* literature (tractates *against* the Jews) prominent in pre-modern Christianity. Mussner's work demonstrates that in order to move forward in Christian-Jewish relations we need to critically reexamine the past. One area that needs further such attention is the study of the Christian appropriation of specific Hebrew Bible texts, specifically with respect to texts and interpretations that have led to hostility towards Jews. This book strives to meet that need by examining how theological perspectives of the interpreters have shaped the interpretation of Isa 66:1–4. Many Christian interpreters have understood this passage as a prophetic indictment against temple and sacrifice and have used it correspondingly to condemn Judaism. Thus the Christian interpretive tradition of Isa 66:1–4 has contributed to the oftentimes problematic relationship between Jews and Christians. The prophetic oracle reads as follows:[2]

> 1 Thus says the Lord:
> Heaven is my throne and earth my footstool
> Where is the house you would build for me?
> Where is my resting place?
> 2 All these things my hand has made,
> And all these things came into being.
> Yet to this one I will look:
> to one who is humble and broken in spirit and trembles at
> my word.
> 3 One who slaughters an ox kills a man,
> One who sacrifices a lamb breaks a dog's neck,
> One who presents a grain offering (offers) swine's blood,
> One who offers a memorial offering of frankincense
> blesses an idol;
> These have chosen their own ways,
> and in their abominations have taken pleasure.
> 4 So I will choose to mock them
> and bring upon them what they fear;
> because when I called, no one answered,
> I spoke, but they did not listen;

> they did what I consider evil
> and they chose what displeases me.

In the following study I examine Isa 66:1–44 and its reception history. I propose that the anti-cultic use of this text is in fact fundamentally incongruous with its broader literary context. I demonstrate through a critical analysis of interpretations from the Patristic Era, the writings of Martin Luther, and the Modern Era that the anti-cultic interpretation of Isa 66:1–4 derives from factors external to the text and construes its message to reflect the interpreter's theological concerns. The structure of the book reflects the need to limit the amount of material covered, and therefore it can be described as selecting representative texts as a means of illustrating both the range of interpretive possibilities and discernible lines of development. The examination of these Christian interpretations of Isa 66:1–4 in light of their historical and theological contexts will reveal a use of the biblical text for polemical purposes and will expose the theological components of Christian anti-cultic biblical interpretation that exist even to the present day. It is my hope that the light shed on this particular text's role in Jewish-Christian relations will lead scholars and laity alike towards a critical self-awareness with respect to the interpretation of other texts.

In the first chapter, I present a translation and an historical interpretation of Isaiah 66:1–4 that provides a basis in the following chapters for exposing the theological factors that have led to understanding this text as fundamentally addressing the inadequacies of material worship. I propose that Isa 66:1–4 is not critiquing temples or sacrifice as illegitimate in themselves. Rather, the theological position represented in these verses is aligned with the temple cult and criticizes syncretic cultic practices and those whom the prophet identifies as apostates. Furthermore, I think Yahweh himself is laying claim to the rebuilding of the temple in 66:1. The contrast is not between material and spiritual worship but between God's nature and human nature, creator and creature, God's status and human status, God's choices and human choices. The problem is not cultic worship, and the text is certainly not anti-Jewish. The theological controversy is embedded in issues of reconstruction. The prophet is criticizing specific individuals within his community in early post-exilic Judah for what he believes to be their abhorrent worship. By accusing his opponents of assuming God's authority for themselves and choosing their own worship, thereby presumptuously claiming to know the mysteries of heaven and earth, the author grounds his polemic within a theological framework. Subsequent chapters will show it is the polemic fixed within the text that in part accounts for its condemnatory application within the Christian tradition.

In the second chapter, I demonstrate that theological controversies drive the function and interpretation of Isaiah 66:1–4 in the Patristic Era. Interpreters repeatedly employ the polemic in these verses against their own theological opponents and interpret the text accordingly as condemning the opposing view. In the context of Marcionite, Gnostic, and philosophical controversies Isa 66:1–4 regularly functions in defense of God's majesty due to his role as creator. In christological debates, the text is often interpreted to elucidate the relationship between the Creator and Christ. Anti-cultic or more general anti-Jewish interpretations emerge in situations in which the authors struggle with developing a Christian reading of Jewish scripture, as well as with the relationship between Jews and Christians overall.

In the third chapter, I show that Martin Luther's theology and 16th century theological struggles shape his interpretation of the Isaiah passage. Luther adapts traditional interpretations of Isa 66:1–4 to defend his central theological principle, justification by grace through faith. He connects his anti-cultic and anti-Jewish interpretations with his attack on the Roman Catholic Church, grounding these interpretations in his own theology of justification. For example, he charges that Roman Catholic worship and the Jerusalem temple cult commit a common sin of works righteousness that denies God's majesty.

The fourth chapter makes evident that Protestant anti-cultic theology is reflected in interpretations of Isa 66:1–4 in the Modern Era, including in historical-critical scholarship. This anti-cultic attitude is rooted in the theology of Martin Luther. Protestant scholars have dominated modern biblical scholarship until recently. This is especially true for German scholarship of the late 19th and early 20th centuries, which is still influential today. Aversion to ritual dominates this scholarship. Sometimes these attitudes take the form of a preference for prophetic and Deuteronomistic material (which is often identified closely with Christianity) over Priestly material (which is identified with Judaism). Other times they take shape as criticism of the temple cult as a Canaanite corruption of "pristine-Yahwism." Modern critical scholarship attempts to examine Isa 66:1–4 in its original historical context and understand what the prophet likely would have meant given his religious, social, and historical setting. The dominant view maintains that historical critical analysis reveals the author's rejection of the temple or a specific temple program in vv. 1–2, while in vv. 3–4 there is a rejection of cultic practices themselves which are de-legitimized on the basis of charges of misuse or apostasy. I believe this historical critical reading reflects the influence of Protestant theology, which is grounded in animosity towards material forms of worship.

In conclusion, I will discuss the implications of this study for biblical exegesis as well as for important issues in church and synagogue relations and in Christian identity.

A significant amount of scholarship exists on the subject of the relationship between Jews and Christians, including Christian hostility towards Judaism. My intention is to compliment the important, comprehensive works on this subject, such as those by Krister Stendahl, Rosemary Radford Ruether, and James Carroll. While they deal thematically in a broad manner, I ground the discussion in the interpretation of a specific biblical text. Such an approach is important for several reasons. First of all, it allows for a detailed study of how a passage can be and indeed has been manipulated for polemical purposes, thus shedding light on Christian anti-cultic theology overall. Examining Isa 66:1–4 in particular in this way is essential because these verses, when interpreted as anti-cultic, are considered the harshest of their kind in the Hebrew Bible. There are other prophetic passages critical, in one way or another, of the temple cult (cf. 1 Sam 15:22–23; Isa 1:10–17; Jer 7:1–5; Amos 5:2; Hos 6:6; Mic 6:6–8; Pss 40:6–8; 50:7–15; 51:16–17). However, only Isa 66:1–4 is generally thought to repudiate completely the temple cult. Furthermore, the meaning of these verses still presents a challenge to biblical scholars. Finally, this work presents significant theological implications. Since its earliest times, Christianity has struggled with how to understand the Hebrew Bible. I believe that the following study, informed throughout by theological reflection, can highlight this continuing problem and offer fresh possibilities for understanding Isa 66:1–4 in a way that is less divisive. While I offer my own translation and exegesis of the text, I will also move beyond questions of interpretation and weigh theological concerns in order to contribute to the ongoing effort to strengthen the foundation of a genuine relationship between Judaism and Christianity predicated on historical honesty and theological integrity.

A Note about Terms

When discussing the early period of Christianity a difficulty arises with respect to how to talk about Judaism and Christianity. In the modern era the terms denote two distinct religions with divergent—if sometimes intertwined — histories. However, since Christianity began as a Jewish sect, the earliest Christians were also Jews. The separation into two distinct religions was a gradual and complex process.[3] Thus while I have chosen to use the terms "Judaism" and "Christianity" as well as "Jews" and "Christians" when speaking about the first and second centuries of the common era, I recognize that the definitions of these terms are somewhat problematic in this period as these categories were still emerging and the lines between them are often blurred.

Notes

1. My concern for Jewish-Christian relations and thus the development of this project is undoubtedly influenced by my own Lutheran heritage.
2. Translations are my own unless otherwise noted. See the Appendix for Isa 66:1–4 according to the MT, LXX, and Vulgate. Also included are translations according to Luther, the KJB, NJB, NRSV, and JPS.
3. A comprehensive overview of the emergence of Christian distinctiveness can be found in James D.G. Dunn, *The Partings of the Ways* (2d ed.; London: SCM, 2006).

CHAPTER 1

Exposition and Exegesis of Isaiah 66:1–4

My purpose in this chapter is to identify a plausible range of interpretation for Isaiah 66:1–4 that is respectful to the ancient voice of the author. This explication of the text will allow me to proceed with the evaluation of the reception of Isa 66:1–4 in the Christian tradition by discerning deviation from this plausible range. I seek to offer a critical reading of the text that narrows the credible interpretation and sets the parameters for my critique. Specifically, I will demonstrate that the theological position represented in Isa 66:1–4 is one aligned with the Israelite cultus and that any anti-cultic reading derives from factors external to the text.

While there may be a range of plausible interpretive layers with regards to a given biblical text, any credible interpretation must respect and make sense within the literary context and socio-religious setting of the text. Since a complete reconstruction of the original setting of the Isaiah passage is beyond the scope of this project, I am adopting here the dominant contemporary views on Isaiah in critical scholarship as the framework for my analysis of Isa 66:1–4. While scholars have differed considerably with respect to the exact dating and division of the oracles as well as the identity of the community of origin, I think we can speak, if not of a consensus, at least of a widely held view with regards to the basic framework of the book of Isaiah. Most Hebrew Bible scholars since the time of Bernhard Duhm (*Das Buch Jesaia*, originally published in 1892) have accepted a division between Isaiah 1–39 and 40–66, assigning only the first 39 chapters to the 8th century prophet Isaiah ben Amoz. Many of these scholars would also agree that chapters 40–66 cannot be attributed to the same author, and thus they assigned chapters 40–55 to the so-called "Second Isaiah" written in anticipation of a return from exile, and chapters 56–66 to "Third Isaiah" (TI). The literary unity of TI is not generally accepted; TI is usually considered to be the work of several post-exilic prophets. Relevant exceptions to the dominant view as well as specific variations in reconstructions will be discussed in chapter four.

While 56–66 may not have originated as a literary unity, they do, I believe, present a unity of thought and provide an appropriate literary context within which to understand Isa 66:1–4. The late 6th century B.C.E. and competing plans for restoration provide the immediate historical context.

We begin with a discussion of textual and translation issues and an analysis of these verses in light of the Hebrew Bible and the rest of TI. The MT and my translation are as follows, beginning with vv. 1–2:

1 כֹּה אָמַר יְהוָה

הַשָּׁמַיִם כִּסְאִי וְהָאָרֶץ הֲדֹם רַגְלָי

אֵי־זֶה בַיִת אֲשֶׁר תִּבְנוּ־לִי

וְאֵי־זֶה מָקוֹם מְנוּחָתִי:

2 וְאֶת־כָּל־אֵלֶּה יָדִי עָשָׂתָה

וַיִּהְיוּ כָל־אֵלֶּה נְאֻם־יְהוָה

וְאֶל־זֶה אַבִּיט

אֶל־עָנִי וּנְכֵה־רוּחַ וְחָרֵד עַל־דְּבָרִי:

1 Thus says the Lord:
Heaven is my throne and earth my footstool
Where is the house you would build for me?
Where is my resting place?
2 All these things my hand has made,
And all these things came into being.
Yet to this one I will look:
to one who is humble and broken in spirit and trembles at my word.

The oracle opens with a message formula and proclaims God's greatness and majesty over all creation. It continues with two rhetorical questions. While exegetical issues abound, the only textual difficulty in v. 1 concerns מָקוֹם, for which we would expect a construct. However, the absence of a construct is easily resolved by reading מָקוֹם in apposition to מְנוּחָתִי or by understanding an implied אֲשֶׁר from the preceding parallel line.

Examining the image of God's throne and footstool elsewhere in the Hebrew Bible helps us understand what it may mean for TI to proclaim heaven itself as God's throne and the earth as God's footstool. In Psalms 11:4 and 103:19, God's throne is *in* heaven. In Jeremiah 3:17, Jerusalem is God's throne and the locus of God's presence, while according to Jeremiah 49:38, God will set his throne in Elam and assume power there. In Ezekiel 43:7, God proclaims the temple to be the place where he will dwell, calling it both his throne and the place of the soles of his feet. The prophets Micaiah, Isaiah ben Amoz, and Ezekiel all have visions of Yahweh's throne (1 Kgs 22:19–22, Isa 6:1–9, Ezek 1:4–28; 10:1–22; 43:1–12). Micaiah sees God sitting on the throne in the midst of a heavenly court. Isaiah's vision incorporates temple imagery, yet God transcends the temple with only the hem of his robe filling it. Ezekiel sees "something like a throne" and something "resembling a throne" (4:26; 10:1). The imagery is clearly temple-oriented, but God is portrayed as transcendent as Ezekiel sees only "the appearance of the likeness of the glory of the LORD" (4:28) and "the glory of the LORD" (10:4; 43:4, 5).

Only in Isa 66:1 is the earth God's footstool. However, the footstool is elsewhere associated with God's resting place. In 1 Chronicles 28:2, David's intended temple is to be a house of rest for the Ark of the Covenant, God's footstool. According to Psalm 99:1–9, God's footstool is the place of worship, namely Zion, the holy mountain. In Psalm 132:7–8, God's footstool is the place of worship and his dwelling place. It is also God's resting place. Solomon recites from this Psalm in the prayer dedicating the temple in 2 Chronicles 6:41f. In Lamentations 2:1, the footstool is the *people* Israel, the daughter Zion. The cloud of divine presence rests upon the tabernacle in Numbers 9:22. In Psalm 95:11, "my rest" is the land of promise. In Isaiah 60:13, the sanctuary is where God's feet rest.

In the Hebrew Bible, heaven and earth comprise God's creation; God's throne and footstool are most often linked with the temple; they are items associated with a king and the seat of his power, and they represent the sphere of God's influence. God's resting place and house are associated with God's presence. The declaration "Heaven is my throne and earth my footstool" asserts God's kingship over all creation at the same time it proclaims God's intimate relationship with it.

The questions that follow the initial proclamation in v. 1 do not challenge the connection between God's throne and footstool and the temple; rather they further assert God as creator and remind the people of Israel of their creature status. אֵי־זֶה has been translated as *where* or *what*. The LXX and Vulgate both interpret it as *what* (ποῖον / *quid*). Clearly the *where* indicates a question of locality while *what* indicates one of quality. However, I am not convinced the force of meaning changes depending on which interrogative is chosen. I read *where* as a more appropriate inquiry for a place, but the ambiguity accords well with the thrust of the verse: if God is Lord of all creation and also present within it, then there is no place where God's presence is not, and there is no thing that is independent of God. Especially since the rhetorical questions follow creation imagery, the force of them in 66:1 echoes the questions God puts to Job in Job 38–41. Here, too, we even find the double use of אֵי־זֶה, in this case asking about the location of the dwelling of light and the place of darkness (38:19). Clearly Job cannot answer the question. In both the Job and Isaiah passage the questions compel recognition of God's majesty and creative powers while humbling and silencing the listener: Look at my creative power; what can you do? There is nowhere you can build that is not already mine; there is nothing you can build that is not already mine. Considered in light of the rest of TI where Yahweh himself brings victory (59:16) and restoration (60:1–22), it is clear that 66:1 does not negate the temple but rather asserts Yahweh as the one who is restoring it.

Isaiah 66:1, as generally noted, resonates with 1 Kings 8:27, where Solomon answers his own rhetorical question:[1] "But will God indeed dwell on the earth? Even heaven and the highest heaven cannot contain you, much less this house that I have built!" Here even heaven proves to be insufficient to contain God and yet temple worship is affirmed. Solomon has built a temple and yet asks whether God will dwell on earth. Of course, God is not confined to the temple; the temple is completely inadequate before God's majesty if heaven itself is inadequate. Yet even so, the prayer calls heaven God's dwelling place (vv. 30, 39, 43, 49) and affirms the prominence of the temple in the human relationship with God, asking for God's response to those who call upon him there. The prayer requests God cast his eyes upon the temple, and in characteristic Deuteronomic tradition, considers the temple to be the place upon which God has caused his name to dwell (v. 29). The temple is emphasized as the place of prayer for the common person, but the prayer is framed with priestly imagery and duties. 1 Kings 8:12–13 asserts the temple as God's dwelling place, associating it with the cloud of darkness (cf. Exod 13:21; 19:16). Solomon completes the temple dedication by offering sacrifice (vv. 62ff.).

There are additional similarities between the 1 Kgs 8 passage and TI, especially with Isa 56:3–8. Twice in 56:7 the temple is called a house of prayer; this corresponds to the association of prayer with the temple in Solomon's dedication. Also, as Solomon asks God's attention on even the foreigner who comes to the temple (8:41–43), TI proclaims acceptance of foreigners into the cult.

Reading TI alongside 1 Kgs 8 illuminates a common challenge to the definition of the cultic community and suggests a similar theology of the temple. The fact that in 1 Kgs 8:29 Solomon asks that God's eyes be open to the temple while in Isaiah 66:2 God says he looks upon the one who is humble, contrite in spirit, and trembles at God's word does not alter this impression. We should not interpret this difference to mean TI is claiming that God does not look upon the temple any longer. Rather, as we will see below in our discussion of

66:2, TI is not contrasting temple worship with the faithful heart and spiritual worship but rather contrasting creator with creature and the righteous with the wicked. There is nothing in 66:1 that repudiates the temple. Asserting God's presence beyond the temple does not presuppose anti-temple theology. God's majesty and creative power is declared as opposed to humanity's. As becomes clearer in v. 2, TI puts human beings in their place as creatures and contrasts God's majesty with his concern for the lowly.

In 66:2 there are two text-critical issues. The MT reads וַיִּהְיוּ כָל־אֵלֶּה: "and all these things came to be." The LXX has ἔστιν ἐμὰ πάντα ταῦτα: "and all these things are mine." Some translations assume haplography in the Hebrew and read accordingly in agreement with the LXX (וַיְהִי לִי).[2] However, we can read the MT without emendation, as I have chosen to do. Furthermore, other versions do not suggest haplography. The Vulgate has *facta sunt universa ista.* Especially given the creation language in Isa 65–66, יָדִי עָשָׂתָה וַיִּהְיוּ כָל־אֵלֶּה calls to mind the refrain of Genesis 1:1–2:4a (וַיְהִי־כֵן): in Genesis 1:7, God made (עָשָׂה) the dome (called שָׁמַיִם in the subsequent verse) and it was so (כֵּן וַיְהִי).

The second textual issue involves וּנְכֵה. This construct form only occurs here and in 2 Samuel 4:4 and 9:3. Other Hebrew manuscripts read וּנְכָא, and 1QIsa reads וּנְכָאִי. Isa 57:15 (see below) reads דַּכָּא "contrite". The LXX has ἡσύχιον "meek" and the Vulgate has *contritum* "contrite". I read נֵכֵה; however, I think either reading is possible without great variance in meaning.

The disjunctive וְאֶל־זֶה contrasts God's majesty with humanity's lowly status, while affirming God's presence with those who confess God's almighty status. Isa 66:1–2 clearly echoes Isa 57:15, where the one who dwells in the high and holy place also dwells with the contrite (דַּכָּא) and humble in spirit:

כִּי כֹה אָמַר רָם וְנִשָּׂא שֹׁכֵן עַד וְקָדוֹשׁ שְׁמוֹ

מָרוֹם וְקָדוֹשׁ אֶשְׁכּוֹן וְאֶת־דַּכָּא וּשְׁפַל־רוּחַ

לְהַחֲיוֹת רוּחַ שְׁפָלִים וּלְהַחֲיוֹת לֵב נִדְכָּאִים:

For thus says the high and lofty one who dwells forever and whose name is holy: In the high and holy place I dwell *but also* with the contrite and humble in spirit to revive the spirit of the humble and to revive the heart of the contrite.

Here too we have a message formula, contrasting God's majestic place with his dwelling with the lowly ones who are faithful. This TI passage reinforces the notion that the contrast in 66:2 is not between the human-made temples and the humble, as if to say God dwells in the human heart *instead* of in the temple, as some early and modern interpreters read. The contrast is between creator and creature, between God's majesty and God's willingness to humble himself for Israel's benefit: God the transcendent dwells among his people.

It is with this understanding of vv. 1–2 in mind that we turn to vv. 3–4:

3 שׁוֹחֵט הַשּׁוֹר מַכֵּה־אִישׁ

זוֹבֵחַ הַשֶּׂה עֹרֵף כֶּלֶב

מַעֲלֵה מִנְחָה דַּם־חֲזִיר

מַזְכִּיר לְבֹנָה מְבָרֵךְ אָוֶן

גַּם־הֵמָּה בָּחֲרוּ בְּדַרְכֵיהֶם

וּבְשִׁקּוּצֵיהֶם נַפְשָׁם חָפֵצָה׃

4 גַּם־אֲנִי אֶבְחַר בְּתַעֲלֻלֵיהֶם

וּמְגוּרֹתָם אָבִיא לָהֶם

יַעַן קָרָאתִי וְאֵין עוֹנֶה

דִּבַּרְתִּי וְלֹא שָׁמֵעוּ

וַיַּעֲשׂוּ הָרַע בְּעֵינַי

וּבַאֲשֶׁר לֹא־חָפַצְתִּי בָּחָרוּ׃

3 One who slaughters an ox kills a man,
One who sacrifices a lamb breaks a dog's neck,
One who presents a grain offering (offers) swine's blood,
One who offers a memorial offering of frankincense blesses an idol;
These have chosen their own ways,
and in their abominations have taken pleasure.
4 So I will choose to mock them
and bring upon them what they fear;
because when I called, no one answered,
I spoke, but they did not listen;
they did what I consider evil
and they chose what displeases me.

Verse 3 has presented significant challenges to translators and interpreters. Four acts the Torah deems legitimate are juxtaposed with four illegitimate acts. However, the relationship between each pair is ambiguous. Is a priest *also* committing injustice and participating in idolatry? Or is the one who partakes in the legitimate cultic act now considered to be *like* one who does something abominable, and is the verse thus condemning the cult? The LXX and the Vulgate read a comparative relationship between each pair (ὡς/*quasi*). The Vulgate thereby equates the illegitimate with the legitimate and condemns cultic practices. The LXX, however, introduces the verse with ὁ δὲ ἄνομος. Therefore, the text equates these practices only for the lawless one. 1QIsa reads כ only between the first two pairs. However, this suggests the same relationship for the remainder of the series and thus has the same effect as the Vulgate. Each is an interpretive reading, and we are not forced to adopt either one. J. A. Alexander effectively read the first participle as the subject and the second as the predicate. This reading was proposed more recently by Alexander Rofé and has been adopted by Brooks Schramm and others.[3] It is an acceptable reading for the MT, and I have adopted it here. Furthermore, not only does the resultant meaning not put this verse at odds with either the rest of TI or the Hebrew Bible, it makes the most sense in the context of TI.

The TI corpus speaks favorably of both temple and sacrifice elsewhere. Yahweh proclaims eunuchs will be given a name in the temple (56:5). The sacrifices of foreigners will be accepted (56:7; 60:7; 66:20). Yahweh himself will glorify the sanctuary (60:7). God promises his people will drink wine in his holy courts (62:9). The temple is presented as the locus of the voice of Yahweh (66:6). Clearly, an anti-cultic stance in 66:1–4 makes no sense in this context, even if TI did not originate as a literary unity.

Instead of condemnation of cultic worship, a review of TI reveals repeated criticism of idolatry, syncretism, immorality, rebellion, wickedness, injustice, and poor leadership: 57:3–13, 17; 56:10–12; 58:3–14; 59:2–8; 65:1–12. Accepted cultic rituals are critiqued only in the midst of injustice, such as fasting while oppressing workers (58:3). Overall the problem in TI is characterized as the unfaithful following their own way (56:11; 57:17; 65:2; 65:12) which is contrasted with God's ways (56:11; 57:17; 58:13; 64:5; 65:2). This same assessment is echoed in 66:3–4.

Isaiah 65:12 provides even more insight to 66:3–4, as it is nearly verbatim to v. 4:

וּמָנִיתִי אֶתְכֶם לַחֶרֶב וְכֻלְּכֶם לַטֶּבַח תִּכְרָעוּ

יַעַן קָרָאתִי וְלֹא עֲנִיתֶם דִּבַּרְתִּי וְלֹא שְׁמַעְתֶּם

וַתַּעֲשׂוּ הָרַע בְּעֵינַי וּבַאֲשֶׁר לֹא־חָפַצְתִּי בְּחַרְתֶּם

I will destine you to the sword, and all of you shall bow down to the slaughter; because, *when I called, you did not answer, when I spoke, you did not listen, but you did what was evil in my sight, and chose what I did not delight in.*

It is clear from the context that in 65:12 the unfaithful are criticized for syncretism: for sacrificing in gardens, for eating swine's flesh, for offering incense on the mountains, for following after pagan deities (see 65:2–7). It is likely that a similar critique is meant in 66:3–4. Jack Murad Sasson has identified a close textual parallel to 66:3 in the Hittite literature that lends support to the view that the illegitimate practices in this verse refer to specific pagan practices, a finding which supports reading this verse as also criticizing syncretism.[4] While the Hittite material dates to an earlier period and therefore does not corroborate the existence of these practices in the postexilic period or even in Judah, linking the illegitimate practices in v. 3 with actual cultic practices does lend credence to the view that v. 3 is condemning observed forms worship and not simply employing metaphor. TI does not introduce a new kind of transgression from Yahweh in 66:3–4 (namely, cultic worship) but condemns essentially the same abuses denounced repeatedly in chapters 56–66: idolatry, syncretism, injustice, and immorality, here manifested as killing a man, breaking a dog's neck, offering swine's blood, and blessing an idol.

Isaiah 66:3–4 is thus intricately related to vv. 1–2. Isaiah 66:1–4 condemns those who labor in vain to be independent from Yahweh and create the world on their own terms. The iniquities that have been barriers between human beings and God (59:2) are clearly not the legitimate practices of the sacrificial cult. The problem is theologically framed as assuming God's authority for oneself: choosing one's own worship and one's own interests and thereby presumptuously claiming to know the mysteries of heaven and earth.

These verses put the creature in his/her place. Humanity's role is not to create or to choose its own way. The declaration that heaven is his throne and the earth his footstool identifies Yahweh as creator and lord. "Where is the house you would build for me?" asks "Who are you?" or "Who do you think you are?" The answer, of course, is that we are not the one whose throne is heaven and footstool the earth. We are silenced before God's majesty as Job is silenced before the whirlwind, and so God answers for us: "My hand made…." Similarly, as our status is contrasted with God's, so are our choices. Sacrifice is not self-chosen, nor is the cult, but idolatry is. So is injustice, for God's throne has its foundation in justice (Ps 89:14). As in other passages in the Hebrew Bible that critique the cult (1 Sam 15:22–23; Isa 1:10–17; Jer 7:1–5; Amos 5:2; Hos 6:6; Mic 6:6–8; Pss 40:6–8; 50:7–15; 51:16–17), the problem is not ritual but the accompanying attitudes and behaviors of the participants and the community as a whole. In fact, far from criticizing the idea of the cultus, Yahweh lays claim to it in TI: "A voice from the temple; the voice of the LORD" (66:6). The temple is the locus of God's emanating presence.

When examined in its immediate and broader literary contexts, it is clear that Isaiah 66:1–4 is not fundamentally opposed to temple or cult but challenges those whom the prophet deems to be unfaithful individuals within the covenant community. This theological critique is not abstract; rather it is grounded within a specific historical controversy. Throughout the biblical text we glimpse conflicting views of community priorities and values in ancient Israel. Texts of the early post-exilic period, such as TI and Haggai, as well as socio-religious reconstructions of this period, such as those by Paul Hanson and Brooks Schramm, suggest controversy running through this period embedded in issues of community reconstruction. The specific views of Hanson and Schramm, among others, will be discussed in chapter four. What is important to note here is that neither Hanson nor Schramm would argue that TI would condemn the temple cult as *categorically* illegitimate. As such, in neither reconstruction is temple worship at stake, and thus in that sense each allows for my reading of Isa 66:1–4, one that explicitly denies anti-cultic theology in the text.

Cultic and spiritual worship are not at odds in 66:1–4, nor are prophet and priest. The program for restoration presented in Ezekiel 40–48 reveals a priestly party dedicated to the orthodox worship of Yahweh and averse to syncretism. We likely have a similar dispute in TI. It is reasonable to assume and in fact Isa 56–66 supports the notion that elements of Canaanite religions that plagued so many pre-exilic prophets had not simply disappeared after the return from exile. Ezra-Nehemiah's condemnation of inter-marriage with "people of the land" illustrates the post-exilic community continued to struggle with indigenous religious practices. A variety of pre-exilic traditions continued to play a role in the religious life of Israel,[5] and the practices traditionally criticized by the prophets are no exception. At odds again in the post-exilic period, as is the case throughout history and across religious traditions, is the proper way to respond to the divine. Here the conflict takes shape between the self-identified "true" Yahweh worshippers, namely those who advocate the traditional cult, and those who would, according to TI, worship Yahweh with both elements of the traditional cult and pagan practices and who behave in other ways the prophet deems unacceptable; for example, they are too exclusionary or economically oppressive. Third Isaiah grounds the accusation against the syncretic forms of worship and their practitioners in theological argument that allows TI to use harsh polemic to cast his opponents as God's opponents.

If I am correct and Isaiah 66:1–4 is not criticizing priestly theology, then what are the factors that produced different understandings of this text throughout the history of its reception, particularly interpretations that find here condemnation of the temple and cultic worship? I believe the root cause for the misunderstanding of these verses is controversy that is both embedded in the text and present in the communities receiving the text. Theological controversy, such as that reflected in TI, is the historical norm, not the exception. TI employed polemic to cast those who believed differently as apostates. In the text's reception the polemic overwhelmed the meaning of the text as interpreters saw their own controversies reflected on the biblical page. As we will see in the following chapters, prominent Christian exegetes in the Patristic Era employed this text for the purpose of polemic against their own adversaries. The controversies of their day shaped the function of the text, and, similarly, the theological struggles of the 16th century shaped Martin Luther's interpretation and application of it. Modern biblical scholarship, which is rooted in Protestant theology, has inherited Luther's anti-cultic theology, and this theology, together with the debates of historical-critical scholarship, has directly influenced the reception of Isa 66:1–4 in the Modern Era. Exposing the function of the text in theological and historical controversies throughout the history of its interpretation highlights the anti-cultic and anti-Jewish readings as impositions on the text.

Notes

1. Jon Levenson has argued an exilic date for 1 Kings 8. Cf. "From Temple to Synagogue" in *Traditions in Transformation* (ed. Baruch Halpern and Jon D. Levenson; Winona Lake, IN: Eisenbrauns, 1981), 143–166.

2. For example, see the NRSV, NJB, and NLT.

3. Joseph Addison Alexander, *The Later Prophecies of Isaiah* (New York: Wiley & Putnam, 1847), Alexander Rofé, "Isaiah 66:1–4: Judean sects in the Persian Period as Viewed by Trito-Isaiah," in *Biblical and Related Studies Presented to Samuel Iwry* (ed. A. Kort and S. Morschausen; Winona Lake: Eisenbrauns, 1985), and Brooks Schramm, *The Opponents of Third Isaiah* (Sheffield: Sheffield Academic Press, 1995). For a more detailed discussion of their interpretations and translations see chapter four.

4. See Jack Murad Sasson, "Isaiah LXVI 3–4a," *VT* 26 (1976): 199–207. His work is discussed further in chapter four.

5. For a discussion of the continuation of variant streams of pre-exilic tradition in the early post-exilic period, see Paul D. Hanson, "Israelite Religion in the Early Postexilic Period," in *Ancient Israelite Religion* (ed. by Patrick D. Miller, Paul D. Hanson and S. Dean McBride; Philadelphia: Fortress Press, 1987), 477–508. Although this article does not discuss continuation of Canaanite traditions, and in fact Hanson considers the charges of apostasy in Ezekiel 44 to be without historical basis, I believe that the bridge Hanson identifies between pre- and post-exilic theology allows for the possibility of the continuation of Canaanite traditions as well.

CHAPTER 2

Isaiah 66:1–4 in the New Testament and Patristic Era

The Book of Isaiah figured prominently as a text in early Christianity, being cited second only to the Book of Psalms by New Testament and patristic authors.[1] The words of the prophet provided the emerging religion with an abundance of christological imagery and a source of criticism of institutional religion that could be directed against Judaism. The frequency of occurrences in this same literature of Isa 66:1–4 indicates that these verses, especially verse 1, shared in the book's overall popularity. The function of these verses in Christian writings indicates that they helped meet the needs for christological imagery and cultic criticism as well.

Necessarily, an examination of how these four verses functioned in early Christianity is an examination of four individual verses rather than of a single unit.[2] While the Book of Isaiah as a whole was a rich source of biblical citations and allusions for Christians, individual verses and passages drew attention and provided specific exegetical motifs. Christian interpreters, as their Jewish counterparts, interpreted texts not only in isolation from their historical context, as modern interpreters might expect, but also in isolation from their immediate literary context. Instead, interpreters often clarified a verse in one book with passages from other books of the Bible. Thus a verse from the prophet Isaiah, such as 66:1, could conceivably be better understood in light of a text from the Pentateuch, such as the creation story in Genesis 1, than from the surrounding material in Isaiah, including verses 2–4, as we will see below.

James Kugel, referring here to ancient Jewish interpreters, explains this verse-centeredness:

> …it is generally true that the basic unit for the midrashist is the biblical verse, or the troublesome or suggestive word or phrase within it. That is, our midrashists did not as a general rule seek to explicate larger units—a whole pericope or chapter—at one blow, and even when they wished to comment on some larger theme, those comments took the form of narrow observations about a single stimulus in the text, a word or phrase.[3]

Table 1. Biblical texts often cited with Isaiah 66:1 in the Patristic Era

Text	Isa 40:12	Isa 64:1, 2	Jer 23:23–24	Acts 17:24	1 Tim 6:15–16
Barnabae 16	X				
Clement of Alexandria, *Protrepticus* 78,2	X	X	X		
—— *Stromata* 2,6,3			X		
—— *Stromata* 5,74,5				X	
—— *Stromata* 5,124,1	X	X	X		
Irenaeus, *Demonstratio* 45	X				
Tertullian, *Adv. Praxeam* 16,6				X	X
Novatian, *De Trinitate* 3,3	X				
Origen, *Eph. cat* 9, 400,71	X				
—— *Joannis Com.* 6,201			X		
—— *De Oratione* 23,3			X		
—— *De Principiis* 2,1,3			X		
Eusebius, *Demonstratio* 9,12,4			X		
—— *Comm. in Isaiam* 2,56		X			
—— *Interpretatio* 3,8			X		
—— *Preparatio* 3,10			X		
—— *Preparatio* 13,13	X	X	X		
Gregory of Nazianzus *Orat.* A 42,8			X		
—— *Orat.* B 2,74	X				
Gregory of Nyssa, *Contra Eunomium* 162	X				
Hilary Poiters, *Ps.* 126,6				X	
—— *De Trinitate* 1,6	X				
—— *De Trinitate* 4,8					X
Ambrose, *Ep.* 29,8				X	
Didymus, *?Trin.* A 2,1	X				
Augustine, Letter 120.14					X
—— Sermon 5.13			X		
—— *De Trinitate* 2.17					X
Numbers Rabbah XII,3			X		
John Cassian, *Institutes* 8,3	X				
Theodoret, *On Divine Prov.*	X		X		

The same holds true for early Christian interpretation. As Rowan Greer has pointed out, method was not a distinctive characteristic of Christian exegesis; rather it was the function of the exegesis that distinguished Christian use of the Bible from its Jewish counterpart. The particularly Christian function of the Bible centered on three areas: proving or explaining Christ, refuting Jewish cultic practices, and explaining Christian virtues.[4] As we will see, Isa 66:1–4 is used by Christian interpreters to do each of these three things.

This function of the Bible for Christians was not pre-determined or formally established. It arose out of particular needs of the Church in response to disputes over Jewish law, Marcionism, Gnosticism, and philosophical issues, as well as in response to a variety of other conflicts within the Christian community in attempts to refine Christian beliefs. Thus biblical interpretation in general, and the interpretation of Isa 66:1–4 in particular, shifted to meet these changing needs.

In this chapter we will study the interpretation of Isa 66:1–4 in the New Testament and Patristic Era (here defined as the first through eighth centuries) by examining representative texts to see both how these verses were interpreted (the range of interpretive possibility) and to understand why they were interpreted in the ways they were (the particular concerns that shaped the approach to these verses). This analysis will expose theological exegesis that reveals to us something about the writer and community out of which these interpretations emerged rather than about the biblical text itself. As we will see, this is no less true for the anti-Judaic polemic in connection with these verses.

Isaiah 66:1

New Testament authors draw on 66:1 twice: Luke cites it in Acts 7:49 and the author of Matthew alludes to it in Matt 5:34–35. *Biblia Patristica*, which is by no means an exhaustive index, lists 74 occurrences of the verse. While this is only about half as many as listed for Isa 7:14 and 53:7, which *Biblia Patristica* lists 149 and 156 times respectively, 66:1 was clearly a popular verse throughout the New Testament and Patristic Era. Scholars have proposed that it was used in Christian *testimonia*.[5] In addition to the verse's popularity, there are several other indications that there were early *testimonia* which included Isa 66:1. First of all, citations of the verse do not always agree with any known scriptural version. In fact, I have found no complete citation of Isaiah 66:1 that agrees in its entirety with the LXX or the Vulgate. Reference to the verse is usually in the form of a partial citation (most often 66:1a) or an allusion. Secondly, these variants sometimes occur in multiple authors that are not literarily dependent on one another.[6] Furthermore, Isa 66:1 often occurs alongside the same series of quotations in independent authors. For example, Acts 7, *Epistula Barnabae* and Athenagoras' *Legatio* read ἢ τις τόπος instead of the LXX's ἢ ποῖος τόπος. As Table 1 illustrates, Isa 66:1 appears multiple times alongside one or more of the following biblical texts: Isa 40:12; 64:1–2; Jer 23:23–24; Acts 17:24; 1 Tim 6:15–16. Finally, its early use in several texts can be characterized as anti-Jewish. The form critical analysis that suggests this verse's presence in a testimony source has not, however, addressed the function of the verse beyond its proposed application to an anti-Jewish *testimonia*.

A careful examination of Isa 66:1 in the writings of the early Church will show that the function and interpretation of the verse varies as the Church encounters different theological controversies that drive biblical interpretation overall. This varied use of 66:1 accords with Barnabas Lindars' argument that biblical testimony quotations often underwent shifts in application in response to Christian growth and development.[7] If texts were no longer needed for the original purpose for which they had been selected because the argument had been won, they were adapted for new use. While anti-temple use of 66:1 does occur, such use is not dominant. The verse generally takes on this role for some authors who are struggling with the question of the relationship between Judaism and Christianity: how do Christians justify not adhering to the cultic ritual prescribed by the Scripture they have claimed as their own. Overwhelmingly, however, the verse is used not in arguments with Jews but in Marcionite, Gnostic, and Trinitarian/christological debates. In these contexts Isa 66:1 functions primarily to demonstrate and defend God's role as creator and God's corresponding majesty, and thereby to prove him to be the Father of Jesus or to otherwise clarify the relationship between the Creator and Christ. Whether the verse functions as an anti-cultic prooftext, as a prooftext in defense of God's greatness, or as a christological prooftext, there are theological agendas shaping the interpretation.

Anti-Cultic Use of Isaiah 66:1

Among those texts in early Christianity that can be said to use Isaiah 66:1 to criticize cultic practices or to speak against temples, there are some, such as Acts 7, *Epistula Barnabae*, and Justin's *Dialogus cum Tryphone*, that specifically take issue with Jewish cultic practices. These generally are products of Jewish-Christian debate in which the young sect is struggling to articulate its self-identity. The other anti-cultic interpretations of Isa 66:1, found in such writings as those of Clement of Alexandria and Novatian, do not condemn Jewish practices or attack the Jewish temple and are not grounded in the Jewish-Christian debate.

Clement's *Stromata*, for example, arises out of his debate with pagans. Thus in New Testament and patristic exegesis we find anti-cultic use of Isa 66:1 that is explicitly anti-Jewish as well as anti-cultic use of Isa 66:1 that is more or less neutral with regard to Judaism. We will examine several major works of the former category in detail and then compare these to texts in the latter category.

Luke quotes Isaiah 66:1–2a as part of Stephen's speech in Acts 7:2–53. The text is very close to the LXX,[8] although there are a few minor variations. First, Luke omits οὕτως from the beginning of verse 1. Second, he shifts λέγει κύριος to the middle of this verse. These are both virtually universal variants. In addition, in place of ἢ ποῖος τόπος he writes ἢ τίς τόπος, thus reading "what is the place?" for "what kind of place?"[9] He also makes a change in his use of v. 2a. Instead of beginning the verse with πάντα γὰρ ταῦτα, and thus emphasizing the direct object, "all these things," he begins with οὐχὶ ἡ χείρ, thereby inverting the direct object and subject and changing what is a statement in the LXX into a rhetorical question. This inversion intensifies the contrast between what humans make and what God creates: "What is the place *you* would build for me? Has not my hand made all these things?"

The meaning of the Isaiah passage in this context, as well as the meaning of the speech as a whole, is debated. In fact, the debate over Acts 7 in New Testament scholarship mirrors, in part, the debate over Isaiah 66:1–4 among Hebrew Bible scholars: there is disagreement as to whether the passage implies the rejection of the Jerusalem temple or the perhaps more benign reinterpretation of the temple and God's relationship to it. An examination of the speech as a whole, as well as the larger literary context of Luke-Acts, yields support for both views. The issue is compounded by the possibility that Luke is making use of a Hellenistic Jewish source for the speech that may reflect views not entirely shared by Luke himself.[10]

The speech is essentially a theological review of Israel's history reportedly given by Stephen in answer to the accusation that he spoke against "this holy place and the law." (Acts 6:13) The speech recounts the promise to Abraham, the sale of Joseph and the resulting enslavement of the Israelites in Egypt, deliverance by Moses and the giving of the law, the golden calf incident, the making of the tent of testimony under Moses, the tent's subsequent transport into the Promised Land under Joshua, David's desire to house the ark in Jerusalem, and finally Solomon's construction of the temple:

> [Our ancestors had the tent of testimony] until the time of David, who found favor before God and asked that he might find a dwelling (σκήνωμα) for the house of Jacob.[11] But (δὲ) Solomon built a house (οἶκος) for it. Yet the Most High does not inhabit (κατοικέω) places made with hands (χειροποίητος); as the prophet says, 'Heaven is my throne, and the earth my footstool. What kind of house will you build

for me, says the Lord, or what is the place of my rest? Did not my hand make all these things?' (7:45b–49)

Stephen closes his speech with an accusation of his own: "You are the ones that received the law as dispositions of angels, and you have not kept it." (7:53) He has not given a direct answer to the charges made against him, and many scholars question how Luke uses the speech and if it actually answers the charges. The key to the speech's meaning, though, is clearly tied to the temple; the Isaiah passage is a prooftext for the climax of the speech in v. 48. What is less clear is the point being made about the temple. Is Stephen defending himself by implying that the building of the temple was itself blasphemy in that it went against the law that instead called for the tent (7:44)? Or is he claiming that his accusers misunderstand the temple by thinking that God dwells in it? In other words, is he rejecting the temple itself as idolatrous in its very conception or is he rejecting only the *attitude* toward the temple held by his adversaries?[12] We will examine both possibilities to attempt to ascertain how Isa 66:1 is functioning here.

Many scholars have held that Stephen's speech is nothing less than a denunciation of the temple and that Isaiah 66:1–2a is used as a scriptural proof for this attack.[13] While a few scholars argue that Stephen presents the temple as the last, and in fact a culmination, of a series of Israelite apostasies,[14] most claim that the tent of testimony was an appropriate form of worship, whereas the temple is an apostasy.[15] This latter view arises due to what is seen as a contrast between the temple and tent in Stephen's descriptions. The temple is of human origin (7:47), as opposed to the tent which was divinely initiated (7:44). The use of δέ following the account of David and preceding that of Solomon (7:47) also implies contrast. Δέ can function as a strong adversative and indicate an opposition between what David wanted to do (build a σκήνωμα) and what Solomon did (build an οἶκος). Thus the tent of testimony was acceptable, since it was of divine origin, as was David's wish to build a σκήνωμα (necessarily understood here as tent),[16] since the text says that he found favor with God. The temple, however, a permanent οἶκος rather than a moveable and thus flexible tent, was unacceptable, as indicated by the corresponding citation of Isaiah, the statement that God does not inhabit (κατοικέω) a place made by hands, and the fact that Solomon is not said to have found favor with God.[17]

Central to the argument that Stephen is anti-temple is the notion that Stephen is associating the temple with idolatry. Immediately following the reference to the house built for God by Solomon (the temple), he says that the Most High does not dwell in houses "made with hands" (χειροποίητος). There are a number of reasons for seeing this as a reference to the temple as idolatrous.

First of all, in describing the golden calf incident Stephen's language is similar: "They *made* (ποιέω) a calf in those days and offered a sacrifice to the idol, and they celebrated over *the works of their own hands*" (τοῖς ἔργοις τῶν χειρῶν αὐτῶν) (7:41). His use of χειροποίητος in v. 48 recalls that event and connects the temple to Israel's idolatrous act in the desert.

Second, in the LXX χειροποίητος is frequently used in reference to what is considered idol worship, translating a variety of Hebrew words. For example, the LXX reads χειροποίητος for Hebrew words for idol (גלל in Lev 26:30 and אליל, which also means *worthlessness*, in Lev 26:1). In addition, the LXX uses χειροποίητος to translate the Hebrew word for sanctuary in a situation when it is not a sanctuary belonging to Yahweh (מקדש in Isa 16:12 refers to a sanctuary in Moab). Furthermore, it occasionally uses this word to translate the Hebrew word for god/gods (אל, in Isa 46:6, is a god made of gold).

Finally, a comparison between Stephen's speech and Paul's speech to the Athenians in Acts 17 offers further indication that Luke intends Stephen's use of χειροποίητος in reference to the temple as an accusation of idolatry. Acts 17 clearly uses χειροποίητος in reference to idolatry: the speech is in response to seeing a city full of idols. In addition to its use of χειροποίητος, Acts 17 echoes Acts 7 in a reference to God as creator that recalls Stephen's use of Isa 66:1–2a:

> The God who made the world and all that is in it, he who is Lord of heaven and earth, does not inhabit (κατοικέω) temples made by hands (χειροποίητος) (17:24)

The parallels suggest a common Hellenistic criticism of temple worship as idolatrous.[18]

An examination of Acts 7:48–49 in the context of the rest of the speech, the book as a whole, and in light of the LXX, suggests that the speech in Acts 7 is equating the temple with idolatry. Following the condemnation of the temple with an attack on his audience as "uncircumcised in heart" (ἀπερίτμητοι καρδίαις) drives this point home. The uncircumcised are Gentiles, the vast majority of whom are idol worshipers.

In short, there is nothing redeeming about the temple in Stephen's speech, and there are several reasons to think that Stephen is condemning it. The temple is presented as further proof that the Jews have always resisted the Holy Spirit. Stephen is accused of speaking against "this holy place," and in response he tells them that "this holy place" is essentially equivalent with the golden calf. The implication is that now they are resisting God again by going against Jesus and his followers, putting their trust instead in what they made and what they chose, as they did in the desert with Moses.

As a detractor of the temple and the cult, Stephen would not stand alone within the Jewish tradition. Scripture itself preserves a diverse attitude toward the cult, including some harsh prophetic criticism (Amos 5:21–27; Hos 6:6; Mic 6:6–8; Isa 1:11–17; Jer 7:1–34). The Qumran community, an example from

Stephen's own time, did not participate in temple worship and instead developed their own rituals by which they, in effect, viewed the community itself as the temple (1QS).

Proponents of an alternate view of Stephen's speech argue that it is not undeniably a rejection of the temple. A number of scholars interpret the speech instead as a proclamation of God's transcendence over anything made by human hands. The temple criticism is therefore only a criticism of an unacceptable attitude towards the temple, namely, the notion that God dwells there.[19] This argument finds several problems with the anti-temple interpretation of Stephen's speech.

First of all, while there is a Jewish tradition of censuring the temple and the cult, this disapproval generally concerns some kind of problem in the way in which temple service is being performed and the attitude towards it; the problem is with abuses (a corrupt priesthood, the wrong calendar, absence of justice and repentance), not the institution itself. For example, the Qumran community would have undoubtedly participated in the Jerusalem cult if they had control of it; they do not fundamentally reject temple theology but rather temple leadership. There is nowhere else in the Jewish tradition up to this point a complete refutation of the temple. In this regard, then, Stephen *would* stand alone. However, it must be pointed out that there are subsequent views that do reject the temple (reflected in the Christian *Epistula Barnabae* and the Jewish *Sibylline Oracles* 4).[20] The Hellenistic Jewish source behind the speech may represent the origin of this view within the Jewish and Christian traditions.[21]

The argument that there is in Acts 7 opposition between David and Solomon, and hence between a σκήνωμα and an οἶκος is also questionable. While δέ can indicate contrast, it can also function as a copulative. Francis Weinert understands it in this way and reads 7:47 parenthetically: "though [it was] Solomon [who] built him [God] a house [=Temple]".[22] In this case, the temple would simply be a continuation of the service of what came before, no better or worse than what preceded it. Σκήνωμα (in this case understood as temple) and οἶκος are both hand-made, and the Isaiah passage is applicable to both. The point here is not that both are equally problematic (the view of Leslie Barnard), but rather that the attitude of the worshiper, not the type of building or structure, has been of primary importance at each stage of Israel's cult. God transcends both σκήνωμα and οἶκος, and the claim that God dwells in either is what signifies false worship.

Another challenge levied against the anti-temple theory is that it fails to adequately take into account Solomon's words at the dedication of the temple: "But will God indeed dwell on earth? Even heaven and the highest heaven cannot contain you; much less this house that I have built!" (1 Kgs 8:27) Solomon,

Trito-Isaiah, Paul, and Stephen all echo the theme of God as creator of heaven and earth and contrast the work of God as creator with the work of human beings. Solomon, the temple-builder, does not present the temple as the place where God himself dwells but as the place where God's *name* dwells: "that your eyes may ever be open night and day toward this house, the place of which you said, 'My name shall be there.'" (8:29) Given the context of Solomon's words, they certainly cannot be taken as temple criticism. Stephen may similarly be arguing for a particular interpretation of the temple, an interpretation of the temple presented by Solomon and one apparently not held by Stephen's adversaries. A rabbinic source uses Isa 66:1 in much this same way and also ties the verse together with Solomon's speech:

> So, too, when the Holy One, blessed be He, said to him, *Let them make me a sanctuary, that I may dwell among them* (Ex. XXV, 8) Moses thought: Who is in a position to make a sanctuary in which He can dwell? *Behold, the heaven of heavens cannot contain Thee,* etc. (I Kings VIII, 27) Furthermore, it says, Do not I fill heaven and earth? etc. (Jer. XXIII, 24), and it also says, *The heaven is My throne, and the earth is My footstool,* etc. (Isa. LXVI, 1). The Holy One, blessed be He, told him: 'I do not ask for a sanctuary in accordance with My capacity, but in accordance with theirs. For should I desire it, the whole world could not hold My glory, nor even a single one of my attendants. (*Numbers Rabbah* XII. 3)[23]

According to this interpretation, the temple is not indicative of God's nature but of humanity's. Midrashic literature appeared in written form relatively late (well after 200 C.E.), but it preserves an earlier oral tradition that could pre-date Luke and even Stephen.[24] Stephen's view, then (when understood as transcendence), is not unique within the Judaism of his day. The confrontation in the speech, as well as the need for explanation in the rabbinic material, indicates the view is not universal either.[25]

An examination of the speech within the larger context of Acts suggests the possibility the speech is not functioning as anti-cultic rhetoric for Luke. First of all, Luke's introduction to the speech presents it in the context of accusations that Stephen is speaking "against this holy place and the law." (6:13) Luke tells the reader, however, that these accusations are made by false witnesses. Furthermore, the Jerusalem temple is not criticized in the rest of Acts. Quite the contrary, Luke presents Jesus' followers as seemingly active participants in the temple (2:46, 3:1). Paul even claims that Jesus appeared to him while praying in the temple (9:17–18). This is in accordance with Luke's favorable presentation of the temple in his gospel (for example, Luke 2:25–38, 41–52).

The transcendence theory has several problems of its own, however. While 1 Kgs 8 and rabbinic sources may reflect transcendence, we can only read Stephen in this way if it makes sense within the context of Luke-Acts. While

Luke does occasionally present the temple in a positive light, Stephen's speech seems to initiate a shift away from the temple. Luke presents the temple community as largely rejecting the gospel message, and this rejection is in fact the impetus for the gospel to spread away from the Jerusalem cult and out into the Gentile world.

Perhaps the most significant problem with the transcendence theory is the difficulty in explaining Stephen's use of χειροποίητος and the resulting association of the temple with idolatry. E. Larsson argues that there is no reason to assume Luke intended his readers to connect Acts 7 with Paul's speech in Acts 17 because of the use of χειροποίητος in both. He sees χειροποίητος in Acts 7:48 as contrasting the work of human hands with the work of God's hand, as indicated with Isa 66:1, and simply emphasizing that God transcends what is made by humans.[26] His argument suffers, however, by severing the two texts from one another; the parallels between the two Acts passages are too strong to deny. D. Sylva also counters the notion that the use of χειροποίητος in 7:48 indicates a denunciation of the temple. He connects this verse with the accusation in 6:14 and the accusation against Jesus in Mark 14:58 (which also uses χεῖ ροποίητος). He claims Luke is correcting the mistaken belief that Christians proclaim Jesus will replace the temple built with hands with one that is not (ἀχειροποίητος). Stephen's message is instead meant to show that God transcends the temple.[27] Neither Larsson nor Sylva accounts for how the use of χειροποίητος connects the temple with the idolatry of the golden calf incident within the speech.

In the end, I am convinced that Isa 66:1 functions for Luke as a prooftext for condemnation of the Jerusalem cult. The implications of this polemical use of the Isaiah passage are complex. There are three layers to consider with regard to the theological ramifications of the use of Isa 66:1–2a in Acts 7. 1) Stephen (or the Hellenistic Jewish source likely behind the speech) and 2) Luke, whether or not having divergent views of the temple cult, represent separate stages in Christian development and therefore Isa 66:1 functions differently for each. 3) The present context of the speech in the New Testament is a third layer for consideration. There are most certainly different implications for cultic criticisms in each layer.

Stephen's speech in its original historical context of Hellenistic Judaism may well have been anti-temple, but it clearly cannot be classified as anti-Jewish. It is a polemical speech, but it is not anti-Jewish polemic; Stephen and the Hellenistic Jews, most likely influenced by anti-cultic views of Greek philosophy, were involved in an internal debate with other Jews. Their condemnation may have been harsher than earlier critics of the cult, including Amos and Third Isaiah, whose texts they use, but Stephen's speech is a Jewish speech and stands *within* the tradition of diversity found in Scripture.

However, we do not read Stephen's speech in its original context. Luke has adopted it and imparts it to us within his own framework of the story of the early Church. The larger literary context of Acts shapes the speech so that Isaiah 66:1–2a functions as a prooftext for the rejection of the Jewish cult. Luke presents Jews, except for those who now follow Christ, as having gotten it wrong all along: "you *always* resist the Holy Spirit" (7:51). Luke, a non-Jew, uses Scripture to castigate Jews who do not accept Jesus as Christ. This is no longer a clear case of internal conflict, but it can scarcely be considered anti-Jewish either. Luke is probably writing between 75 and 80 C.E. Jews have not and are not becoming followers of Jesus in large numbers, and Luke, most likely a God-fearer with close ties to Jewish Christians, is disappointed at what must seem to him a rejection of their heritage. Still, Christianity and Judaism had not yet completely gone their separate ways, nor had they reached the point of intense mutual hatred reflected in John's Gospel. Christianity is a fledgling religion, a sect not quite standing on its own. In this context, it is evident that Luke is not using Isaiah 66:1–2a in condemnation of Judaism.

The theological danger for this passage lies in its present context as part of the New Testament. As part of Christian Scripture, Stephen's criticism takes on a different force than it would in isolation, and even than it would have in Luke's own time when Christians were in the minority and still closely connected to Judaism. But taking the text out of a Jewish context does not automatically make it anti-Jewish. After all, if Christians share in the biblical tradition, then they also share in the failings therein, common human failings. Taken to heart they can be the impetus for an honest evaluation of how their faith is implemented. The danger comes, I think, when Christian readers identify with Stephen, "the first Christian martyr," as one of "us," while seeing the opponents, the Jewish leaders, as wholly "other."

Epistula Barnabae is another example of anti-cultic use of Isaiah 66:1. The citation of v. 1 in *Barn.* 16 differs from the LXX in only one word: τίς for ποῖος. We saw this same variation in Acts 7:49. *Barnabae* is the first text known to cite Isa 66:1 alongside Isa 40:12. Form criticism has been central in research on the *Epistula Barnabae*, with many scholars arguing that the author of the epistle made use of various material from midrashic traditions to Christian *testimonia*, thus there is a possibility that these texts had already been linked as a commentary on God's creative power prior to *Barnabae*.

Earlier in the epistle, Barnabas[28] condemns Jewish sacrifice, circumcision, food laws, and Sabbath observance. In chapter 16, he takes on the Jerusalem temple itself, condemning the cult and warning against hoping for its reconstruction. The polemical nature of this section is clear. Jews are called wretches and are compared to heathens and idol-worshipers. Their view is contrasted with God's by use of scriptural proofs designed to demonstrate that God's majesty, incorporating both heaven and earth, ridicules the idea of a building serving as God's temple.

> Moreover I will also tell you about the temple and how those wretches erred when, instead of putting their trust in their God who had made them, they put it in the building, as if it were the house of God [or: when they were the house of God]! In fact, they almost resembled the heathen in consecrating him by the temple. But learn how the Lord speaks in superseding it: Who has measured heaven with a span or the earth in a handful? [Isa. 40:12] Is it not I? says the Lord. Heaven is my throne and the earth my footstool. What kind of house will you build for me, or what is the place of my rest? You know that their hope is vain. (16:1–2)

Offering an alternative Christian view in 16:6–10, he insists that the only true temple is the spiritual temple, which he identifies as the heart of the believer ("In our little house—in us—there really dwells God," 10:8). Barnabas compares the heart of an unbeliever with a temple built by hands (χειροποίητος) and a nest of idolatry, and he thereby reinforces his claim of God's rejection of the Jewish temple:

> I find, therefore, that there is a temple. Learn how, then, will it be built up in the name of the Lord: before we believed in God, the habitation of our heart was corrupt and weak, like a temple really built by hand; in fact, it was a nest of idolatry and a haunt of demons, because it was opposed to God. (16:7)

The material temple, thus the Jerusalem temple, is not only worthless ("their hope is in vain") but is juxtaposed with idolatry. In chapters 4 and 14, the Jews have already been essentially called idolaters with references to the golden calf incident (an incident Stephen also referred to). Here, by associating unbelievers with the material temple, which of course the audience will associate with Jews given 16:1–5, Barnabas has effectively characterized Jews as idolaters and unbelievers at enmity with God.

Epistula Barnabae is one of the harshest pieces of *Adversus Judaeos* literature in early Christianity. In Paul's epistles, the apostle had argued that the old covenant and its commandments had been fulfilled in Christ. Implicit in this argument, shared by many early Christian writers, is the notion that there had in fact been a valid covenant with the Jews. In *Barnabae*, however, the author argues that the Jews never received the covenant, having turned to idols and thus already proved themselves unworthy of it while Moses was still on the mountain. Furthermore, he insists the Jews had completely misunderstood Scripture by literally implementing the cultic ritual described there, such as circumcision, dietary laws, and sacrifice. For example, in 9:4, Barnabas writes that God "…did not speak of a circumcision to be performed in the flesh; no, they went against the commandment, being deluded by a bad angel." He offers instead an esoteric and often christocentric interpretation of Scripture, frequently employing allegory or typology, and he juxtaposes this reinterpretation with an exhortation to his audience to choose the morally upright Way of Light over the Way of Darkness.

The unidentified author of this epistle was probably writing in Alexandria[29] around 117–119 C.E.[30] In the early reign of the emperor Hadrian, Jews had found a more lenient Roman policy than previously, as well as an emperor committed to peace. As orders to rebuild Jerusalem were issued, hopes of a reconstructed temple soared to the extent that rumors may have suggested the construction was already underway.[31] This hope, coupled with the relatively favorable religious and political conditions under the new emperor, created an enthusiasm among Jews that fed a missionary fervor. The resulting attraction to the Jewish faith threatened competition for converts and encouraged Judaizing tendencies among Christians.[32] Barnabas wrote to confront what he believed to be a Judaizing threat, struggling to clarify the authority of Jewish Scripture while condemning the Jewish practice based upon it with the warning to his fellow Christians not to "go astray as they did" (2:9). The result is an anti-Jewish polemic that pits "us" (the Church) against "them" (Jews) and appeals to a reinterpreted Scripture for proof: "How could those people grasp and understand these things? But we rightly understand and explain the commandments in the sense which the Lord intended" (10:12). It is within this framework that Isaiah 66:1 is used to condemn the Jewish temple cult.

Barnabas' view is undoubtedly harshly anti-cultic and anti-Jewish. The epistle's view of Judaism and Scriptural interpretation, however, was by and large rejected by Christianity. While the text enjoyed early popularity in the struggle for Christian self-definition over and against Judaism, in the face of Gnostic controversy and Christianity's attempt to embrace the Jewish Scripture as its own, Barnabas' interpretations proved to be of little use. Anti-Jewish exegesis, however, continued.

Justin Martyr cites Isaiah 66:1 in his *Apologia I* and his *Dialogus cum Tryphone*. The citations are virtually identical to one another, and in both cases he uses an abbreviated and inverted form of the verse which otherwise differs only slightly from the text of the LXX: ποῖον μοι οἶκον οἰκοδομήσετέ λέγει κύριος ὁ οὐρανός μοι θρόνος καὶ ἡ γῆ ὑποπόδιον τῶν ποδῶν μου (*Apologia I*, 37.7–9).[33] Justin's variation of the text has nothing in common with the variants in Acts and *Barnabae* and does not hint at literary dependence. However, his use of the text is similar to theirs.

In the *Apologia I*, Isa 66:1 demonstrates Justin's concept of prophetic revelation. Following a section in which Justin proclaims Christ as foretold by the prophets, he begins in chapter 36 to clarify the modes of this prophecy for his readers. He explains that the prophet is not speaking of his own accord, but rather the Word of God prompts a prophet to speak sometimes in the prophet's own voice but other times in the name of the Father, in the name of Christ, or in the name of the people. Justin demonstrates each of these cases with what he considers to be prooftexts for his claim.

He quotes Isa 66:1, along with Isa 1:3, 4; 1:11–15 and 58:6–7, to illustrate the prophecies uttered in the name of the Father. This function of these verses here is seemingly benign and there is not inherently an anti-cultic force to his point, nor does Justin provide exegesis to the text to suggest he is reading 66:1 anti-cultically. In fact, he offers no explanation of the text apart from the introduction as to the purpose of these prooftexts (examples of prophecy in the name of the Father). Nevertheless, the use of 66:1 here provokes anti-cultic and anti-Jewish sentiment because of the texts he cites alongside it both here and in the subsequent section. On the surface, it appears Justin is simply collecting verses in which God speaks in the first person, however, a closer examination of the verses reveals he is grouping together verses around the theme of prophetic indictment, which he is directing towards Jews: the first verse (Isa 1:3,4) sets the tone for how to understand the subsequent passages by accusing Israel of not understanding and being a sinful nation; God then criticizes Jewish sabbath days, fasts, feasts and sacrifices (Isa 1:11–15), which Justin contrasts with a call for social justice (*"but* loose every bond of iniquity"). In the next chapter, too, the first text in the series is reproachful: "I stretch my hands to a rebellious and contradicting people, who walk in a way that is not good." (Isa 65:2) Here Justin is listing prophecies he claims to be in the voice of Christ. He puts forth subsequent texts as describing Jesus' mistreatment at the hands of the Jews at his crucifixion (Isa 50:6; Pss 21:17–19; 3:5; 21:8).[34] In light of this overtly critical context, 66:1 reads as criticism of the temple and of the Jewish concept of God.[35]

In *Dialogus cum Tryphone*, Isa 66:1 functions straightforwardly as an anti-cultic text. Central to the *Dialogus* is the debate of the Mosaic Law. Trypho argues that if Christians indeed are God-fearers, then they cannot ignore God's commandments and expect to have a hope for salvation (*Dial.* 8, 10). Justin uses Scripture, the very locus of that Law, to counter Trypho's objections to Christian practice and belief, prefacing his discussion with the implication that Trypho, a Jew, does not know the meaning of Jewish Scriptures: "you have been instructed by teachers who are ignorant of the meaning of the Scriptures" (*Dial.* 9). Justin maintains that Torah observance is unnecessary for Christians for two reasons: First, the old Law has been abrogated by Christ, who is the new Law (*Dial.* 11).[36] Second, the Law was only for Jews and was never in fact necessary for salvation; God instituted the Law because of Israel's sinful nature:

> [A]ll these men [Adam, Enoch, Noah, Melchizedek, Abraham, David] though they kept no sabbaths, were pleasing to God. The same can be said of Abraham and his descendants down to the time of Moses, when your nation showed itself to be wicked and ungrateful to God by making a golden calf as an idol in the desert. Wherefore, God, accommodating his laws to that weak people, ordered you to offer sacrifices to his name in order to save you from idolatry.... Moreover, you were commanded to keep sabbaths by God so that you would be forced to remember him, as he himself said, "that you may know that I am God who redeemed you." (*Dial.* 19)

In *Dial.* 22, Justin continues his explanation through Scriptural proofs as to why Christians do not observe the Mosaic Law. Here, Justin reiterates the notion that sacrifice was instituted because of Israel's sinful propensity to idolatry, and he offers as textual evidence Amos 5:18–26; 6:1–8, Jer 7:21–22, and Ps 49:1–23.[37] Sacrifices are unacceptable and God has no need of them, he concludes; the temple was similarly unacceptable, as proven by Isa 66:1, since it served the same purpose as sacrifice:

> For indeed the temple, which is called the temple in Jerusalem, he [God] called his house or court, not as if he needed it, but because, by giving yourselves to him in that place, you might not worship idols. And [to prove] that this is so, Isaiah said: "What is this house you build for me? says the Lord. Heaven is my throne, and the earth is my footstool." (*Dial.* 22)

Isa 66:1 clearly serves here as a condemnation of the Jewish cult and of the Jewish people. According to Justin, the cultic institution in its very inception was built on Jewish idolatry.

Justin was writing in the middle of the second century. His *Apologia I* was written between 150 and 155 C.E. and *Dialogus* shortly thereafter. At this time, Christians were condemned by the state, by philosophers, and by Jews, and they were in the midst of internal Christian controversy, most notably with Marcionites.

Justin wrote his *Apologia* to pagans as a defense or explanation of the Christian belief in the hope of attracting converts. In addition to addressing criticisms from the state and philosophy, it also takes up the question of Christianity's relationship to Judaism. Because Justin claims a connection to Judaism in the acceptance of the authority of Scripture, Justin must not only explain why Christians do not follow the Mosaic Law, he must demonstrate this through Scripture itself. The *Dialogus* takes up this concern directly with Judaism in the form of a dialogue between Justin and his Jewish counterpart, Trypho.[38] Here Justin attempts both to explain Christianity against Jewish criticisms that Christians do not observe all the commandments and to demonstrate that Israel's hope is fulfilled in Christ.[39] In the background of both of these writings is the Marcion controversy. Since Marcion did not recognize the Jewish God who created the world as the Father of Christ, he argued that Jewish Scriptures hold no value for a disciple of Christ. Marcion agreed with the Jewish view that Christians had no claim to Scripture, and in fact he proposed a canon of his own. Justin is caught between defending the role and authority of Scriptures against Marcion's claims and justifying his rejection of the Mosaic Law against Jewish objections (or what potential Jewish converts might object to). These theological controversies are driving Justin's biblical interpretation and thus his interpretation of Isa 66:1.[40] Justin uses Scripture to argue that there is in fact only one God, the creator of all, and Christians, although they do not follow all of the commandments prescribed in Scripture, do in fact worship him. Scripture points to Christ and therein lies its authority and primary value.

Justin, like Barnabas, claims that Jews are ignorant of the true meaning of this Scripture: "But these Jews, though they read the books, fail to grasp their meaning" (*Apol.* 31; cf. also *Dial.* 9). Justin, however, does not think the cultic commandments were meant to be understood allegorically. He acknowledges that God did mean for the Jews to observe the Law, but he thinks it was ordered to curb the sinfulness of the Jews. Overall, the tone in Justin's writings is not as harsh as we find in *Barnabae.* In the *Dialogus,* Trypho is often addressed as friend, his arguments are acknowledged as reasonable, and in the end, the two agree to disagree. It is important to note, however, that this is not a true dialogue; Justin is presenting Trypho as a straw-man for his argument.

Ending the dialogue with a parting of ways is a fitting end in that going their separate ways is a historically accurate representation of Jewish-Christian relations. Perhaps Justin himself has already recognized this as inevitable and intended for the *Dialogus* to explain the parting of ways. At the time Justin is writing, the animosity is present on both sides, as each strives to forge its own identity as independent from the other. Justin's anti-cultic polemic stems from the attempt to define Christianity as something other than Judaism while still maintaining ties to the Jewish tradition and in fact claiming Jewish Scripture for Christians. In the process, Justin criticizes the Jewish interpretation he does not accept. Jews, according to Justin, are also condemning beliefs they do not share, marking belief in Christ as something wholly other by cursing his followers in the synagogue daily (*Dial.* 16, 96).[41]

In Justin's writings we glimpse a mutual struggle between these two religions for understanding and self-definition that is grounded in scriptural interpretation.

While Acts, *Barnabae*, and Justin employ an anti-cultic use of Isa 66:1 that is critical of Judaism, Clement of Alexandria's anti-cultic application is not. Clement refers to Isa 66:1 several times, only two of which can be classified as anti-cultic and neither of which are anti-Jewish.[42] In *Stromata* 5.11.74.5, Clement writes:

> But certainly, the Word, prohibiting the construction of temples and all sacrifices, intimates that the Almighty is not contained in anything, by which he says, "'What house will you build me?' says the Lord. 'Heaven is my throne,'" and so on. Similarly respecting sacrifices: "I do not desire the blood of bulls and the fat of lambs." [Ps 50:13] (*Str.* 5.11.74.5)

The location of λέγει κύριος in the middle of the verse is found both in Justin and in Acts.[43] Clement's citation shares with Justin's its inverted as well as its abbreviated form, although Clement's is shorter still.

Clement cites this verse in a section in which he argues that true knowledge of God arises from the mind alone and through withdrawal from the corporeal world or the objects of the senses: "Now the sacrifice which is acceptable to God is unswerving abstraction from the body and its passions. This is the really true piety." (5.11.1) His view echoes Plato's dualism of the corporeal and incorporeal worlds, and in fact Clement tries to demonstrate that this Greek philosophical view is not only harmonious with but also dependent on Scripture.[44] God is above and beyond both time and space. Scripture demonstrates this conception of God in its repudiation of temples and sacrifices. Clement cites Acts 17:24–25 as a companion text to Isa 66:1 and Ps 50:13. He considers Scripture to be in agreement with Greek philosophical criticism of temples and sacrifice.[45]

However, even with his criticism of material forms of worship, Clement does not use Isa 66:1 to criticize the *Jewish* material cult. In fact, he holds up Moses and the Jerusalem temple as models for the proper understanding of God. First of all, he indicates that the construction of only *one* temple illustrates the concept of the unity of God (74.3). Secondly, because Moses does not set up an image, his temple demonstrates that God is invisible and cannot be circumscribed (74.4). Finally, echoing the temple theology of 1 Kings 8, Clement understands this temple to have led the Jews to "the conception of God by the honor for his name in the temple" (74.4). Clement's view is thus complex, for while he dismisses the value of temples and sees Isa 66:1 as prohibiting them, he acknowledges that the Jerusalem temple embodies an acceptable and, in fact, proper notion of God.

Clement makes similar use of Isa 66:1 in *Stromata* 2.5.4–2.6.3. Here again Clement argues that knowledge of God does not come through the senses:

> But he who is far off has come near – an unutterable marvel! "I am a God who draws near," says the Lord. He is in essence remote ("for how is it that what is begotten has approached the unbegotten?"). But he is near in power which holds all things in its embrace. "If one does something in secret," he says, "will I not also see him? [Jer 23:23][46] For the power of God is always present, in contact with us, in inspection, in beneficence, in instruction. When Moses was persuaded that God is not known by human wisdom, he said, "Show me your glory;" and entered into the thick darkness where God's voice was, that is, into the inaccessible and invisible ideas concerning existence.[47] For God is not in darkness or in place, but above both space and time, in qualities of objects. Wherefore, neither is he at any time in a part, either as containing or as contained, either by limitation or by section. "For what house will you build to me?" says the Lord. No, he has not even built one for himself since he cannot be contained. And even though heaven is called his throne, not even there is he contained, but he rests delighted in the creation.

Central to this passage is Clement's view of God as beyond the grasp of human senses. While using 66:1 to convey this aspect of God's nature, Clement also admonishes the idea of a temple (house). The message is more subtle here than in *Stromata* 5.11, but it is clear nonetheless. There is a contrast between the incorporeal realm and the imperfect corporeal realm (specifically, a material cult).

In the *Stromateis*, Clement presents a Christian apology which argues for the antiquity of biblical (and thus Jewish) theology in relation to Greek philosophy. In this context, he uses Isa 66:1 to help put forth a biblical basis for an anti-cultic view found in contemporary Greek philosophy, but he does not condemn Jewish practice in the process. In fact, overall anti-Jewish polemic in Clement's writings is minimal.[48] This could in part be because he is defending Jewish Scripture and Christianity's claim to it in the face of Marcionites and Gnostics who would question its worth.[49] However, this controversy does not prohibit strong anti-Jewish polemic in other patristic authors. The Marcionite debate stands in the background of Justin's writings, for example. Furthermore, Tertullian wrote a treatise against Marcion (*Adversus Marcionem*), as well as a scathingly anti-Jewish one (*Adversus Judaeos*). J. Carleton Paget traces Clement's lack of vehement anti-Jewish polemic to a depleted Jewish population in Egypt after the Trajanic revolt.[50] The theological issues compelling Clement's biblical interpretations are not centered on direct debates with Jews or Judaizers, and thus anti-Jewish polemic is not necessary in his attempt at Christian self-definition (he is not defining Christianity against Judaism) and does not drive his interpretation of Isa 66:1 or his biblical interpretation overall.

The emergence of Latin as a dominant language for patristic writings did not seem to diminish the prominence of Isa 66:1. Church Fathers such as Ambrose of Milan, Hilary of Poiters, and Cyprian of Carthage all quote or allude to the verse. Novatian, the third century Roman presbyter whose work *De Trinitate* has been called "the first great Latin contribution to theology,"[51] cites

Isa 66:1 in its entirety: *Caelum mihi thronos est, terra autem scabellum pedum meorum; qualem mihi aedificabitis domum aut quis locus requiei meae.* (*De Trin.* 3.3) Novatian's use here of *qualem* (what kind) is unusual among Latin citations of this verse, although it reflects the LXX and can be understood to reflect the Hebrew as well. We usually find *quae* (what),[52] which reflects the Greek variation of τις for ποῖος in Acts, *Barnabae*, and others. The form of Isa 66:1 in Latin writings varies frequently with regard to vocabulary and word order, although these variations do not generally reflect or affect exegesis.[53] In this respect, the verse mirrors the overall lack of textual consistency in Latin translations prior to the Vulgate's ascendance as an authoritative version.[54]

Novatian uses this verse in support of his argument of God's infinite nature in contrast with idols:

> It is he who says through the prophet: "I am God, and there is none beside me." [Isa 45:21–23] He says by means of the same prophet: "I will not give my majesty to another," [Isa 48:11] so that he might exclude all heathens and heretics with their images, proving that he is not God who is made by the hand of an artificer; nor is he God whom heretical ingenuity has devised. For he is not God whose existence requires an artificer. Again, he says through the prophet: "Heaven is my throne, earth the footstool under my feet: what sort of home will you build for me, or what is the place of my rest?" — this to make clear that since the world cannot contain him, much less can a temple enclose him. (*De Trin.* 3.3)[55]

It is the pagan temples and their idols which Novatian dismisses here. His point is to promote God's majesty in contrast with the nature of idols,[56] thereby differentiating the Creator, the Father of Christ, from any handmade so-called god. The tabernacle and the Jerusalem temple are not condemned; in fact, in a later chapter, in which he again makes use of Isa 66:1, he explains them in relation to God's nature: All anthropomorphic representations of God—including "when the earth is considered the footstool of God" (*De Trin.* 6.1)—are for the benefit of human understanding and do not reflect limits of God's nature.[57] God allowed the tabernacle and the subsequent temple even though he cannot be contained in them because human beings' power of perception is finite. This view compares with that of *Numbers Rabbah*.[58] Novatian goes on, however, to quote a passage from the Gospel of John (4:21, 24) in which Jesus describes the temple as imperfect and temporary:

> God is not straitened, but rather the understanding in people's minds is straitened. Accordingly, Our Lord said in the Gospel: "The hour shall come, when neither on this mountain nor in Jerusalem will you worship the Father," and he gave the reason: "God is spirit, and therefore they who worship him must worship in spirit and in truth." (*De Trin.* 6.3–4)

He dismisses the temple as if it is passé, but this dismissal is not explicitly polemical. In fact, it is secondary to his discussion of God's nature, which it serves to illustrate. Novatian is primarily concerned with promoting the doctrine of the Trinity[59] against heretical Monarchianist (cf. *De Trin.* 24ff.), Marcionite, and Gnostic views. The brief reference to the commonly held notion that the destruction of the temple was associated with the coming of Christ serves to further his argument regarding the creator's immaterial and infinite nature. The christological controversy that is dominating Novatian's theology leaves him virtually uninterested in Jews and completely uninterested in cultic issues.

Isaiah 66:1 and the Nature of God

While Isa 66:1 did function as a prooftext for cultic critique in the Patristic Era, writers in the early Church came to understand Isa 66:1 primarily as a text that explicates God's nature as creator and lord of all. Theological controversies are factors behind this function of the verse, as they were in the texts we examined where Isa 66:1 functioned essentially anti-cultically. Patristic authors use Isa 66:1 to defend their various truth claims about God's character, particularly God's majesty and lordship, in the face of criticism from and debate with pagans, Gnostics and Marcionites, and in christological controversies concerning Christ's nature in relation to the Father's. A Jewish interpretive tradition of this verse (regarding God's nature) likely predates Christian use as such.

The earliest evidence of Isa 66:1 functioning as a text demonstrating God's lordship is found in the Gospel of Matthew and predates texts with an anti-cultic interpretation of the verse.[60] In Matthew 5:34–36, Jesus alludes to Isa 66:1a in his prohibition of oaths in the Sermon on the Mount. The Jewish Scripture allows for swearing by the divine name, so long as it is not done falsely (cf. Lev 19:12). The passage in Matthew implies an accepted practice of swearing by heaven or by earth, perhaps so as not to use the divine name in vain, in accordance with Exod 20:7, Deut 5:11; 23:23. As seen in the Antitheses of Matthew 5:21–48, some in the early Church understood Jesus' moral demands as exceeding requirements of both accepted Jewish practice and Scripture. With a reference to Isa 66:1, Matthew attempts to show that the substitution in oaths of heaven, earth, or Jerusalem for God is still an affront to God's majesty:

> But I say to you: Do not swear at all, either by heaven, for it is the throne of God, or by the earth, for it is his footstool, or by Jerusalem, for it is the city of the great King. And do not swear by your head, for you cannot make one hair white or black. (Matt 5:34–36)

This Christian application probably builds on an earlier Jewish interpretive tradition.[61] Matthew not only makes ample use of Jewish Scripture, especially in the

Sermon on the Mount where Jesus is presented as a second Moses, but he also incorporates Jewish exegesis into his Gospel. The use of Isa 66:1 in the form of an allusion and the addition of Jerusalem to a list that seems to be a catalogue of God's possessions suggest that the verse is already well-known and that Matthew is making use of a pre-existing interpretive tradition which demonstrates God as Lord of all in part by inventorying his possessions and thus what he controls. In fact, such an interpretation exists in rabbinic sources:

> Five possessions did the Holy One, blessed is he, take to Himself in his world; and these are they: the Law is one possession, and the heaven and earth are one possession, Abraham is one possession, Israel is one possession and the Temple is one possession…. Whence (do we learn of) heaven and earth? Because it is written, The heaven is my throne and the earth is my footstool; what manner of house will ye build unto me and what place shall be my rest? And it says, O Lord how manifold are thy works! In wisdom thou hast made them all: the earth is full of thy riches. [Ps 104:24] (m.Abot 6:5)

This text, while relatively late as a written source, may well record an oral history of interpretation that predates Jesus, and, together with Matthew's gospel, it suggests an early function of Isa 66:1 in Jewish tradition as a text that demonstrates God's lordship.

In a similar but distinct exegetical tradition, the Talmud uses Isa 66:1 to determine the order of creation and comment on Gen 1:1.[62] Isaiah's association of heaven and earth with standard palace furnishings (throne and footstool) leads to the application of the verse as an architectural explanation of Gen 1:1.

> The House of Shammai say, "Heaven was created first, the earth afterward." The House of Hillel say, "The earth was created first, and heaven afterward." They both adduce supporting reasons for their opinions. What is the reasoning of the House of Shammai? "In the beginning God created the heaven and the earth." [This is to be compared] to a king who made a throne; after he had made it, he made his footstool: "Heaven is my throne and earth my footstool." (yHag. 2:1)

In both of these traditions the same stimulus stands behind the use of this verse, namely the key words of heaven and earth. This latter reading of Isa 66:1 is not unrelated to the texts above proclaiming God's lordship, as that lordship is a function that God no doubt possesses due to his role as creator.

The fact that the interpretive tradition associating Isa 66:1 with Gen 1 was well established in Rabbinic Judaism is evident from their pairing in the Torah readings in the ancient Synagogue. According to the Triennial Palestine Cycle (TC), Isa 66:1 was one possible choice for the *haftara* (prophetic text) read with the first *seder* (Gen 1:1–2:3). Interestingly, the TC lists Isa 66:1–11 as *haftara* for both Exod 26:1–30 (instructions for the tabernacle) and Lev 17:1–18 (restrictions on sacrifice).[63]

The use of Isa 66:1 in the exegesis of Genesis found its way into the Christian tradition, as first evidenced in the writings of Origen. Origen was a biblical exegete who strove to demonstrate the value of Jewish Scripture for Christians. He was greatly influenced in this endeavor by Jewish interpretations, having even consulted Jewish exegetes during his time in Caesarea.[64] In his *Homiliae in Genesim*, Origen links Isa 66:1 with the creation account in Gen 1. He, too, comments on the order of creation, but Origen uses 66:1 to explicate Gen 1:6 rather than 1:1:

> And God said, 'Let there be a firmament in the midst of the water and let it divide water from water.' And it was so done. And God made the firmament." Although God had already previously made heaven, now he makes the firmament. For he made heaven first, about which he says, "heaven is my throne". But after he makes the firmament, that is the corporeal heaven. For every corporeal object is, without doubt, firm and solid; and it is this which "divides the water which is above heaven from the water which is below." (*Homiliae in Genesim* 1,1)[65]

Origen, like Clement, was an Alexandrian influenced by Plato. He applied Plato's view of a dualistic world comprised of a material and an immaterial realm to Scripture, where he often identified twofold meanings, the literal and the spiritual.[66] Here, Origen combines this exegetical tradition concerning the order of creation with an allegorical interpretation that identifies the throne with the incorporeal realm.

While Origen incorporates Jewish exegesis, he does not uncritically adopt all he encounters. Later in this same homily on Genesis, Origen criticizes Jewish literalist interpretation of Isa 66:1.[67] The interpretation he speaks of, however, has no similarity to the exegetical tradition he borrows when connecting the verse to Gen 1. He rebukes Jews and others for an interpretation that understands the anthropomorphic characteristics of God in 66:1 (sitting on a throne, feet reaching down to earth) as implying a physical nature of God. Although Origen and the anti-cultic interpretations of Isa 66:1 suggest some Jews may have envisioned God as such, there is no Jewish evidence of such an interpretation with regard to Isa 66:1. However, the Audians, a 4th century Christian sect, apparently used Isa 66:1 as a prooftext for their anthropomorphic view of God.[68]

Nicholas R.M. De Lange does not think Origen is responding to biblical references in a particular Jewish text but rather that he is simply using a standard Christian argument criticizing Jews for literal interpretation of the Bible.[69] Such criticisms are grounded in the Jewish-Christian debate over Torah observance: some Christians insisted followers of Jesus should observe the law of Moses if they claimed Scripture as authoritative, but others countered that Jews are mistaken in their continued literal interpretation of cultic precepts after Jesus.

The connection of Isa 66:1 with Gen 1 is also found in the Gnostic traditions, which often drew heavily upon Jewish themes, especially with regards to Gen 1–3. The Nag Hammadi text *De opificio mundi* weaves Isa 66:1a into a cosmogony which includes, in part, a reinterpretation and retelling of Gen 1–3. An allusion to Isa 66:1 is seamlessly incorporated into an account of the events narrated in Gen 1:6–10:

> When the ruler saw his magnitude—it was only himself that he saw: he saw nothing else, except for water and darkness—then he supposed that it was he alone who existed. His [...] was completed by verbal expression: it appeared as a spirit moving to and fro upon the waters. And when the spirit appeared, the ruler set apart the watery substance. And what was dry was divided into another place. And from matter he made for himself an abode, and he called it heaven. And from matter, the ruler made a footstool, and he called it earth. (*De opificio mundi* 100.29–101.9)[70]

In accordance with Gnostic beliefs,[71] we find different emanations of the deity in this text. The creator of heaven and earth and ruler of the natural world, Yaldabaoth, is himself created (by Pistis Sophia) and thus is not supreme, although he is ignorant of his engendered state. Gnostics generally associated this creator god (the demiurge) with the Jewish God. In spite of their dependence on the Jewish Bible for source material,[72] Christian Gnostics had an antagonistic relationship to it. They denied that the demiurge, whom they viewed as an evil being who tried to trap human beings in his natural realm, was also the Father of Jesus Christ; rather, in the dualistic world-view of Gnosticism, the two deities were in conflict. Marcion and his followers also denied the role of the Jewish God in salvation. There is, in fact, evidence that Isa 66:1 functioned in defense of both sides of this controversy. Gnostic Christians apparently used the verse to criticize the creator God of Jewish Scripture, while proto-orthodox Christians cited Isa 66:1 in response to criticism of the Jewish God.

For example, in Irenaeus' *Adversus haereses* (*Haer.*) we find Isa 66:1 working in both of these ways. First, Irenaeus quotes 66:1a alongside Matt 5:34 to argue, against Marcionites, that the God of the law and the prophets is not only the one Jesus calls Father but is in fact the *only* God. He thus challenges not only their dismissal of the Jewish God, but also their polytheistic beliefs:[73]

> He [the Son] says: "Swear not at all; neither by heaven, for it is God's throne; nor by the earth, for it is his footstool; neither by Jerusalem, for it is the city of the great king." For these words are evidently spoken with reference to the creator, as also Isaiah says: "Heaven is my throne, the earth is my footstool." And besides this Being there is no other God; otherwise he would not be termed by the Lord either "God" or "the great King;" for a Being who can be so described admits neither of any other being compared with nor set above him. For he who has any superior over him, and is under the power of another, this being can never be called either "God" or "the great King." (*Haer.* 2,5)[74]

Origen similarly cites Matthew's allusion to Isa 66:1 as proof God's relation to Christ.[75]

Giving evidence of Isa 66:1's role in the other side of the controversy as a prooftext for the Gnostic viewpoint, we find in Irenaeus refutation of an interpretation of Isa 66:1 that discredited the creator. Such use of Isa 66:1 by Gnostics is not surprising considering the evidence in *On the Origin of the World* that they associated this verse with creation and thus the creator they disdained. Gnostics understood the idea of having heaven as a throne and earth as footstool to imply the creator's limits of space and time rather than to prove his Lordship:

> Again, as to their [the Gnostics] malignantly asserting that if heaven is the throne of God and the earth his footstool and if it is declared that the heaven and earth shall pass away,[76] then when these pass away the God who sits above must also pass away, and therefore he cannot be the God who is overall; in the first place, they are ignorant what the expression means, that heaven is [his] throne and earth [his] footstool. For they do not know what God is, but they imagine he sits after the fashion of a human being, and is contained within bounds, but does not contain. (*Haer.* 3,1)

Tertullian also uses Isa 66:1 against the Marcionites to battle their criticisms of God. According to *Adv. Marc.* 2,25, Marcionites found fault with God because of his query as to Adam's whereabouts in Gen 3:9. Tertullian finds in Isa 66:1 a rebuttal:

> Moreover, seeing he grasps the whole world in his hand like a nest, seeing the heaven is his throne and the earth his footstool, do you suppose that some small corner of paradise had escaped his notice, or that wherever Adam was, even before God called him, he was not in full view while hiding, no less than while taking the forbidden fruit? (*Adv. Marc.* 2,25)[77]

With an allusion to 66:1, Tertullian denies that the incident is evidence of God's weakness and instead proclaims it "an indication of God's majesty and of God's instruction of humankind." (2,25) This association of Isa 66:1 with God's majesty and his limitlessness nature is also found in christological debates.

By the fourth century, Christianity had become an established religion, secure in its status in the empire.[78] As Christians rose to prominence, debate centered on attempts to establish fixed theological doctrine regarding the nature of Christ and his relationship to the Father. The theological scene was one in which opponents were now internal as the Church struggled with views eventually deemed heretical in light of the Doctrine of the Trinity. In the second and third centuries, arguments about Christ's relationship with the Father were in large part caught up in Gnostic and Marcionite disputes, but even here we see contributions to the later questions taken up at the Council of Nicea. Isa 66:1 played an important role in christological and theological controversies.[79]

In *Adversus Praxean*, Tertullian uses Isa 66:1 to challenge the Monarchianist views of Praxeas, whose theology he accuses of having "crucified the Father" (*Adv. Prax.* 1). Praxeas was a Modalist; he held that the Father, Son, and Holy Spirit were only temporary roles of one Godhead:

> Moreover, how comes it to pass, that the Almighty Invisible God, whom no man hath seen nor can see; He who dwelleth in light unapproachable {1 Tim. 6:16}; He who dwelleth not in [temples] made with hands {Acts 17:24}; from before whose sight the earth trembles, and the mountains melt like wax {Joel 2:10; Ps 97:5}; who holdeth the whole world in his hand like a nest {Isa. 10:14}; whose throne is heaven, and earth his footstool {Isa. 66:1}; in whom is every place, but himself is in no place; who is the utmost bound of the universe; —how happens it, I say, that he [who, though] the Most High, should yet have walked in paradise towards the [cool of the] evening, in quest of Adam; and should have shut up the ark after Noah had entered it; and at Abraham's tent should have refreshed himself under an oak…. unless all these events happened as an image, as a mirror, as an enigma [of the incarnation]. (*Adv. Prax.* 16)[80]

The majesty of God the Father, as evidenced by Isa 66:1 and companion texts affirming the same theological point, precludes the possibility of identifying the Father with any anthropomorphic representations. Tertullian asserts instead that the theophanies in Jewish Scripture were actually manifestations of the Son[81] which served to prepare humanity for the incarnation. He thereby defends Christ's independence as a separate person of the Trinity.

In *De Trinitate*, Hilary of Poiters uses Isa 66:1 in his own attempt to present the doctrine of the Trinity as biblically based,[82] and he refutes his opponents' use of the same verse to deny the divinity of the Son. For Hilary, the verse serves to illustrate God's majesty and omnipotence and to interpret in part Exod 3:14 (*ego sum qui sum*), which he understands to be God's own testimony about himself. Isa 66:1, together with 40:12, is, like Exod 3:14, a statement "suitable to human understanding" that is worthy of God's incomprehensible nature.[83] The image of heaven as his throne and earth as his footstool present these things as an extension of God, and yet according to Isa 40:12, God holds heaven in his palm and the earth in his hand as one who is external to them. Interpreted alongside 40:12, Isa 66:1 shows that God permeates all things while at the same time all is subject to him:

> Thus, He Himself with his whole being contains all things that are within Him and outside of Him, nor is He, the infinite One, separated from all things nor are all things not present within him who is infinite. (*De Trin.* 1.6)[84]

It is crucial to note, however, that for Hilary God's infinite nature does not prevent the divinity of the Son or suggest in any way the Son's inferiority. Hilary was a leader in the christological controversy of the fourth century as a defender of the idea that the Son is of the same substance as the Father (*homoousion*) in opposition to the Arian view rejecting the divinity of the Son (*homoiousion*). Whereas he interprets Isa 66:1 in reference to the Father, he argues that the Son shares the Father's infinite nature.

Hilary's opponents apparently used Isa 66:1 as one of several texts they believed contradicted the notion of Christ's divinity because they proclaim God the Father as solely divine. Hilary recounts their argument from Scripture that God alone is, for example, good (Mark 10:18), mighty (1 Tim 6:16), immutable (Mal. 3:6) and inconceivable (Isa 66:1).[85] He maintains that by asserting these properties to be God's alone they falsely deny them to the Son and thereby belittle him. While Hilary would accept their interpretation of Isa 66:1 as proof of God's inconceivable nature, he would deny that such an understanding precludes the divinity of the Son as well.[86]

An allegorical interpretation of Isa 66:1 allowed Ambrose of Milan to understand the verse as referring directly to Christ, particularly to his divine and human natures. Ambrose, who is influenced by Origen[87] and known for the role of allegory in his exegetical writings, depends on allegory in his doctrinal writings, such as *De Spiritu Sancto*. The latter half of the fourth century saw a rise in controversy over the divinity of the Holy Spirit.[88] In *De Spiritu Sancto*, Ambrose defends the Trinity, specifically the worship of the Holy Spirit, and he does this in part through a defense of the worship of both the human and divine natures of Christ.[89]

Ambrose argues, contra Apollinarianism, that even in two natures Christ is not divided but is one, and so Christ in the mystery of the Incarnation is to be worshiped along with divine nature. Since the Incarnation is the work of the Holy Spirit (Luke 1:35), the Holy Spirit is also to be adored. Psalm 99:5 serves as a prooftext for the worship of Christ according to the flesh: "Worship at his footstool, for it is holy." Ambrose uses Isa 66:1 to read the footstool mentioned in the psalm as Christ.[90] Isa 66:1 equates earth with God's footstool, but since the earth is a creature of God, it cannot be the earth itself the psalm is imploring us to worship. Rather, Ambrose identifies the earth with what Christ took on of the earth through the Incarnation: his birth according to the flesh. The throne and footstool of 66:1 refer not to God the Father's nature but rather they *symbolize* the Son's divine and human nature.

For Gregory of Nyssa, Isa 66:1 refers directly to the Son and his role as creator. Gregory alludes to Isa 66:1 in *Contra Eunomium*, where he condemns the bishop's Arian-like views[91] and insists that the incomprehensible nature of the Father is shared by the Son. Eunomius, according to Gregory, defined the Son as "the image and seal of the energy of the Almighty" or the "seal of the Father's works," with works being interpreted as the created world. Gregory insists, however, that the Gospel presents creation as the works of the only-begotten Son,

> who is contemplated in the eternity of the beginning of existent things (John 1:18), who is in the bosom of the Father, who sustains all things by the word of his power, the creator of the ages, from whom and through whom and in whom are all things, who sits upon the circle of the earth, and has meted out heaven with the span, who measures the water in the hollow of his hand (Isa 40:12), who holds in his hand all things that are, who dwells on high and looks upon the things that are lowly, or rather did look upon them to make all the world to be his footstool,[92] imprinted by the footmark of the Word…. (*Contra Eunomium*, 2,12)

Gregory goes beyond the usual Christian application Isa 66:1 to explain theophanies as referring to the Son; he interprets texts which refer to the creator, and which Christians generally associated with the Father, to be speaking of the Son and his creative power.[93] While this christological interpretation of Isa 66:1 is not prominent, as we will see, patristic writers frequently use Isa 66:2a in a similar way (Christ's role in creation as the hand of God).

Isaiah 66:1: Conclusion

Isaiah 66:1 was a well-known verse in early Christianity. Examination of its function in the New Testament and Patristic Era has revealed clear theological components to Christian interpretation of the verse. As we have seen, its predominant function was not as a condemnation of the Jewish cult but as a defense or explanation of God's nature.

The texts most often cited alongside it as fellow prooftexts (cf. Table 1) are not texts that criticize or even mention the Jewish temple or cultic practices but texts that proclaim God's role as creator and lord of all.[94] The key terms that bring most of these texts together to bear on this theological point are "heaven" and "earth" (Isa 40:12; 64:1–2;[95] Jer 23:23–24; Acts 17:24). These texts speak to God's act of creation and/or God's power over creation (Isa 40:12; 64:1–2; Acts 17:24) as well as God's presence in relation to that creation (Jer 23:23–24; 1 Tim 6:15–16). Clearly Isa 66:1 was fundamentally associated with creation and not with temple and cult, although the verse itself may call all of these things to mind.[96]

Examination of Isa 66:1 in various Jewish and Christian literature, suggests that the verse had broad usage for discussions of God's majesty and that the text was later adapted for anti-cultic use, as first seen in Acts. Employing Isa 66:1 as anti-cultic polemic directed towards Jews is a minority interpretation. However, the interpretation is used in texts which have a prominent place within the history of Christianity: Acts, Justin's *Dialogus cum Tryphone*, and *Epistula Barnabae*. In each of these writings, Jews and the Jewish cult are associated with idolatry, and in fact each author points to the golden calf incident as proof. While Clement's and Novatian's application of Isa 66:1 can also be classified as anti-cultic, there is a noticeable difference between the verse's function here as opposed to its use by Stephen (Luke), Barnabas, and Justin, where it was coupled with varying degrees of Jewish criticism. Clement and Novatian demonstrate that even an anti-temple interpretation of Isa 66:1 does not necessitate anti-Jewish polemic.

The Christian use of Isa 66:1 to condemn Jewish practice and belief is most prominent in the Christian struggle with and against Judaism for self-identity in the first two centuries of the Common Era.[97] Christianity's position on the Law and cult were central to the conflict. Once Christianity established itself as independent from Judaism and, through various methods of biblical interpretation such as allegory and typology, established its claim to the Jewish Scriptures without adopting the Law, theological needs shifted away from cultic issues to doctrinal ones. To a certain extent, so, too, did the interpretation of this verse shift away to meet those needs. However, the anti-Jewish interpretation of 66:1 was not lost. Eusebius, for example, drew on earlier exegetes and their anti-cultic understanding of this verse in his efforts to define boundaries between Judaism and Christianity for the new Christian emperor, Constantine.

Isaiah 66:2

While Isaiah 66:2 is not as broadly employed in the service of various theological controversies as 66:1, we encounter it enough in patristic writings to conclude that it is a well-known verse in its own right. There are 47 occurences if 66:2 in *Biblia Patristica*. However, 66:2a and 66:2b function essentially as independent verses which Christian authors apply to unrelated theological discussions. Writers generally cite or allude to either 66:2a or 66:2b, and their exegesis of either half of the verse is generally independent of the other.

Isaiah 66:2a and 66:2b have separate and dissimilar interpretive traditions from 66:1 based upon distinctive vocabulary in 2a and 2b that serves as interpretive clues for the early Christian commentator. There are, however, a couple of exceptions to the independent exegetical developments of these verses. Writers sometimes quote 66:2a together with 66:1.[98] In such cases 2a usually functions as part of 66:1 and falls into categories discussed above, such as Stephen's speech in Acts 7 and Hilary's *De Trin.* 4.8. In addition, as we will see below, there are several instances when an interpretive tradition of 66:1 influences the exegesis of 66:2 and results in an interpretation of the verse against a cultic backdrop.

Isaiah 66:2a

While the interpretation of 66:2b is diverse, in general we find two commonalities in almost all patristic references to 66:2a:[99] the hand is identified as Christ, and Christ's role in creation is emphasized. We see this illustrated, for example, in the Christian Nag Hammadi text *The Teachings of Sylvanus*:

> Only the hand of the Lord
> Has created all these things.
> For this hand of the Father is Christ,
> and it forms all.
> Through it, all has come into being
> Since it became the mother of all.[100]

In the fourth century Trinitarian debates, this interpretive tradition served the defense of the unity of the Godhead in general and, specifically, the divine status of the Son. For example, in Ambrose's treatise *De Spiritu Sancto*, he identifies both the Son and the Holy Spirit with the hand of God and argues that their works, along with those of the Father, are of one body and indistinguishable:[101]

> And yet since we read that the Son is the hand—for it is written: "Has not my hand made all these things?" and elsewhere: "I will cover thee with my hand, I have placed my hand under the covering of the rock," [Exod 33:22] which refers to the mystery of the Incarnation, because the eternal Power of God took on itself the covering of a body – it is certainly clear that Scripture used the term hand both of the Son and of the Holy Spirit. (3.5.33)[102]

To make his case, Ambrose cites several other texts speaking of God's hands and fingers: Pss 19:1; 102:26; 8:3; 92:4; 119:73. In Cyprian's *Ad Quirinum*, where he uses 66:2a as a prooftext in defense of the testimony that Christ is the hand and arm of God, Cyprian also cites several other texts referring to God's hands or arms, but none of the texts are from the Book of Psalms; all are from Isaiah: 26:11; 41:15–20; 52:10; 53:1. Neither the passages from Psalms nor the ones from Isaiah appear with other citations of 66:2a. Thus despite a common interpretive tradition among patristic authors in which the hand is identified as Christ and understood to be the operative power of God, 66:2a does not seem to have functioned as part of a set of standard prooftexts on this theme. This is no doubt due in part to the multitude of anthropomorphic verses available in Scripture.

Isaiah 66:2b

Patristic authors find in Isa 66:2b ideas that serve several distinct purposes. Most prevalent is the repetition of the words of 66:2b in homiletic discourses teaching and imploring a particular standard of conduct. However, in two distinct traditions under the influence of the interpretive traditions of 66:1, 66:2b functions as a prooftext in opposition to the cult: Origen, Ambrose, and Augustine, for example, appeal to a rewritten version of 66:2b to reject temple theology in favor of the individual, and Irenaeus cites it as an anti-cult prooftext that puts forward ethical requirements instead of a material cult. Ironically, while these latter two uses of 66:2b take issue with Jewish practice and belief, only in its application to Christian moral conduct do we find 66:2b engaged in anti-Jewish polemic. In general, though, the christianization of the verse is most often neutral with regard to Jewish-Christian relations.

In our examination of Isaiah 66:1, we saw that one of Christianity's earliest difficulties was whether or not to adopt Jewish Scripture as its own, especially once it became clear that Christianity would not consider itself to be bound to the Law of Moses—except for what Christians generally considered to be natural law, embodied in the Decalogue. One of the ways the Church claimed the authority of Scripture while rejecting its cultic instruction was by adopting the text as a moral guidebook. An analysis of the exegesis of 66:2b in patristic writings reveals the verse's value in this role. The words of 66:2b were often put to use teaching Christian virtue.

In this context, an early and dominant function of 66:2b in the Patristic Era is as a prooftext to reinforce the Christian application of the "Two Ways" doctrine. Proponents of this moral philosophy assert that there are two opposing paths before each individual, one good and leading to life and the other wicked and leading to death. Each person must choose the direction they will walk. The topos is not unique to Christianity.[103] In fact, some Jewish Two Ways document (now lost to us) probably stands behind the source for the Two Ways material in the Christian tradition, such as that found in *Barnabae* and the *Didache*.[104] Mirroring Christian appropriation of Jewish Scripture, the Jewish doctrine of the Two Ways would then have been christianized and, in the process, sometimes used against Jews. The polemical application of the doctrine creates an anti-Jewish association with 66:2b as well.

The Jewish origin of the Two Ways doctrine eventually found in Christianity is evident. The idea of two paths is present in a variety of texts in Scripture: "Thus says the LORD: Behold, I set before you the way of life and the way of death." (Jer 2:18) "But the path of the righteous is like the light of dawn, which shines brighter and brighter until full day. The way of the wicked is like deep darkness; they do not know over what they stumble." (Prov 4:18–19) "Blessed is the man who walks not in the counsel of the wicked, nor stands in the way of sinners, nor sits in the seat of scoffers…for the LORD knows the way of the righteous, but the way of the wicked will perish." (Ps 1:1, 6). The idea is perhaps most developed in Deuteronomy:

> See, I have set before you today life and prosperity, death and adversity. If you obey the commandments of the LORD your God that I am commanding you today, by loving the LORD your God, walking in his ways, and observing his commandments, decrees, and ordinances, then you shall live and become numerous, and the LORD your God will bless you in the land that you are entering to possess. But if your heart turns away and you do not hear, but are led astray to bow down to other gods and serve them, I declare to you today that you shall perish; you shall not live long in the land that you are crossing the Jordan to enter and possess.

> I call heaven and earth to witness against you today that I have set before you life and death, blessings and curses. Choose life so that you and your descendants may live, loving the LORD your God, obeying him, and holding fast to him; for that means life to you and length of days, so that you may live in the land that the LORD swore to give to your ancestors, to Abraham, to Isaac, and to Jacob. (30:15–20)

We find the doctrine in full expression in post-biblical Judaism in 3.18–4.26 of the Qumran *Community Rule* (1QS):

> He set for him two spirits in which to walk until the time of his visitation, namely the spirit of truth and of deceit. Truth came forth through a spring of light but through a spring of darkness deceit comes forth. In the hand of the Prince of lights is the dominion of all the sons of righteousness; in the ways of light they walk. But in the hand of the angel of darkness is the dominion of the sons of deceit and in the ways of darkness they walk. (1QS 3.17–20)

Although we do not find in 1QS specific reference to 66:2b, the characteristics listed in association with the way of light are clearly related to those in the Isaiah passage: in 66:2b, God looks upon the one who is humble (עָנו) and the one who trembles (הרד) at his word (דבר). In 1QS, God loves the one with a spirit of humility (ענו)[105] and the one whose heart fears (פחד) God's precepts (משפטים). In early Jewish and Christian exegesis, a particular word or phrase was often the stimulus to associate a text with an existing motif.[106] From the common use of ענו and the similar theme of fear or trembling at God's words or precepts, we can clearly see why 66:2b would eventually be coupled with the Two Ways doctrine.

Epistula Barnabae contains the earliest known Christian version of the doctrine of the Two Ways and perhaps the first allusion to Isa 66:2b in association with this doctrine. In *Barn.* 18–21, we find a hortatory address in which the author exhorts his audience to walk on the path of light, which brings glorification in the kingdom of God. To a long list of characteristics one must strive for or against, *Barnabae* includes being meek (πρᾶος), being quiet (ἡσυχιός), and trembling (τρέμων) at "the words which you have heard." The LXX reads ταπεινὸν (humble), not πρᾶος, in Isa 66:2b.[107] However, this variation is not surprising considering that in other instances the LXX uses πρᾶος when translating the Hebrew ענו. Other Greek authors, including some who are clearly not dependent on this same interpretive tradition, use πρᾶος when referring to Isa 66:2b as well.[108] The Latin citations of the verse exhibit even greater variations; the particular translation of the first two qualities was particularly fluid. For example, while the Vulgate reads *pauperculum* and *contritum* for ענו and נכא, Latin citations of 66:2b read in most cases *humilem* or *mansuetum* for ענו and *quietum* or *modesto* for נכא, but there are other possibilities as well.

The material in *Barnabae* 18–21 is similar to the Two Ways doctrine in 1QS.[109] There is no significant christianization of the doctrine itself at this stage. However, in the larger context of the condemnation of Judaism in *Barnabae*, the doctrine, and therefore Isa 66:2b, functions as Christian anti-Jewish polemic. The Two Ways material itself is not anti-Jewish. In fact, this section of the epistle (chapters 18–21) is notably different from the first seventeen chapters in that it is without outright condemnation of Jews. However, the remainder of the epistle shapes the reading of these chapters. While the author of the epistle (or even a later editor) may have appended the Two Ways material to the epistle from another source, the larger context is clearly not arbitrary and therefore to be ignored. The theme of the Two Ways is present in the earlier part of the epistle. For example, in *Barn.* 5.4, the author refers to the Way of Holiness and the Way of Darkness. In *Barn.* 4.10, he urges his audience to detest the practices of the wicked way. The presence of this common theme indicates that the author/editor expects his audience to understand chapters 18–21 in light the epistle as a whole, and one thing he clearly expects his audience to understand is that the Way of Darkness is associated with the way of the Jews.

Barnabae 1–17 presents a dichotomy between Jewish practices and scriptural interpretation on the one hand and what the author considers appropriate Christian practice and interpretation on the other. This dichotomy is presented in such a way as to suggest Jews and Christians are on divergent paths with regard to the Two Ways doctrine. For example, the author wants his audience to be on guard against the "Black One," lest they, too, lose the covenant as the Jews did (4.9–10). This implies that Barnabas believes the Jews to have already fallen under the influence of the Black One. This Black One, also mentioned in *Barn.* 20, parallels the dark angel (מלאך חושך) in 1QS. In 9.3, Barnabas explicitly says a "bad angel" (ἄγγελος πονηρός) deluded the Jews. This calls to mind the Spirit of Deceit (עול) in 1QS.

Given the overall opposition between Jews and Christians in chapters 1–17, coupled with explicit overtones to the Two Ways doctrine, Barnabas must have intended his audience to associate the characteristics of those on the dark path in chapter 20 with the Jews. These characteristics include the absence of those qualities that recall Isa 66:2b: In the Way of Darkness "…are things which lack the fear (ἄφοβος) of God. Those who walk this way…are utter strangers to meekness (πρᾶος) …." (20.1,2) Thus in the larger context of the epistle as a whole, the Doctrine of the Two Ways (and thus Isa 66:2b) is used to present Christian *as opposed* to Jew.

One of the occurrences of Isa 66:2b in Cyprian of Carthage's writings is similar to that in *Barnabae* in its association of the verse with the doctrine of the Two Ways and in its anti-Jewish framework. In *Epistula* 13, Cyprian instructs Christians and especially Confessors, who have even greater moral responsibilities in that they are examples to others:

> We must persevere along the straight and narrow road of honor and glory. It befits every Christian to be peaceable and humble and to show that tranquility comes from right living in accordance with the word of God who has regard for no man unless he is humble (*humilem*) and peaceable (*quietum*) and trembles (*trementem*) at his teachings. (3.1)[110]

Cyprian does not teach about two different paths or ways in this epistle. His exhortation to persevere along the straight and narrow road, however, is clearly a reference to that doctrine. Consider, for example, Matthew 7:13–14, which presents two ways, and the way leading life is by way of a narrow gate. While the similarity to Matthew is too faint to be considered an allusion, the language is further indication that the road Cyprian is referring to is meant to be understood against the backdrop of the Two Ways topos and that Cyprian is drawing on a pre-existing tradition associating 66:2b with that topos.

Immediately following his call to Confessors to be moral examples, Cyprian claims that Jews have become alienated from God (3.2). With a reference to Romans 2:24, he contrasts what he sees as Jewish boastfulness with the principles of right conduct he says he knows his Christian audience by and large adheres to (empty words vs. righteous action). This is the only reference to Jews in the brief letter,[111] but it presents us with a similar situation to the one we encountered in *Barnabae*. As in *Barnabae*, Cyprian does not interpret the verse itself to condemn Jews; he references it to exhort Christians to be models of good behavior. The association of Isa 66:2 with the Doctrine of Two Ways and its adaptation for Christian use is not intrinsically anti-Jewish. However, the larger context of both epistles suggests the authors' view that Jews do not exhibit these qualities. This anti-Jewish function of 66:2b is a result of the overall framework of the epistles not the specific interpretation of the verse. More often than not, patristic writers used Isa 66:2b in ways similar to Barnabas and Cyprian but without this polemical framework.

Isaiah 66:2b served in a variety of specifically Christian contexts to discuss and to teach appropriate behavior. For example, in addition to using the verse to instruct Confessors, Cyprian applies the verse to lapsed Christians as well. In the *Didascalia Apostolorum*, he applies 66:2b to promising young leaders: an individual too young to be a bishop (under age 50) could serve as such if he exhibited the qualities put forth in this verse. This adoption of the verse for Christian use is eventually coupled with an adaptation that merged the verse with the teaching of Christ, most notably, with Jesus' pronouncement of the blessed state of the poor (πτωχοὶ) and meek (πραεῖς) in the Sermon on the Mount, found in Matthew 5:3 and 5:5, respectively.[112]

Extant textual evidence suggests the link between Isa 66:2b and Matt 5:5 is quite early and rooted in the Greek tradition, while the association with Matt 5:3 is more difficult to establish but may be later and rooted in the Latin tradition. Consider, for example, that the Greek texts of the *Didache* and the *Didascalia Apostolorum* cite Isa 66:2b with Matt 5:5. The Latin text of Cyprian's *Ad Quirinum* also makes reference to Matt 5:5, but the author reads *humilem* for 66:2b and *mites* for Matt 5:5, thus indicating the connection pre-dates the Latin or is based on an unknown Latin translation. The Latin authors Hilary of Poiters, John Chrysostom, Augustine, and Gregory the Great all read 66:2b with Matt 5:3. While this would be in accordance with the Vulgate's reading of *pauper* in both Isa 66:2b and Matt 5:3, Hilary reads *pauper* only for Matt 5:3 and reads *humilem* for the Isaiah passage. This again suggests the possibility of a pre-existing association of these verses. However, the Greek evidence for associating 5:3 with 66:2b is not overwhelming. The LXX reads ταπεινὸν for עני in 66:2b, but עני can be translated into Greek as πρᾶος and πτωχὸς as well, and thus correspond with either Matt 5:5 or 5:3. As we have seen, several Greek writers read πρᾶος when citing 66:2b. There are no instances where a Greek interpreter reads πτωχὸς, yet the Greek translation by Symmachus does use πτωχὸς to translate עני in 66:2b. In the end, the difficulty explaining the origin of the association of Isa 66:2b with Matt 5:3 may have more to do with the Matthew passage than the Isaiah one. Matt 5:3 and 5:5 shared a close interpretive tradition; some textual traditions even set the verses side by side.[113]

The *Didache* is the earliest known text pairing 66:2b with the Beatitudes:

> But be meek (πρᾶος), for the meek shall inherit the land. [Matt 5:5] Be patient, merciful, guileless, and mild (ἡσυχιός) and gentle, and in every regard fearful (τρέμων) of the words which you have heard. Do not exalt yourself or allow insolence in your soul. Do not let your soul cling to the proud, but associate with good and humble (ταπεινὸν). (3.7–9)

Niederwimmer sees this as a reference to Ps 37:11 rather than Matt 5:5; however, since Matthew is also citing the Psalm, it is difficult to determine whether this is an OT or NT reference. There are several reasons, however, to see this as a gospel reference. The *Didache* is a Christian text probably from the late-first to late-second century. Like *Barnabae*, it also teaches the differences between the Way of Life and the Way of Death, and it is most likely ultimately dependent on the same Jewish Two Ways tractate as *Barnabae*. There is no evidence that the Jewish tractate included a reference to Ps 37:11. Considering this, as well as the fact that the *Didache* includes several other references to Matthean material, it is reasonable to conclude that the verse is part of the christianization of the material overall. In fact, in the *Didache*, the material is more christianized than *Barnabae* in both context (it serves to teach baptismal candidates) and content (the author frequently intersperses gospel references, although they may be from an oral tradition). Furthermore, the *Didascalia Apostolorum* and Cyprian both explicitly link 66:2b with Matt 5:3.[114] If the *Didache* is not reading Matthew 5 with Isa 66:2b, later Christian tradition certainly is, and it is dependent on the *Didache*.

There is a significant variant in the Old Latin version of Isa 66:2b: God says "I rest upon" (*requiescam*) rather than "I look upon" (*respiciam* in the Vulgate; נבט in the MT; ἐπιβλέπω in the LXX).[115] There is no evidence of this textual variant in either Hebrew or Greek; some Latin manuscripts, however, read *requietionis* in 66:1 (*quis iste locus requietionis meae*), which I believe is the key to this deviation. The presence of *requiescam* in 66:2b is a midrashic-like re-wording of the text that pulls together verses 1 and 2 to allow for a reading 66:2b in direct response to the question in 66:1: the *place* of God's rest is *in the one* who is humble, etc. Isa 57:15 may be influencing this reading as well.

We find this variant picked up in Ambrose and Augustine, among others,[116] with important interpretive results, namely, the rejection of the temple theology in which the temple is a miniature of the world and thus the place where God finds rest in a re-enactment of the rest on the seventh day of creation. Jon Levenson in *Sinai and Zion* expounds this biblically based temple theology:

> Since the creation of the world and the construction of the Temple are parallel, if not identical, then the experience of the completed universe and that of the completed sanctuary should also be parallel. In fact, the two entities share an interest in *rest* as the consummate processes that produced them. In the case of creation, God "rested" on the seventh day, the primordial Sabbath, after he had completed his labors…, and he commands his servants to rest *in imitatione Dei* in similar language. The same root describes his experience in the Temple as well:

> 13 For YHWH has chosen Zion,
> He has desired it for his seat:
> 14 "This is my resting place forever;

> Here I shall be enthroned, for I
> desire it." (Ps 132:13–14)[117]

Temple and world stand together as microcosm/macrocosm, and human beings, created in the image of God, participate in the creative act themselves through Sabbath observance. The rendering of 66:2b in Ambrose and Augustine reveals, however, a divergent Christian theology in which the individual replaces the Jewish temple. The inter-relatedness of creation, the Sabbath (performed *in imitatione Dei*) and human beings (created *in imagine Dei*) is also reworked. Human beings, created in the image of God, do not rest on the Sabbath to imitate the creator, but rather as the image of God they are the perfect locus of God's rest.

We only first see it clearly expressed and developed in the works of Ambrose. He links both Isa 66:1 and 66:2b with the themes of creation, the image of God, the divine Sabbath, and an abode:

> Although he [humankind] is compared in body with the beasts, in mind he is counted among the celestial beings, for, even as we have borne the likeness of the earthly, so we bear the likeness of the heavenly. How is he not heavenly who was made to the image and likeness of God? Rightly is heaven first and last in the creation of the world, for in heaven there is what is beyond heaven, there is the God of heaven. Lastly, of him it is understood: "heaven is my throne," for God does not sit above the element of heaven but in the heart of man. For this reason the Lord also says: "We will come to him and make our abode with him." [Jn 14:23] Heaven, therefore, is the first of the works on earth; man is the close or end or last. [*Epistularum liber sextus* 29 (43) 8][118]

> Moreover, he [God] did not find rest when he had created such irrational creatures as fish and the various species of wild beasts. He found rest, however, after he had made man to his own image. Give ear to him as he states on whom he finds rest: On whom shall I rest but on him that is humble and gentle and that trembles at my words. (*Hexaemeron* 6, 8, 49)[119]

> Surely we should now make our contribution of silence, since God has rested from the work of the world. He found repose in the deep recesses of man, in man's mind and purpose, for he had made man with the power of reasoning, an imitator of himself, a striver after virtue, and one eager for heavenly grace. God finds comfort in these traits, as his own testimony declares: Or on whom shall I find repose but on him who is humble and peaceful and who trembles at my words? (*Hexaemeron* 6, 9, 75)

Augustine's works reflect similar themes, although without the creation imagery. He connects both Isa 66:1 and 66:2b with the idea of God dwelling in humanity and relates the Sabbath commandment to 66:2b:

Remember the Sabbath day to sanctify it (Ex 20:8). This third commandment imposes a regular periodical holiday – quietness of heart, tranquility of mind, the product of a good conscience. Here is sanctification, because here is the Spirit of God. Well, here is what a true holiday, that is to say, quietness and rest, means: *Upon whom,* he says, shall my Spirit rest? Upon whom is humble and quiet and trembles at my words. (Sermon 8.6)[120]

When sins are forgiven in the sacraments, the house is cleaned out, but it needs an occupant, the Holy Sprit, and the Holy Spirit only lives in the humble of heart. God, you see, says, *Upon whom shall my Spirit rest?* And he answers the question, Upon the humble and the quiet and the one who trembles at my words. (Sermon 72A.2)

It's by being humble, in fact, and God-fearing that he becomes God's throne. And when he has become God's throne, isn't he already heaven? It says in the scriptures, *Heaven is my throne, while the earth is the stool of my feet.* So if heaven is God's throne, be heaven in order to carry God. (Sermon 360B.7)

Most interesting and illustrative of the reworked theology, as well as the influence of 66:1, is Augustine's commentary on David's words in Ps 132:3–4.[121] These verses refer to the King's desire to build a permanent temple for Yahweh, as expressed in 2 Samuel 7, but Augustine reinterprets them to be speaking of God's dwelling in the human heart:

"O Lord, remember David in all his meekness." In this temper he vowed his vow, and there should be a house of God: "I will not come within the tabernacle of mine house, nor climb up into my bed." I will not suffer mine eyes to sleep, nor mine eyelids to slumber." This seems not enough; he adds, "Neither the temples of my head to take any rest, until I find out a place for the Lord; a habitation for the God of Jacob." [Acts 7:46] Where did he seek a place for the Lord? If he was meek, he sought it in himself. For how is one a place for the Lord? Hear the Prophet: "Upon whom shall my spirit rest? Even upon him that is poor and of contrite spirit and trembles at the word of God.... (*Enarrationes in Psalmos* 132.2)[122]

While there is no evidence of a common exegetical tradition, there is a faint echo here in Ambrose and Augustine of the theology we find in *Barnabae.* He used Isa 66:1 to condemn the material temple, which he contrasted with the heart of the faithful human being as the true temple of God. The writings of Ambrose and Augustine reflect a later stage in Christian thought when the idea that the human heart, not the temple, was God's dwelling place had already taken hold. We see in their writing not simply a statement to that effect but a complex reworking of a Jewish exegetical tradition to reflect the Christian view that the Jewish cult has been replaced by the incarnation as the locus of revelation.

In *Aduersus haereses*, Irenaeus criticizes the material cult as unnecessary and worthless with respect to righteousness, and he characterizes Jewish observance as slavish (17.11). In this setting, Isa 66:2b serves as an anti-cultic prooftext demonstrating that true sacrifice is an afflicted heart:

> "Thou hast not [brought to] Me the sheep of thy holocaust, nor in thy sacrifices hast thou glorified me: thou hast not served me in sacrifices, nor in [the manner of] frankincense hast thou done anything laboriously; neither hast thou bought me incense with money, nor have I desired the fat of thy sacrifices; but thou hast stood before me in thy sins and in thine iniquities." [Isa 43:23,24] He says therefore, "Upon this man will I look, even upon him that is humble and meek and who trembles at my words."… From all these it is evident that God did not seek sacrifices and holocausts from them, but faith, and obedience, and righteousness, because of their salvation." (*Haer.* 4.17.3.4)

Earlier in this chapter, Irenaeus quotes Ps 51:17 ("The sacrifices of God are a broken spirit; a broken and contrite [*humilem*] heart"), and this verse may be one factor behind his inclusion here of Isa 66:2b.[123] However, there are indications an interpretive tradition for Isa 66:1 is a factor as well. His criticism of the cult draws on texts familiar to Christians in the cultic debate, such as Isa 1:11; 58:6; Jer 7:21–24; Hos 6:6 and Mal 1:10–11. In this context, Isa 66:2b is functioning in criticism of the Jewish cult in a manner more analogous to what we would expect for 66:1. While 66:2b frequently is cited in Christianity in conjunction with passages from the beatitudes, some of the texts cited here, such as Jer 7:21–24, Isa 1:11, and Isa 58:6, are texts associated with 66:1 and its suspected role in Christian *testimonia*.[124] Furthermore, Irenaeus' criticism of the cult is in part based upon a concept of a God who has no need of anything from human beings. (17.1) This is also an idea associated with 66:1.[125]

The criticism of the cult is not directed at Judaism, and thus cannot be considered anti-Jewish polemic. Irenaeus is defending his interpretation of Christianity against Gnosticism and the charge that the demiurge is weak and not the supreme divine being. In response, he strives to show that the material cult described in Jewish Scripture is not indicative of a limited, ineffectual creator in need of human service.

I think the inclusion of 66:2b in this cultic context is in part dependent on Irenaeus' familiarity with an anti-cultic association of 66:1, and, furthermore, it is evidence that, despite the verse-centered interpretive methods of early Christianity, the interpretive tradition of a particular verse influenced the interpretation of surrounding verses. For although 66:2b is located between verses that directly address the material cult, this verse itself is devoid of direct cultic reference and, as we have seen, was not used in direct criticism of the cult. Isa 66:2b developed its own interpretive tradition, which was primarily in the service of

Christianity's use of Scripture as a moral guidebook. Irenaeus incorporates the moral interpretation of 66:2b into an anti-cultic context associated with 66:1. The text around which he pulls both of these ideas together is Jer 7:24. This verse is frequently cited with 66:1, but it also calls to mind the Two Ways theme: "walk in all my ways whatsoever I have commanded you, that it may be well with you".

Isaiah 66:3, 4

Isaiah 66:3 does not hold nearly the prominence in the Patristic Era that verses 1 and 2 do. Its use is rare and the use of 66:4 even more so. The Hebrew of 66:3 ambiguously juxtaposes acceptable and offensive cultic practices; a variant Greek text not only resolves the ambiguity, but also explicitly assumes a situation that is at most implicit and arguably absent in the Hebrew: according to the LXX translation received by the Church, the *lawless* one (ἄνομος) who performs a legitimate cultic rite *is like* (ὡς) one who commits an egregious act. The ὡς defines the relationship between each pair of actions as one of comparison. However, with the presence of the qualifying adjective "ἄνομος", the verse is clearly not a condemnation of sacrifice or the material cult in itself.[126] The Greek verse claims that a cultic act is worthless, even profane, if one is impious or not in right relation with the Law. While the Vulgate lacks this adjective, Latin writers knew and accepted this version of the verse. For example, Irenaeus and Basil of Caesarea both qualify the one who performs these acts as *iniquus*. This variation is key to Christian interpretation of this verse.

In *Aduersus haereses*, Irenaeus navigates the narrow early Christian position between Judaism and Gnosticism. We have already discussed and recognized this situation as critical to Christian biblical interpretation, and here, too, the use of Isa 66:3 serves Irenaeus' attempt to steer between these two poles. In defense of Gnostic criticism of the Jewish God, particularly with regard to sacrifice, Irenaeus argues that sacrifice is for human benefit, not God's.

> … not that he stands in need of sacrifice from us, but that he who offers is himself glorified in what he does offer, if his gift be accepted. For by the gift both honor and affection are shown forth towards the King. (*Haer.* 4.18.1)

That God is not appeased by sacrifice is demonstrated by the story of Cain and Abel:

> For at the beginning God had respect to the gifts of Abel, because he offered with single-mindedness and righteousness; but how had not respect unto the offering of Cain, because his heart was divided with envy and malice…. (*Haer.* 4.18.3)

Isa 66:3 serves as his concluding prooftext:

> Sacrifices, therefore, do not sanctify a person, for God stands in no need of sacrifice; but it is the conscience of the offerer that sanctifies the sacrifice when it is pure, and thus moves God to accept [it] as from a friend. "But the sinner," he says, "who kills a calf for me is as if he slew a dog." (*Haer.* 4.18.3)

To explain this passage and his argument further, Irenaeus identifies the oblations of the Church, that is offerings such as goods and possessions for the needy, as a pure sacrifice grounded in love and therefore acceptable to God. The offerings of the Church are contrasted with those of Jews, whose hands are "full of blood" and who have not "received the Word," and therefore whose offerings are not pure.[127]

Basil of Caesarea uses 66:3 to make a similar point regarding the status of the offerer, although in this case it is in response to internal Church debate. In his treatises *De Baptismo* and *Asceticon Magnum*, Basil takes up the question of whether it is possible for a sinner or arrogant individual to perform a meritorious act that finds favor with God. In both cases he insists this is not possible, and he puts forth Isa 66:3, along with 2 Cor 6:14–15 ("What partnership is there between righteousness and lawlessness?"), as a prooftext.[128]

As we have seen with 66:1, for example, patristic use of Isa 66:3b–4 also illustrates Christian manipulation of the biblical text for application to various conflicts. In *Ad Hermammonen*, Dionysius directs the accusatory words to the Roman leader Valerian, in condemnation of his persecution of Christians:

> For Valerian was prompted to these acts by this man [Macrianus], and was by this means exposed to contempt and reproach, according to the word spoken by the Lord to Isaiah: "They have chosen their own ways, and their own abominations in which their soul delighted; I also will choose their mockeries. (in Eusebius, *Historie Ecclesiasticae* 7.10)

It is not surprising that we also find these words directed towards Jews. In his *Commentarius in Isaiam*, Eusebius understands Isa 66:4—as he did 66:1–3—as God's condemnation of Jewish conceit: "for they did not submit (παρέχω) themselves to the one calling." (56) Eusebius' criticism of Judaism, as is often the case with the criticism of others before him, is in the context of identity issues: one of his tasks is to clarify the boundary between Christianity and Judaism for the new Christian emperor, Constantine. All Christian condemnation of Judaism does not fall within this context of identity issues, but clearly the anti-

Jewish interpretation of Isa 66:1–4 has its roots in this context, which included the effort of the Church to appropriate the Jewish Scriptures as its own.

Notes

1. See *Biblia Patristica: index des citations et allusions bibliques dans la littérature patristique* (ed. Jean Allenbach et al.; 7 vols.; Paris: Editions du Centre national de la recherche scientifique, 1975–) and the index to *Novum Testamentum Graece* (ed. Nestle and Aland; Stuttgart: Deutsche Bibelstiftung, 1993).

2. Although sometimes Isa 66:1–2a is cited as a whole, as is 66:3–4a, citation of v. 4 alone is rare.

3. James L. Kugel, *In Potiphar's House: The Interpretive Life of Biblical Texts* (Cambridge: Harvard University Press, 1990), 255.

4. James L. Kugel and Rowan A. Greer, *Early Biblical Interpretation* (Philadelphia: Westminster, 1986), 127.

5. For example, Pierre Prigent's work on Barnabas showed that a book of *testimonia* likely stands behind Barnabas' use of Isa 66:1. See Prigent, *Les Testimonia dans le christianisme primitif: l'Epître de Barnabé I–XVI et ses sources* (Paris: J. Gabalda, 1961). Rendel Harris' *testimonia* hypothesis (a single Testimony Book ante-dating Paul and consisting of scriptural passages collected for the purpose of anti-Jewish apologetic) is no longer accepted in its entirety. However, while the form and function of a book of *testimonia* is debated, most scholars seem to agree that there was some kind of early Christian testimony source(s) that Barnabas and others drew upon. The earliest extant Christian collection of *testimonia* is Cyprian's *Ad Quirinium*, also known as *Testimonia* (3rd century). *4QTestimonium* and *4QFlorigelium* are known examples of Jewish counterparts to the hypothetical first century Christian *testimonia*.

6. For example, ἤ τις τόπος instead of ἤ ποῖος τόπος (LXX) in Acts 7, *Epistula Barnabae*, and Athenagoras' *Legatio*.

7. Lindars, *New Testament Apologetic* (Philadelphia: Westminster, 1961).

8. Luke most likely made use of a Greek Bible similar to the LXX. See Joseph A. Fitzmyer, *Acts of the Apostles* (AB 31; New York: Doubleday, 1998).

9. This same variation occurs in several other Greek texts, such as *Epistula Barnabae* and Athenagoras' *Legatio*. The Latin equivalent occurs in Novatian's *De Trinitate*.

10. Most scholars agree that Stephen's speech is not Luke's original composition. See the commentaries.

11. "[A] dwelling place for the *house* of Jacob" is awkward, and in fact, later texts read θεός for οἶκος. This would make the Acts passage more harmonious with Ps 132:5 where David says, "until I find a place for the Lord, a dwelling place for the Mighty One of Jacob." Also, it solves the problem of the antecedent for the αὐτός in the following verse. For an interpretation of the speech centered on reading the text as "house of Jacob" rather than "God of Jacob," see Delbert Wiens, *Stephen's Sermon and the Structure of Luke-Acts* (N. Richland Hills, TX: Bibal 1995).

12. A third possibility is that Stephen (or Luke) is suggesting the idea of something replacing the temple (such as Jesus or the community) as the locus for God's presence, as the temple replaced the tent of testimony. I think this third possibility is less likely, because there are no

such claims in the text, but cf. Luke Timothy Johnson, *The Acts of the Apostles* (Collegeville, MN: The Liturgical Press, 1992) and Donald Juel, *Messianic Exegesis: Christological Interpretation of the Old Testament in Early Christianity* (Philadelphia: Fortress, 1987).

13. See, for example, Marcel Simon, "Saint Stephen and the Jerusalem Temple," in *JEH* 2 (Jl – O 1951): 127–142; Leslie W. Barnard, "Saint Stephen and Early Alexandrian Christianity," in *NTS* 7 (1960): 32–45; Charles K. Barrett, "Attitudes to the Temple in the Acts of the Apostles," in *Templum Amicitiae* (JSNTSupp 48; ed. W. Horbury; Sheffield: JSOT Press, 1991): 345–367; Hans Conzelmann, *Acts of the Apostles* (Hermeneia; Philadelphia: Fortress, 1987); James D. G. Dunn, *The Acts of the Apostles* (Petersborough: Epworth, 1996); Joseph A. Fitzmyer, *Acts of the Apostles*; Ernst Haenchen, *The Acts of the Apostles: A Commentary* (Philadelphia: Westminster, 1971); and Albertus F. Klijn, "Stephen's Speech—Acts VII.2–53" in *NTS* 4 (1957–1958): 25–31.

14. Leslie W. Barnard sees Stephen as an extremist who was strongly anti-cultus. See Barnard, "Saint Stephen and Early Alexandrian Christianity."

15. The Letter to the Hebrews also views the tabernacle favorably as opposed to the temple.

16. In the LXX, σκήνωμα can mean either tent or temple.

17. Viewed in this light, the account by Stephen follows 2 Samuel 7, where David desired to build Yahweh a house, but the prophet Nathan tells him that God prefers a tent and would build David a house instead. The promise in 2 Samuel 13, that David's son would build the temple, is probably a later addition to the prophecy to reflect the historical reality. Stephen does not include God's concession with regard to the temple in his version of the story.

18. Cf. Joseph A. Fitzmyer, *Acts of the Apostles*, 608. The temple criticisms in Acts have parallels with criticisms of pagan temples by Greek philosophers: "What house fashioned by builders can contain the divine form within enclosing walls?" (Euripides).

19. See, for example, John Kilgallen, "The Function of Stephen's speech (Acts 7,2–53)," in *Biblica* 70:2 (1989): 173–193 and *The Stephen Speech: A Literary and Redactional Study of Acts 7,2–53* (Rome: E. Pontificio Instituto Biblico, 1975); Edvin Larrson, "Temple Criticism and the Jewish Heritage: Some Reflections on Acts 6–7," in *NTS* 39 (1993): 379–395; Dennis Sylva, "The Meaning and Function of Acts 7:46–50," in *JBL* 106/2 (1987): 261–275; Francis Weinert, "Luke, Stephen, and the Temple in Luke-Acts," in *BTB* 17 (Jl 1987): 88–90; and Delbert Wiens, *Stephen's Sermon*.

20. *Epistula Barnabae*, a Christian text, is discussed below. *Sibylline Oracles* 4, a Jewish text possibly from the late 1st century C.E., rejects temple worship in general: "I am not an oracle monger of false Phoebus, whom vain men called a god, and falsely described as a seer, but of the great God, whom no hands of men fashioned in the likeness of speechless idols of polished stone. For he does not have a house, a stone set up as a temple...." (4–8) "Happy will be those of mankind on earth who will love the great God, blessing him before drinking and eating, putting their trust in piety. They will reject all temples when they see them; altars too, unless foundations of dumb stones (and stone statues and handmade images) defiled with blood of animate creatures, and sacrifices of four-footed animals." (24–29) Translated by John Collins, *The Old Testament Pseudepigrapha*, (ed. James H. Charlesworth; 2 vols.; New York: Doubleday, 1983), 1:384.

21. There could possibly be a testimony source standing behind the speech in Acts.

22. Francis Weinert, "Luke, Stephen, and the Temple in Luke-Acts," 89–90.

23. We find a similar view in the writings of the 3rd century presbyter Novatian. See below.

24. Barry W. Holz, ed. *Back to the Sources: Reading the Classic Jewish Texts* (New York: Summit Books, 1984) provides an introduction to rabbinic sources.

25. There is substantial biblical evidence suggesting that, by Stephen's day, Israel had long since ceased viewing the temple as the literal dwelling place of God (in addition to 1 Kgs 8:27, cf. 2 Sam 8:13; 2 Chr 6:18, 21; Jer 7:14; 29:13–14). Graham I. Davies argues, however, that while this view indeed existed, it was not as widespread in Second Temple times as is usually thought. He cites as evidence Joel 2:27, Matt 23:21, 1QS 28.7–10, Josephus, *Jewish War* 6.299, *a.Sukkah* 5.4, and Ps 135:21. See "The Presence of God in the Second Temple and Rabbinic Doctrine," in *Templum Amicitiae* (JSNTSupp. 48; Sheffield: JSOT Press, 1991): 32–36.

26. Edvin Larsson, "Temple Criticism and the Jewish Heritage," 394, esp. n.38.

27. Dennis Sylva, "The Meaning and Function of Acts 7:46–50," 270–271.

28. *Barnabae* is an anonymous text that later came to be associated with the Barnabas who accompanied Paul. The use of Barnabas here refers to the anonymous author.

29. There are several arguments for an Alexandrian origin, including its use of the allegorical method, its early and favorable reception there by Clement of Alexandria and Origen, and it presence in the Codex Sinaiticus. The question of origin is disputed, however, with Syria-Palestine and Asia Minor usually offered as alternatives. Martin Shukster and Peter Richardson argue for Syria-Palestine, Klaus Wengst for Asia Minor. See Shukster and Richardson, "Temple and Bet Ha-midrash in the Epistle of Barnabas," in *Anti-Judaism in Early Christianity* (ed. Stephen G. Wilson; 2 vols.; Waterloo: Wilfrid Laurier University Press, 1986), 17–31 and Wengst, *Didache (Apostellehre): Barnabasbrief, Zweiter Klemensbrief, Schrift an Diognet* (Darmstadt: Wissenschaftliche Buchgesellschaft, 1984).

30. The epistle is thought to have been written anywhere between 70 and 150 C.E. The only internal clues as to the date of its origin are 4:3–5 and 16:4, and both are problematic. Chapter 4 quotes the vision of the "Ten Kings" passage from Daniel 7, and attempts to date the epistle based on this passage involve trying to determine to which Roman emperor Barnabas might be referring with this passage. Cases are made for Vespesian (Hvalvik), Nerva (Shukster/Richardson), and Hadrian (Paget). Hvalvik argues that this text is taken over from an earlier tradition and is not relevant for dating the text. See Reidar Hvalvik, *The Struggle for Scripture and Covenant: The Purpose of the Epistle of Barnabas and Jewish Christian Competition in the Second Century* (Tübingen: J.C.B. Mohr, 1996), 25–26. *Barnabae* 16 mentions the rebuilding of a temple. Exactly what he means here is open to interpretation. A spiritual temple (Williams and Prigent), a plan or hope to rebuild the Jewish temple (Alon and Paget), and a pagan temple to Jupiter in *Aelia Capitolina* (Hvalvik and Windisch) have all been proposed. A spiritual or pagan temple makes the least sense in the context of *Barnabae* 16:1–5.

31. Gedaliah Alon, in *The Jews in Their Land in the Talmudic Age (70–640 C.E.)* (trans. G. Levi; 2 vols.; Jerusalem: The Magnes Press, 1980, 1984), demonstrates that while there is no specific evidence pointing to a Roman edict or plan to rebuild the Jewish temple, there is a tradition in both Jewish and early Christian sources suggesting it was *believed* the temple would be rebuilt.

32. Some scholars have argued that the *Adversus Judaeos* literature was purely academic in the sense that it was for internal use only and did not reflect any threat or ongoing controversy between Christians and Jews (Harnack is the main proponent of this school of thought).

However, in *Versus Israel: A Study of the Relations between Christians and Jews in the Roman Empire (135–425)* (trans. H. Keating; New York: Oxford University Press, 1986), Marcel Simon has shown that Jews did indeed present a missionary threat to Christianity and were a much more active group in the first four centuries than previously thought. He demonstrates that *Adversus Judaeos* literature would have been used to combat Judaizing tendencies among Christians. Albert Baumgerten has recently discussed challenges to Simon's reconstruction. His conclusion, however, calls for a scaling back of Simon's "conflict theory" rather than a complete rejection of it. See "Marcel Simon's *Versus Israel* as a Contribution to Jewish History," in *HTR* 92 (O 1999): 465–478.

33. The only additional difference from the LXX is καὶ ἡ γῆ for ἡ δὲ γῆ. In *Dialogus cum Tryphone*, the first μοι is moved to the end of the question and the subjunctive replaces the indicative οἰκοδομήσετε.

34. In *Commentari in Isaiam* 93, Procopius of Gaza (6th cent.) ties an anti-Jewish interpretation of Isa 66:1 with the Jews' loss of favor due to their rejection of Christ.

35. Pierre Prigent also notes that the texts in *Apologia* i, 37 unite around an anti-ritualistic polemic See *Justin et l'Ancien Testament* (Paris: J. Gabalda, 1964), 262. Likewise Oskar Skarsaune considers these to be anti-cultic testimony clusters. See *Proof from Prophecy: A Study in Justin Martyr's Proof Text Tradition* (NovTSup LVI; Leiden: E.J. Brill, 1987), 158.

36. Michael Hollerich compares Justin's view of the temple and his treatment of Isa 66:1 to Eusebius's view. See *Eusebius of Caesarea's Commentary on Isaiah* (Oxford: Clarendon Press, 1999), 41–46. Eusebius' emphasis on a new heaven and a new earth—and thus a new Jerusalem—is in agreement with Justin's view of God's provisional presence in the temple.

37. Stephen also quotes from Amos 5 in Acts 7:42–43. Prigent sees in the opening of *Dialogus cum Tryphone* 22 an allusion to Isa 1:11–13, which is explicitly quoted in *Apol.* 37. He believes that there was an anthology of anti-ritualistic texts that would have included Isa 1:11–13 and 66:1.

38. The intended audience of the *Dialogus cum Tryphone* is debated. Theodore Stylianopoulos argues in *Justin Martyr and the Mosaic Law* (SBLDS 20; Missoula, MT: Society of Biblical Literature and Scholars Press, 1975) that it is in fact written to Jews. Cf. the above discussion as to whether or not *Adversus Judaeos* literature was solely for internal use.

39. Christians have always acknowledged the validity of the moral law in Scripture.

40. This is not to disregard the influence of the tradition of interpretation that lies behind his use of any biblical text, including Isa 66:1, which shows signs of having functioned in *testimonia* literature for anti-cultic purposes. Still, Justin has his own agenda and picks, chooses, and edits accordingly.

41. Some date the curse from Birkat Minim to this period. See Philip Alexander, "'The Parting of the Way' from the Perspective of Rabbinic Judaism," in *Jews and Christians: The Parting of the Ways: A.D. 70 to 135* (ed. James Dunn; Grand Rapids: Eerdmans, 1999), 6–7. However, the dating is controversial and the text does not specifically refer to Christians. Lee Martin McDonald's words are directed in part to this period: "Both groups at various times in their histories have been guilty of shameful acts towards each other." See McDonald, "Anti-Judaism in the Early Church Fathers" in *Anti-Semitism and Early Christianity: Issues of Polemic and Faith* (ed. C. Evans and D. Hagner; Minneapolis: Fortress, 1993), 250–251.

42. Clement also applies this verse to a discussion of God's nature without the anti-cultic dimension. For example, in *Stomata* 5.14.124.1, he presents Orpheus as in agreement with

Isa 66:1. In *Protrepticus* he finds the *Sibylline Oracles* to be "in remarkable accord with inspiration" (incl. Isa 66:1; 40:12; 64:1,2; Jer 23:23 and Ps 97:5): There is one God, who sends rain, and winds, and earthquakes, thunderbolts, famines, plagues, and dismal sorrows, and snows and ice. But why detail particulars? He reigns over heaven, he rules the earth, he truly is." (78,2) The *Sibylline Oracles*, a Jewish text modeled after pagan Sibylline books were accepted by many early Christians as genuine. See John J. Collins, "Introduction to the *Sibylline Oracles*," in *Old Testament Pseudepigrapha*, 381ff.

43. Annewies van den Hoek sees this as evidence that Clement took the quotation directly from Acts. See *Clement of Alexandria and his Use of Philo in the Stromateis* (Leiden: E.J. Brill, 1998). I think the inversion suggests instead a book of *testimonia* as a possible source.

44. Alexandrian Christianity, and especially Clement, was greatly influenced by Philo, who also sought to synthesize Greek paideia with Scripture. Cf. Annewies van den Hoek, *Clement of Alexandria*.

45. Clement quotes passages from Euripides, Zeno, and Plato, which all speak to the worthlessness of temples.

46. Clement quotes this verse again with Isa 66:1 in *Protrepticus* 78,2. The use of Isa 66:1 in connection with the theme of a God both far off and near surfaces again.

47. Clement's interpretation of Moses' entering into darkness in Exodus 25 as an entrance into the incorporeal realm shows Philonic influence and raises the question as to whether he, as Philo, understood the tabernacle and thus maybe even the Jerusalem Temple to be a representation of the incorporeal reality (cf. *De Opificio Mundi*).

48. This is not to say his writings are devoid of anti-Jewish statements. Cf. Clement, *Strom.* 2.21.2, 2.42.4–5, 6.41.2, etc.

49. Annewies Van den Hoek argues for this in "How Alexandrian was Clement of Alexandria: Reflections on Clement and his Alexandrian Background," in *HeyJ* 31 (Ap 1990): 179–194.

50. J. Carleton Paget, "Clement of Alexandria and the Jews," *SJT* 51 (1998): 86–97.

51. Johann Quasten, *Patrology* (3 vols.; Brussels: Spectrum, 1950–1986), 2:217.

52. In addition to the Vulgate, see, for example, Hilary, *De Trinitate* 4.8, and Cyprian, *Ad Quinium testimonia adversus Judaeos* 2.4.

53. Variations include, for example, *thronos/sedis* and *subpedaneum/scabellum*.

54. For a discussion of Scripture's translation into Latin, cf. Benjamin Kedar, "The Latin Translations," in *Mikra: Text, Translation, Reading and Interpretation of the Hebrew Bible in Ancient Judaism and Early Christianity* (ed. M.J. Mulder and H. Sysling; Philadelphia: Fortress, 1988), 299–338.

55. Trans. by R. De Simone.

56. He contrasts God's infinite nature with human limits. In fact, he puts forth Isa 66:2 to illuminate the proper qualities by which an individual fully recognizes God's greatness.

57. See a similar view in Theodoret of Antioch's 4th century commentary on Ps 138: Let us enter his tabernacle, let us worship in the place where his feet stood. He changed the time. He means we go in there and adore, believing the Temple has been accorded a divine apparition; this is the sense of where his feet stood. We believe, after all, that the divinity is not only incorporeal but also uncircumscribed. The divine scripture speaks in more corporeal terms about it, however, accommodating the language to human ears. Theodoret cites along with this idea Isa 66:1, Acts 17:24, and 2 Chr 6:18.

58. *Numbers Rabbah* xii.3 is discussed above. For a similar view in Christianity of the conception of God in terms of human experience, cf. Cyril of Jerusalem, *Catechesis* 6.

59. Novatian, writing a century prior to the council of Nicea, essentially presents what became the orthodox view of the Trinity. He presents his treatise, however, as a defense or explanation of the Rule of Faith.

60. If Luke borrowed Stephen's speech from elsewhere, as many scholars believe he did, Acts 7 could represent a source earlier than Matthew. However, Matthew is also making use of earlier material.

61. I refer here to a tradition claiming heaven and earth as God's possessions based on Isa 66:1 and am not making a claim as to the source of the antithesis itself. Ulrich Luz gives a brief overview of scholarly opinion concerning the origin of the Antitheses in Matt 5:21–48 in *Matthew 1–7: A Commentary* (trans. W. Linss; Edinburgh: T&T Clark, 1989), 275–279.

62. *Exodus Rabbah* VIII also reads Isa 66:1 together with Gen 1:1: "On the first day, he created the heavens and the earth; they were also created for His glory, for it says: Thus saith the Lord: The heaven is my throne…."

63. Charles Perrot, "The Reading of the Bible in the Ancient Synagogue," in *Mikra* (ed. M.J. Mulder and H. Sysling; Philadelphia: Fortress, 1988), 137–159. The *sederim* are the Torah readings of the Sabbath. The Triennial Palestine Cycle covered the entire Torah over a three year period.

64. For Origen's relations with the Jews see Nicholas R.M. De Lange, *Origen and the Jews: Studies in Jewish-Christian Relations in Third-Century Palestine* (New York: Cambridge University Press, 1976).

65. Trans. by R. Heine.

66. Origen actually speaks of a threefold meaning of Scripture, but more often than not he gives two interpretations for any given passage. For an introduction to Origen's exegetical approach see J. Carleton Paget's "Christian Exegesis in the Alexandrian Tradition," in *Hebrew Bible/Old Testament: The History of Its Interpretation* (ed. M. Saebo; vol I/1; Göttingen: Vandenhoeck & Ruprecht, 1996).

67. *Homiliae in Genesim* 1,13. See also *De oratione* 23,3.

68. Cf. Epiphanius, *Panarion* 70.6.1.

69. Cf. De Lange, *Origen and the Jews*, 44.

70. Trans. by H.G. Bethge.

71. Gnosticism was a varied tradition not a single sect. Thus, there was no single belief system. There were, however, certainly shared characteristics. The Nag Hammadi texts were collected by Christians, but they have various origins; many of the texts are non-Christian. Jewish and Neoplatonist themes permeate many Gnostic texts. Cf. James M. Robinson's introduction in *The Nag Hammadi Library in English*, 2–26.

72. For example, in addition to Gen 1–3, *On the Origin of the World* makes extensive use of Isaiah (esp. chapters 43–47), Ezekiel, and Deuteronomy. It also alludes to Psalms, various minor prophets, and the historical books. See Craig Evans *et al*, eds. *Nag Hammadi Texts and the Bible* (NTTS XVIII; New York: E.J. Brill, 1993).

73. The Christian apologist Athenagoras also cites Isa 66:1 to argue for monotheism (*Legatio* 9.2).

74. Trans. by Alexander Roberts and James Donaldson.

75. *De Principiis* ii, 4,1.

76. Later in the passage Irenaeus makes it clear that the Gnostics were referring to 1 Cor 7:35.

77. Trans. by Ernest Evans.

78. Julian (361–363 C.E.) did not succeed in his attempt to weaken the Church and re-establish paganism's dominance.

79. This is not to say Isa 66:1 is used only in this way at this time. The text still serves to illustrate God's majesty aside from the christological debate. Cf., for example, Eusebius, *Orations in praise of Constantine*, where it illustrates both Constantine's and God's kingship.

80. Trans. by Ernest Evans.

81. Irenaeus also uses Isa 66:1 to deny the notion that theophanies could have been the Father, Creator of all, who is not circumscribed in space. Cf. Irenaeus, *Demonstatio* 45.

82. G.M. Newlands discusses the role of scripture in Hilary's theology in *Hilary of Poiters: A Study in Theological Method* (Bern: Peter Lang, 1978).

83. *De Trin.* 1.5–6.

84. Trans. by S. McKenna.

85. *De Trin.* 4.8.

86. For example, see *De Trin.* 2.8–11.

87. In addition to his platonic allegorical interpretation of Isa 66:1, mentioned above, Origen also employed a christological allegory of the verse. However, unlike Ambrose, he understands the verse as referring to both Christ and the Church: "And it is not absurd for him to be properly speaking the Father's throne, since he is called allegorically "heaven;" and his church, called "earth," is the stool of his feet." (*De Oratione* 23.4)

88. For example, see also Basil's *De Spiritu Sancto*.

89. *De Spiritu Sancto* 2.11.

90. Other texts suggest the psalm's reference to the footstool indicates the ark: cf. 1 Chr 28:2; 2 Chr 9:18; and Ps 132:7.

91. Specifically, Eunomius was an Anomean, a 4th century proponent of a doctrine similar to Arianism. He held that Christ, as "generate," was of a different nature from God.

92. Isa 66:1 is the only reference to the earth as the footstool. Other passages suggest the ark as to be the footstool of God. Cf. 1 Chron 28:2; 2 Chron 9:18; Ps 132:7.

93. Gregory even applies Eph 4:6 to the Son ("he is above all and through all and in all"), which is clearly referring to the Father.

94. Acts 17:24 is a possible exception. It does mention temples and says that the Lord of heaven does not dwell in them. However, Paul is not referring to the Jerusalem temple but rather the temples he sees in Athens.

95. Isa 64:1–2 refers only to heaven, but the mountains stand in for the earth as the other realm of creation.

96. See Jon Levenson, "The Temple and the World," in *JRel* 64 (1984): 275–298. Levenson has demonstrated that in the Jewish tradition the temple and creation are linked: "the Temple is a visible, tangible token of the act of creation, the point of origin of the world, the 'focus' of the universe." (283) His position will be discussed further in chapter four.

97. Interestingly, in the powerfully anti-Jewish writings of the 4th and 5th centuries (during a period of intense Jewish proselytizing) we do not find anti-Jewish interpretation of Isa 66:1

among prominent writers such as Chrysostom, Cyril, and Augustine. This most likely reflects Christianity's sense of identity by this time as distinct.

98. There are no incidences when 66:1–2 is cited in full.

99. This assessment excludes citations of v. 2a as part of 66:1.

100. Trans. from the Coptic by Jan Zandee, *Nag Hammadi Codex VII,4* (Nag Hammadi and Manichaean Studies 30; The Coptic Gnostic Library; Leiden: E.J. Brill, 1966), 74.

101. Also in accordance with the Council of Nicea's stance on the Trinity, Gregory of Nyssa uses 66:2a in his defense of Christ's divine status in his treatise *Contra Eunomium* (3.5). Cf. also Athanasius' *Orationes contra Arianos* 2.71 and 4.26.

102. Trans. by R. Deferrari.

103. See Kurt Niederwimmer, *The Didache: A Commentary* (Hermeneia; Minneapolis: Fortress, 1998). He demonstrates the nearly ubiquitous presence of this topos in the ancient world.

104. For form critical analysis of *Barnabae*, see Pierre Prigent *Les Testimonia dans le christianisme primitive: l'Epitre de Barnabe I–XVI et ses sources* and Robert A. Kraft, "Barnabas' Isaiah Text and the 'Testimony Book' Hypothesis," in *JBL* 79 (1960): 336–350. Niederwimmer presents a detailed analysis of the development of the Two Ways material in the Christian tradition as well as a discussion of its Jewish roots.

105. The Qumran community identified themselves as ענוים. The importance of this quality for the theology of the community is reflected in the frequency of its appearance in 1QS: 2:24; 3:8; 4:3; 5:3; 5:25; 9:22; 11:11.

106. We also find Isa 66:2b in association with ענוים theology in Rabbinic writings: When a man is rich and has a poor relative, he does not acknowledge him; for when he sees his poor relation, he hides himself from him, being ashamed to speak to him, because he is poor. Solomon said this, *All the brethren of the poor do hate him* (Prov 19:7).... If one, however, is rich, all cleave to him and love him, as it says, *But the rich hath many friends* (Prov 19:20). With God it is not so, for the poor are his people. When he sees a poor man, he cleaves to him. A proof? Read what it says: *Thus saith the Lord; the heaven is my throne*, and what does it say after this? – *But on this man I will look, even on him that is poor and of a contrite spirit.* [*Exodus Rabbah* XXXI.13]

107. See below for more on the use of πρᾶος with 66:2b.

108. Cf. Clement of Alexandria, *Stromata* 2.101.2 and Origen, *Fragmenta in Lucam* 163.

109. Jean Daniélou compares *Barnabae* and Essene Judaism, including the Two Ways material. See *The Theology of Jewish Christianity* (vol. 1 of *A History of Early Christian Doctrine before the Council of Nicea*; trans. J. A. Baker; Philadelphia: Westminster, 1967), esp. 35f.

110. Trans. by R. C. Clarke.

111. The derogatory remark is, however, in accordance with what we might expect from Cyprian given the views expressed in Book One of his treatise *Ad Quirinum*, also known as *Testimoniorum libri adversus Judaeos*.

112. Niederwimmer traces the overall Christianization process of the Two Ways material.

113. Daniel Harrington discusses the similarity btw. Matt 5:3 and 5:5 in *The Gospel of Matthew* (SP 1; Collegeville, MN: Liturgical Press, 1991).

114. *Didascalia Apostolorum* 4 and *Ad Quirinum* 3.5.

115. John Cassian (*Institutes* 31) quotes the verse with *requiescam*, according to the Old Latin, and then quotes the verse again with *respiciam* according to the Vulgate with the introduction: "according to those copies which express the Hebrew accurately."

116. Cf. for example John Cassian and *Pseudo-Makarios*.

117. Jon Levenson, *Sinai and Zion: An Entry into the Jewish Bible* (Minneapolis: Winston Press, 1985), 144.

118. Trans. by R. Deferrari.

119. Trans. by J. Savage.

120. Trans. by E. Hill.

121. Note the reference to both Isa 66:1 and Ps 132:4 in Acts 7.

122. Trans. by E. Hill.

123. John Chrysostom also quotes these two verses together. Cf. *Homily on the Gospel of Matthew* 65.6.

124. For the use of Jer 7:23–24 and Isa 66:1, cf. Table 1. Justin Martyr (*Apologia I*) cites Isa 66:1; 1:11; and 58:6. Pierre Prigent sees these as an anti-cultic testimony grouping (see above).

125. See, for example, Justin's *Dialogus cum Tryphone* 22.

126. There are additional variations in this verse in the LXX; however, they do not seem to affect interpretation. The LXX compares only three pairs while the Hebrew relates four. The first pair in the LXX (sacrificing a bull/killing a dog) is actually a mingling of the first two pairs in the Hebrew (slaughtering a bull/killing a man and sacrificing a lamb/breaking a dog's neck).

127. Athanasius also uses Isa 66:3 in an attack on Jewish worship as hypocritical. Cf. *Epistula* 19; *Epistulae festales* 347.

128. *De Baptismo* 7. Cf. a similar discussion in *Asceticon Magnum* 29.

CHAPTER 3

Isaiah 66:1–4 and Martin Luther

Martin Luther is one of the major biblical theologians of the Church. His writings continue to be influential in Christianity even almost 500 years after his death. As a professor of the Bible and as a biblical theologian, rather than as a systematic theologian, Luther centered his work on the exposition of the Bible. As Althaus noted in his work on Luther's theology: "His theological thinking is nothing more than an attempt to interpret Scripture. Its form is basically exegesis."[1] Most of that exegesis, at least with regard to teaching, was of the Old Testament,[2] his understanding of which has endured in Protestant Christianity and its academic heir, modern biblical scholarship. As we will see, this is no less true for his interpretation of Isaiah 66:1–4.

Medieval biblical exegesis was characterized by the *quadriga*, a four-fold understanding of scripture: the literal, allegorical, moral, and anagogical.[3] While Luther adopted this method in his earliest teaching, he soon rejected the *quadriga*. He saw in the ancient interpreters a more pristine interpretation, although not necessarily accurate and most definitely not authoritative. He favored what he considered to be a more literal interpretation of the text. His break with this medieval method depends on a number of factors, including the influence of the work of Nicholas of Lyra (although in the end Luther rejected his ideas as overly influenced by rabbinic exegesis) and the humanists' emphasis on the original languages of scripture. His own work was methodologically in a decidedly different direction, one that incorporated and was further shaped by his theological views.

Luther's exegesis is informed by his belief that Scripture contains both Law and Gospel. Law prepares us for the Gospel message and provides a civil function. Gospel saves us. Both are found in the Old Testament. Thus for Luther, Christ, who embodies the Gospel, is the central theme of all Scripture: *"Tolle Christum e Scripturis, quid amplius in illis invenies?"*[4] The message of Scripture, Luther believed, spoke directly not only to ancient Israel but also to his own historical situation.

The work of Christ, according to Luther, is salvation, which accounts for the central place of the doctrine of salvation in his theology. Luther believed that reconciliation between human beings and God is by grace alone through faith. There is no way to earn justification or righteousness. He saw both Jewish and Roman Catholic worship, as well as that of Enthusiasts (radical reformers), as an attempt at self-justification.

A significant amount of scholarship exists on the subject of Martin Luther and the Jews.[5] His harsh, anti-Jewish rhetoric has been used to back Nazi anti-Semitic atrocities, on the one hand, and has been a source of great embarrassment to many of his followers, both in his time and our own, on the other. In the end, there is no way to justify his views, expressed most horrifically in *On the Jews and Their Lies*, which endorses brutal crimes against Jews. What we seek here is to understand how his views concerning Jews intersect with his interpretation of Isaiah 66:1–4. What will become evident from his interpretation of these verses is the following: Luther often uses Jews as historical (biblical) examples of sin that parallel the sins of the Roman Catholic Church in his own time. He attacks contemporary Jews as well, but his criticisms generally take on what will become a distinctly Protestant flavor: they are guilty of works-righteousness.

It is important to note that Luther's views are not in line with what we found in the anti-Jewish *Epistula Barnabae*: sacrifice, law, and circumcision are not problems in themselves. Luther's literal hermeneutic leaves him little room but to accept their historical validity, and he believes they could have remained valid as signs of God's covenant *if* Jews had accepted Christ. However, for Luther these things have no salvific value; yet sacrifice, law, and circumcision are more than signs in the Hebrew Bible.

Before examining Luther's interpretation of Isa 66:1–4, we will briefly examine the commentary in the *Glossa Ordinaria* with respect to these verses in order to highlight further both Luther's dependence on tradition and his divergence from it. The *Glossa Ordinaria* was the standard medieval Bible commentary and a primary resource for preaching and teaching. It provided an (unofficial) authoritative foundation for interpretations of a passage by explanations tied to important words or phrases; part of a verse was quoted, followed by notes which could serve as the basis for further commentary.

The commentary on Isa 66:1–4 is succinct. Yet we are able to discern both continuity with patristic themes and slight variations from them. Examples echoing patristic exegesis include: the nature of God renders a temple ineffectual; God dwells in human beings; God no longer wants animal sacrifice; the sacrificial system was a temporary dispensation to keep Jews from idolatry.

Interestingly, even similar themes may not result from the same trajectory of interpretive tradition. For example, in the Patristic Era the interpretive tradition associated with this text of the Christian as God's resting place is rooted in a variant present in some Latin manuscripts whereby *requiescam* is read for *respiciam* in v. 2: The place of God's rest is not the temple; God rests in the human heart. In the *Glossa Ordinaria*, however, the replacement of the temple with the individual is expressed by way of the assertion that the just soul (*anima justi*) is the throne (*sedes*) of God. The theme seems to have migrated to verse 1, perhaps through some association with Ps 89:14: "Righteousness and justice are the foundation of your throne…" (*iustitia et iudicium praeparatio sedis tuae*).

Variations from interpretations found in patristic texts include a lengthy explanation of the reference to dogs in v. 3. Deuteronomy 23:18 is offered for clarification: *Non offeres in domo Dei tui mercedem meretricis, neque pretium canis* ("You shall not offer in the house of your God the wages of a prostitute or the price of a dog").[6] The commentary seems to relate more to the text from Deuteronomy (explaining the connection between dogs and prostitutes) than to Isa 66:3 (where breaking a dog's neck is juxtaposed with sacrificing a lamb): dogs and prostitutes are similarly problematic because they indulge their lust.

Another interpretation offered by *Glossa Ordinaria* and not found in patristic texts involves the connection of John 11:48 to Isa 66:4. The Romans fulfill the judgment that "I will bring upon them what they fear": *Venient Romani, et tollent nostrum locum et Gentem* ("the Romans will come and destroy both our holy place and our nation").

Martin Luther adapts traditional (patristic) interpretations of these verses to wage his own theological battles, namely against Roman Catholics, Enthusiasts (*Schwärmer*), Jews, and Antinomians. In Luther's writings Isa 66:1–4 speaks to many of the same themes these verses did in the Patristic Era (God's nature, Christ's role, Jewish worship), but we find Luther shaping these themes to confront the specific controversies of 16th century Christianity. Luther's central theological principle, justification by grace through faith, is a driving force behind his interpretation and application of the biblical text.

Luther cites or alludes to portions of Isaiah 66:1–4 at least thirty-eight times, not including his commentary on Isaiah 66. As was the case among patristic authors, he refers most frequently to verses 1 and 2. In fact, these two verses are among the twenty most-often cited verses of Isaiah in Luther's writings.[7] These references are present in polemical writings, such as *The Jews and Their Lies, The Last Words of David*, and *This Is My Body*, as well as in expository lectures and sermons, such as lectures on Psalms and Lenten sermons. The type of work the verses appear in is not indicative of the function of the verses.

Luther's knowledge of prior interpretations is evident from his use of them, especially the interpretations of Luke and Hilary, both of whose interpretations of 66:1–2a he mentions. Also, the themes from ancient interpretation of this material recur in Luther's early writings seemingly apart from careful exegesis on Luther's part. Clearly the meaning of these verses is sometimes assumed based upon received tradition. Yet Luther shapes these interpretations with his own theological views.

Luther lectures on Isaiah in the middle of his career, between 1527 and 1530. Here we find his most extensive comments on Isa 66:1–4 in all of his writings and, since the text is the focus of his work here, certainly his most thought-out comments on the text. Luther addresses each verse, and in fact sections of the verses, individually. This is not unusual in his commentaries, although he also occasionally comments on multiple verses at once. Despite his treatment of these verses independently, his use of them elsewhere suggests his understanding of them is not so neatly defined. In fact, the verses work together for Luther. In other words, Luther often presents these verses in ways that suggest he is examining them in context of, at the very least, surrounding verses in Isaiah. Although he knows of the prooftexting tradition, and to a certain extent uses it himself by pulling verses out of context to relate them to others, the verses blend for him more than we saw in patristic writings.

Nevertheless, due to the nature of the structure of his commentary, and in order that we might more easily compare his interpretation of these verses to those interpretations we encountered among patristic writings, we will use Luther's discussion of each individual verse in the lectures on Isaiah as a framework for discussing his use of these verses elsewhere. Instances in which he uses verses together will be discussed after all of those verses have been dealt with through his commentary. As in early Christianity, 66:2a often functioned with 66:1. A prominent example is Acts, to which, in fact, Luther often refers. We will address 1–2a as a unit.

Luther and Isaiah 66:1–2a

Isaiah 66:1–2a in Luther's Lectures on Isaiah

haec dicit dominus: coelem sedes mea, terra autem scabellum[8]

Luther understands this verse as a condemnation of the temple cult. He compares the verse's meaning here to Stephen's use of it in Acts 7:49, and he interprets them both as saying essentially the same thing: temple worship is on par with illegitimate sacrifices. However, Luther recognizes temple criticism as problematic. He describes the prophet's words as a "rash outrage" against the "temple *of God*" (italics mine). Stephen was considered to be a heretic because of his presumed temple criticism, and even Luther considers the prophet's words to be troubling. Temple worship is not the same thing as sacrificing in the fields and mountains, after all. *Unlike* the temple cult, such sacrificing is self-chosen worship. With regard to the temple, Luther believes God made a promise, found in Haggai 2:9:

> "The glory of this present house will be greater than the glory of the former house," says the Lord Almighty. "And in this place I will grant peace," declares the Lord Almighty.

Unlike some of his patristic predecessors, Luther does not consider the temple to be idolatrous in its very inception, nor does he find the true meaning of the cult in allegory. Luther acknowledges the validity and holiness of the temple cult, believing them to have been established by God. Luther explains this apparent contradiction of Isaiah's denunciation of the temple with the Word of God by explaining two kinds of promises in the Word of God. On the one hand, there are absolute promises such as those concerning Christ. These promises are unconditional and unalterable. He offers as an example the promise of the blessings to all nations through Abraham's offspring in Genesis 22:18. The promise regarding the temple, however, is not such a promise according to Luther. Rather, the temple promise was a conditional promise. So while Luther's emphasis on the literal interpretation of the Bible leads him to accept the validity of temple worship at one point in history, he does not believe the temple retained that validity. Luther finds his proof for this interpretation in Jeremiah 7 and God's rejection of reliance on the temple. The futile cry "the temple of the LORD" shows not only that the promise was conditional but also that the Jews did not understand this: they had a false confidence in the temple. The Babylonian destruction of the temple underscores this point.

Luther does not clearly state here what the Jews did to bring about the destruction of the First Temple, although he ties the Roman destruction of the Second Temple to the Jews' rejection of Christ. Later, in the next section of the commentary but also in response to 66:1a, he gives two reasons for God's withdrawal of the promise: they do not keep the commandments and they spurn faith and Christ. Thus, he suggests that not keeping commandments (and by this he probably means idolatry) led to the first destruction, as he already indicated that the rejection of Christ lies behind the destruction of the Second. These two sins are interrelated for Luther, because he considers rejection of

Christ to be a violation of the First Commandment, since he considers the Gospel a version of that commandment.[9]

His discussion of Jews in this section is historical in nature: he speaks of the Jews and Babylonians as well as the Jews and Romans. While his claim that if they accepted Christ the promise would have remained does suggest that Jews today are outside of God's promise, he does not actually say anything specific regarding Jews after the destruction of the Second Temple. As such, the historical meaning of the text seems to dominate. However, in reality there is confusion between Isaiah's situation and Stephen's (see below), and furthermore, the historical meaning exists within an underlying christological framework.

In any event, the prophet Isaiah's words provide more than a history lesson for Luther. He applies his understanding of this text to the officials of the Roman Catholic Church. He compares them to those in Jerusalem who trusted in the deceptive words: "this is the temple of the LORD." They are falsely confident that the spirit is with them; they, too, trust in a conditional promise, and clearly Luther does not believe they have fulfilled the conditions that would keep the promise in force. The Isaiah text speaks against the papists, who are guilty of false confidence:

> These promises are conditional, not absolute. The Jews, however, did not understand them as being conditional in this way. Thus God threatens that the temple will be destroyed and that Jerusalem will be laid waste by the king of Babylon. When they hear this, the Jews object, "But God promised this temple," not understanding that this promise is conditional. So our papists, who hold the office of the church, exclaim loudly, confident that the Spirit is with them, trusting the promise.[10]

While Luther's exegetical work here is historical in nature, he does not interpret Isa 66:1 within its own literary and historical context but rather through that of Acts 7. This accords with his basic hermeneutical principles, namely that Scripture is its own interpreter and the Old Testament is revealed by the New.[11] Thus, the situation Stephen encounters, in which he is accused of blasphemy but judged by the author of Acts to be a martyr, is applied to Isaiah's situation. The words of both Stephen and Isaiah seem problematic, but in fact, there is truth in them. Stephen is the interpretive key to 66:1 for Luther. Once he establishes this connection with Acts, he makes no specific reference to Isaiah. Explanation is sought elsewhere, specifically in Jeremiah 7, which provides Luther with the false understanding of the temple for which he is looking. His use of Jeremiah 7 suggests that he sees a contrast between the people's claim of a temple and what God actually claims as his temple in 66:1. However, at this point in the commentary, Luther makes no specific references to details in the verse that drive his interpretation.

celum sedes mea[12]

This second section stands as a link between Luther's two major sections of commentary for verse 1. The brief section points forward towards a discussion of 66:1b and God's nature while also restating Luther's position that the Jews lost the conditional promise, thus rendering temple worship invalid. Temple worship, which was never quite congruous with God's nature but nonetheless accepted, is now completely unacceptable due to the Jews' loss of the promise.

First, after citing the first part of the verse, he asks two questions in God's voice: "Why are you so foolish? Do you think that I am enclosed in the temple?"[13] In giving no introduction to these questions, he implies that they are equivalent to what is being said by Isaiah. Here Luther directly engages the text instead of finding meaning in Stephen's use of it. In this context, Luther understands the text to be a clarification of God's nature, given which, the idea of a temple seems to be almost a laughing matter. And yet Luther has just said in the previous section that the temple was divinely ordained. Furthermore, he quotes Psalm 50:8: "I do not reprove you for your sacrifices." Sacrifice in itself, while not necessary, is not intrinsically unacceptable: "Keep my commandments, and then your sacrifices will be acceptable. If you do not keep my commandments, I want none of your sacrifices."[14] The Jews have not met the conditions that would keep their temple worship acceptable.

In this section we find Luther struggling with a number of important ideas. Since he insists on a historical understanding of the text, he cannot write off temple worship as best understood allegorically (cf. Origen). His exegetical methods force him to reconcile temple worship not only with his idea of God's nature, but also with its historical demise. He does this, albeit briefly, in this section: he recognizes the validity of the temple and sacrifice, he shows them to be ultimately inappropriate with respect to God's nature, and he explains their passing as the fault of the Jews.

quae est ista domus[15]

Luther's commentary on this part of the verse revolves around the question of God's nature. First, he responds to those who would answer the question in 66:1 by saying that God's house is in Jerusalem (presumably, those in question are Jews contemporary to Isaiah, although Luther simply refers to them as "they"[16]). Luther indirectly scorns the very idea of a house for God:

> God is inside, outside, below, above the world. He sits outside of heaven and has his feet on the earth. That is, he sits on all creatures.[17]

Luther praises here the exegesis of Hilary of Poitier, who understood 66:1 as an expression of God's incomprehensible nature in terms comprehensible by human beings. That Luther is drawing on tradition rather than doing original exegetical work is clear. Hilary's discussion of this verse is focused on 66:1a;[18] so, too, Luther's summary (above), in its reference to heaven and earth, refers to 1a rather than the beginning of 1b, which he just quoted.

His exegesis of 66:1b commences with an interpretive restatement of the question:

> What are you building for me? Were not the wood, the keys, the stones, yes, the builder himself, mine to begin with and you want to give them to me?[19]

One can almost hear the incredulous tone Luther imagines to be in the text. He characterizes as madness the very notion of giving anything to God except praise suggesting that it effectively puts God on par with cattle:

> Madness possesses us that we want to give God something, when everything is his and he has no need of what we have. We were not created by God to give to him but to give to our neighbors. I can give a cow something, but I cannot give God anything. Away with the sacraments, annual observances, and all our own righteousness by means of which we want to give God something! You must know that you got everything you have from God and that he does not need what you have.[20]

Luther adopts the traditional association of 66:1 with God's nature, namely God's role as creator and Lord of all, in defense of his theology of faith as opposed to works. By calling for an end to "sacraments, annual observances and all our own righteousness," Luther clearly indicates that he interprets this verse in reference to his theological battle with the Roman Catholic Church. Roman Catholic cultic practices are equated with the Jerusalem temple cult, and both are denounced for denying God by making him "a beggar who presumably needs our merits and our works."[21] Isaiah 66:1 is important for Luther; it helps him clarify his doctrine of God, particularly the connection that he establishes between the nature of God and righteousness through faith.

Luther returns to Stephen's speech to conclude his own comments on Isaiah 66:1. Instead of using Stephen's situation as an interpretive key for the Isaiah passage, as he did earlier, Luther holds up as authoritative what he considers to be Stephen's interpretation of Isaiah 66:1: God *wanted* the temple. The temple of Solomon *pleased* God. But God did not want the temple so that he might dwell in it; rather God wanted to be praised in it. We find in Luther's interpretation of Stephen a view similar to those modern scholars who understand Acts 7 not as a rejection of the temple but a rejection of a particular attitude towards the temple.

As for the place of God's rest, Luther does not specifically raise the last question in the verse, "what is the place of my rest," but he answers it nonetheless:

> He does not want to be bound to a handmade temple; he only wants to be praised in it.
> But this cannot happen unless he first dwells in hearts. He cannot be praised in this
> temple unless he has been in our hearts.[22]

The reference to God dwelling in the human heart picks up on an interpretive tradition associated with 66:2 that we saw in the previous chapter and, in fact, points forward to Luther's own interpretation of that verse, as we will see in detail in the discussion of 66:2b.

omnia haec manus mea[23]

Here Luther reiterates the notion that we cannot give God anything and to presume so mocks God and makes of him a beggar. Since God has made everything, all is already God's. We cannot give something to God unless God first gives it to us. Thus Luther writes of God and his creative power: "My hand is a thunderbolt against self-righteousness."[24] It is the nature of God as creator that exposes as folly the notion that we can give anything to him that he needs. In view of Luther's theological position on justification, this reads as evidence against a theology of works-righteousness. In fact, we will see below that Luther incorporates this passage into that theological debate.

Isaiah 66:1–2a in Luther's Other Writings

The theme of God's nature dominates in Luther's use of 66:1–2a. He incorporates this theme in his other writings in one of two different ways, as was the case in his commentary on Isaiah. He uses Isaiah 66:1 as proof of God's uncircumscribable nature and as proof of God as creator and possessor of all.

When Luther uses 66:1 in relation to the first category, regarding God's ubiquitous presence, Luther quotes 1a essentially as a prooftext to argue that since God is represented as simultaneously in heaven and on earth, God is everywhere while contained nowhere.[25] Luther's use of 66:1a echoes the patristic association of the verse with the extent of God's nature. We even find Luther using the text in defense of Christ's two natures, which became a function of the verse in christological controversies of the patristic era as well. For example, in Luther's *Sermonic Commentary on the Gospel of St. John* he cites 66:1a as proof of what he understands the evangelist to be stating in John 3:13, namely that Christ coexists in heaven and on earth.[26]

Yet another echo of traditional interpretation of this verse is found in Luther's citation of Jeremiah 23:23–24 as a companion prooftext for God's nature, as is the case in *This Is My Body* (1527) and *Lectures on Psalms* (1512).[27] The

Jeremiah text, as we saw in the previous chapter, often appeared along Isa 66:1 in patristic writings.[28]

When we consider these similarities with patristic writings, as well as Luther's reference to Hilary's interpretation of the verse,[29] Luther's knowledge and use of tradition with regard to this verse becomes evident. Luther does not adopt this tradition into a vacuum, however. He is not only unconsciously under the influence of the controversies and worldview of his own time, but he also consciously and intentionally interprets the Bible for the contemporary church, to which he believes the Word of God speaks. While some applications of 66:1a as a prooftext in explication of various texts seem relatively neutral regarding controversy, such as its use in explaining Jonah and Psalm 112, there are cases in which Luther's own theological views and the controversies within which he is embroiled reshape traditional interpretations and give them new applications. For example, in his treatise *This is My Body*, Luther again employs 66:1a as a scriptural proof of Christ's dual presence. In this case, however, Luther uses 66:1a to defend his doctrine of Christ's presence in the Lord's Supper against the Swiss reformers, such as Zwingli. Luther's doctrine of the Eucharist was one of consubstantiation. He believed the bread and wine were transformed into the body and blood of Christ at consecration but also that the bread and wine remained bread and wine; the body and blood co-existed with the elements. Zwingli believed that the Lord's Supper *signifies* the body and blood of Christ but does not actually *become* the body and blood:

> *Heaven is my throne and the earth is my footstool.*…What can Isaiah intend with this saying but as St. Hilary also says on this subject, that God in his essence is present everywhere, in and through the whole creation in all its parts and in all places, and so the world is full of God and he fills it all, yet he is not limited or circumscribed by it, but is at the same time beyond and above the whole creation.… In comparison with this it is a trivial matter that Christ's body and blood are at the same time in heaven and in the Supper.[30]

Luther's interpretation of this verse here is very similar to what we find in his lecture on Isaiah 66, even if the function is notably different. In both cases he draws on the association of the text with the view that God's nature is incomprehensible, specifically mentioning Hilary's exegesis of the verse. The idea that God's nature is beyond human capacity to understand, as evidenced by 66:1a, supports the notion that Christ's presence, in contrast with reason, is in the Eucharist. But Luther is saying more than that God's ways and even God's self are often beyond human reason. The controversy was christological at its heart, and so is his understanding of Isa 66:1a. Luther's opponents on this issue, whom he often refers to as "fanatics," held that Christ's ascension into heaven precluded his real presence in the eucharistic meal. Luther counters this with arguments of God's uncircumscribable nature, a characteristic he believes, as did Hilary, is shared by Christ. Christ's presence both in heaven and on earth is ultimately a question of his human and divine nature. The Christ who is capable of being in heaven and incarnate on earth— and we saw that Luther uses 66:1a to argue just this in his commentary on John 3:13—is able to be in heaven and in the bread and wine of the Eucharist. The association of this text with christology in the 4th century allows it to play a role now in the 16th century controversy of the understanding of the Eucharist.

While Isa 66:1a tends to function in Luther's writings as a scriptural proof of God's limitless nature, 66:1b–2a often serves to prove that God's creative powers leave human beings powerless in their wake. As we saw above, Luther believes that God's role as creator prevents us from being able to offer God anything: everything is already God's since it was God who brought all into being. When we encounter this text in Luther's works apart from the commentary on Isaiah, it serves as proof in his theological argument against works, specifically, the works of human hands. He applies this text in criticisms of both Roman Catholics and Jews.

For example, Luther refers to 66:2a in a Lenten Sermon given in 1518 during the controversy over indulgences. In this sermon on John 9:1–38 ("A Man Born Blind Receives Sight"), Luther uses 66:2a in his criticism of the Catholic bishops for what he must have believed to be their own blindness, namely their "trifling veneration" of relics. He argues instead that the suffering and death on the cross are the true relics of Christ, "not the wood, stone, or vesture which he touched."[31] He taunts the bishops' defense of preserving the legacy of Christ and St. Peter:

> O you poor Christ, O you wretched Peter! If you have no inheritance but wood and stone and silver and gold, you are of all the most needy. Ah, but the good God wants what Isaiah speaks of in the last and also the first chapter. *These things are all the works of his hands, which he has made.* Therefore he does not need our goods....[32]

Similarly, in his *Commentary on Hebrews* (1517–18), Luther uses Isa 66:1b–2a in his discussion of Hebrews 5:7 ("In the days of his flesh, Jesus offered up prayers and supplications....") to hold up prayer and praise as a means to justification over and against physical goods. Here he contrasts prayer and praise not with relics but with the "old sacrifices," the calves and goats offered by the priests.[33] Isa 66:1b–2a is one of several texts Luther uses to prove his view of justification:

> "He that offers praise and sacrifice will glorify me." (7:23) And again: "Offer to God praise as your sacrifice" (that is, what else do you offer when you offer yourself than praise of me?") (7:14) In the same vein Isa. 1:11 says: What to me is the multitude of

your sacrifices?" And in the last chapter of Isaiah we read: "*What is this house which you will build for me?*" (They, namely the Jews, would reply: "This house built of stone and wood.") But the Lord continues: "*All these things my hand has made, and all these things were made, says the Lord.*"[34]

This use of 66:2a to contrast the sacrificial system with faith in Christ is relatively neutral. While it is clear that Luther's use of the biblical text is shaped by his theological arguments, he does not use the text to attack contemporary Jews or papists. In Luther's lecture on Psalm 28 (1512), on the other hand, he employs Isa 66:1b–2a in stark polemic against Jews. As the lectures on Psalms are among the earliest works of Luther, the anti-Jewish view he expresses here stands in opposition to claims that Luther's harsh rhetoric against Jews was the product of the "old Luther" and the result of either frustration or mental ill-ness.[35] Here, as we will see, he lashes out against Jews not only for what he considers to be their own idolatry but also for being the model for all idolaters.

In the context of the rest of Psalm 28, the "work of their hands" (v. 4) refers to the unspecified evil done by those with whom the psalmist insists he is not to be counted. The psalm is a prayer of deliverance in which the supplicant pleads for vindication. For Luther, however, τὰ ἔργα τῶν χειρῶν obviously suggests χειροποιέω, which the LXX sometimes uses in reference to idol worship. Luther not only interprets the works in 28:4 as idols; he identifies those accused here of wrongdoing as the Jews, recalling that Scripture often rebukes them for worshiping idols and statues, the works of their hands. This is more than a historical criticism. Luther uses the historical situation of prophetic criticism of idolatry, applied to this verse, to criticize all contemporary Jews as well:

> These idols they worship are mystical today. And the idols or works of their hands, are now those works which they perform according to their own righteousness, not knowing the righteousness of God. And thus they produce their own works in opposition to God and to faith in Christ. This is their idolatry to the present day, an idolatry that had in the past been prefigured in many ways by all the literal idolatries.[36]

Both Isa 66:1b–2a and Stephen's citation of the verse in Acts 7 are brought in as a scriptural proof of his interpretation of the psalm, and thus they, too, become understood as statements against works-righteousness and against Jews, and in the end, against all heretics:

> Therefore the prophet here rebukes them, because they do not have an understanding of the works of God, that is, they do not know and do not want to know the righteousness of God, but seek to establish their own. Likewise they do not understand, that is, they do not believe the works of his hands, namely, the church, which is God's new creature. But they do not understand the works of the prior creation either. Thus we read in Is. 66:1–2: "*What is this house, etc.?...These things were made, says the Lord.*" And Stephen cites these words (Acts 7:48–50), as if to say: "The

very creation of the world ought to teach you that God does not care about the size of your works and that he does not need your works. All he wants is obedience and faith."

All heretics imitate the designs and idolatry of these people. For in ignorance of true righteousness, namely, that of faith alone, they set up for themselves their own righteousness as a spiritual idol and do not submit to the righteousness of God.[37]

In this context, we read God's rhetorical questions in the Isaiah passage as evidence that the Jews did not and do not understand God's ways. Given Luther's earlier statement in this lecture that "the works of creation, justification, redemption"[38] are works that God alone does, when he cites Isaiah, "My hand has made all these things" is heard as God's condemnation of works-righteousness. Luther's interpretation of Stephen's citation of Isa 66:1–2a not only reinforces the reformers' interpretation of Isaiah but also forces the same interpretation on Stephen's speech.

The association of 66:1b–2a with God's role as creator, and thus the idea that human beings are incapable of giving anything of any consequence to the creator, allows the text to fit only superficially with his explication of the psalm. His explanation of Psalm 28:4 centers on the idea that the works of human hands are idolatrous; this is based upon the use of χειροποιέω in the LXX. Thus I think it is ultimately the Acts passage, with its use of χειροποιέω, that brings Isa 66:1b2a into this discussion as a prooftext. Above, in our discussion of his lecture on Isaiah, we saw how Luther used Stephen's situation (being considered a heretic) as an interpretive key for the Isaiah passage. Here Luther uses the occurrence of χειροποιέω in Acts as the interpretive key.

Although Luther in principle rejects allegory in favor of the historical meaning of the text, his method was not modern historical criticism. He does not seek to reconstruct the original historical setting to ground his interpretation. Furthermore, he sees no conflict in using Acts to understand Isaiah. In fact, his application of Acts to the Isaiah text is grounded in his hermeneutical principle that the Old Testament should, whenever possible, be translated and interpreted to be in harmony with the New Testament.[39] Interestingly, Luther never in any of his references to Isa 66:1 draws on the allusion to the verse in Matthew 5. It is Stephen's use of Isa 66:1–2a in Acts 7 that suits his purpose and best aids him in applying Isaiah to his own context and controversies. Using traditional themes of interpretation, Luther applies Isaiah 66:1–2a to his controversies with the Catholic Church, the Swiss Reformers, and Jews.

Luther and Isaiah 66:2b

Isaiah 66:2b in Luther's Lectures on Isaiah

ad quem autem respiciam?[40]

References to Isaiah 66:2b occur in Luther's writings 17 times, which is more than references to any other part of 66:1–4. While the verse sometimes functions independently, at other times, such as here in his lectures on Isaiah, the reformer clearly understands this verse in relation to the first. In such instances, he draws on the patristic interpretation which uses this verse in connection with a reworked temple theology, which understands the human heart as God's true temple. As we saw in the previous chapter, this interpretation is tied with an Old Latin variant (also found in some patristic authors) in which God is said to "rest upon" (*requiescam*) rather than to "look upon" (*respiciam*). Luther's concluding comments on verse 1, in which he claims God wants to dwell (*habitaturum*) in human hearts rather than a handmade temple, recall this interpretive tradition and suggest we might find the variant text in his commentary on verse 2. In fact, in several other writings of Luther we do find 66:2b rendered as "rest upon" or "dwell".[41] However, here in his commentary, as well as in his translation of the Bible into German, he reads the text as "look upon" (*respiciam/ansehen*).

Nevertheless, his commentary on the verse betrays an influence from the variant and its interpretive tradition:

> "This God cannot be contained in heaven and on earth. He has his palace in a humble and contrite spirit." The most beautiful court and palace of God is a contrite heart and a humble spirit. Therefore, we must all strive to be contrite and afflicted.[42]

Luther gives no explanation here to justify his interpretation. The work simply continues with glosses on the vocabulary of the text.

pauperculus[43]

Luther explains the Latin *pauperculus* by means of the Hebrew ענו. He interprets it as meaning "afflicted and wretched" and applies it to Christ and Moses, both of whom he describes as "poor" (*pauper*). Luther illustrates the quality using Christ's life as an example, noting that he "did not associate with the rich and the wise, but with the lowly, the lepers and the sinners."[44] Luther identifies these "associates" of Christ as the ענו upon whom God "looks," as evidenced in his eloquent summary of his comments: "Trembling hearts that are ready to fall into hell, such are the palaces of God."[45]

ad quem?[46]

Luther continues interweaving a reading of "look" with an interpretive tradition based on "rest": "Here we have a description of the workshop and royal palace of God, who lingers with the contrite."[47] Referring to his association of עֲנָו with "poor," Luther clarifies that the godly are not those in physical but spiritual poverty. He insists God only looks upon or dwells in those who recognize there is no works-righteousness. For Luther this text, whether we read "look upon" or "rest", is about justification, and thus he defines the favored characteristics accordingly. In contrast to the godly who know that their only help comes from God, Luther describes the ungodly as hypocrites who smugly go their own way and follow their own traditions. Not surprisingly, those whom Luther identifies in the category of people upon whom God does not look are some of Luther's own opponents: papists, tyrants, and Enthusiasts. He does not elaborate here on what he considers to be their hypocrisy.

pauperculum, contritum, trementem[48]

Luther begins this section by applying these three words to death, the Law, and sin, respectively, thereby reinforcing his interpretation of this verse as one about justification. His comments here, however, center on the phrase "I will look upon," and in fact, for the first time in this commentary on 66:2b, his interpretation actually *depends* on the reading "look":

> To look and to show the face is a Hebraism. When God's countenance is calm, it means mercy and grace. This is called God's face. This face appears to those who are afraid, as if to say, "Do not be afraid. I will show you another face."[49]

Also for the first time in his explication here of 66:2b, Luther offers an explanation of the text in its historical (and literary) context. In pronouncing that God's countenance is upon the unworthy, the prophet casts the temple and its worship aside. The reformer then understands this event within the framework of his theology: "Here there is no room for merit. There is only room for the grace of God."[50]

Isaiah 66:2b in Luther's Other Writings

The most prevalent application of Isa 66:2b in Luther's writings is to discussions of justification and faith in a manner similar to his comments to the text above under the section headed *Ad quem?* In this context he draws primarily on the three characteristics highlighted for God's attention. While these are clearly favored characteristics, whether God looks upon (*respiciam/ansehen*), rests on (*requiescam*), or dwells in (*habitaturum*) those possessing them appears to be irrelevant, as Luther uses all three. The emphasis is simply on the characteristics and the fact that God favors them.

His earliest use of Isa 66:2b in connection with his theology of justification seems to have been in his glosses on Romans (1515–16). He refers to the passage from Isaiah in his discussion of Romans 8:28: "We know that all things work together for good for those who love God, who are called according to his purpose." He interprets this verse along with the rest of chapter 8 as scriptural proof of his view that salvation occurs through God's election and immutable will and not through anything we ourselves do.[51] Luther uses Isa 66:2b along with Luke 12:32, Isa 35:4, and Ps 112:1 to console those in a state of fear to offer comfort to those frightened in the face of this teaching. He concludes that the Word of God accomplished its work in those who fear the Word of God and despair in themselves[52] The rendering of 66:2b here ("Upon whom does my spirit rest except on him who is humble and trembles at my word?") matches neither Luther's own rendering of the text in his Isaiah lectures or Bible translation nor the Vulgate, LXX, or MT. He presents a question in place of the statement in the biblical text; he substitutes "my spirit" for "I"; he uses the Latin variant "rest" (*requiescam*); and he lists only two of the three qualities, excluding "contrite". His version of the text recalls Augustine's[53] and the accompanying interpretive tradition which reads 66:2b as a claim that the human heart is the true temple of God. Despite Luther's appropriation of this version of the text, his application of the verse does not incorporate the theme of God's rest but the idea of trembling before God's word.

We find a similar translation in *Explanations of the Ninety-five Theses*: "My spirit rests upon him, but only upon that one who is humble and contrite in spirit, and trembles at my word." Here, too, we find an interpretation of the verse in connection with the theme of justification, this time in the context of Luther's explanation of thesis seven: "God remits guilt to no one unless at the same time he humbles himself in all things and makes him submissive to his vicar, the priest." The Isaiah text is no doubt brought to bear on the discussion of justification because of its reference to humility, since that quality is specifically mentioned in the thesis. Luther uses 66:2b as a prooftext for his understanding of the process of salvation, which he describes as follows.[54] According to the reformer, humility, contrition, and fear are all precursors to and signs of the infusion of grace, and thus the Isaiah passage is appropriately understood in reference to justification. This interpretation of the text is not dependent on the reading "rest" (*requiescam*). We find the same association of 66:2b with the theme of faith and justification in, for example, the lectures on Galatians (*respiciam*) and in the treatise *Instructions for the Visitors of Parish Pastors* (*ansehen*). The key seems to be that these qualities are associated with favorable attention from God.

In addition to reading Isa 66:2b through the lens of his theological views, Luther also uses this text against his theological opponents, the Jews, in his polemical treatise *On the Jews and their Lies*. In this treatise, Luther criticizes Jews for, among other things, what he calls the "false boast" of circumcision. He accuses Jews of pride and arrogance in their claim to be God's only people through the covenant of circumcision, and he condemns them with Isa 66:2b:

> …be on your guard against such accursed, incorrigible people, from whom you can learn no more than to give God and his word the lie, to blaspheme, to pervert, to murder prophets, and haughtily and proudly to despise all people on earth. Even if God would be willing to disregard all their other sins—which, of course, is impossible—he could not condone such ineffable (although poor and wretched) pride. For he is called a God of the humble, as Isaiah 66 states: "*But this is the man to whom I will look, he that is humble and contrite in spirit, and trembles at my word.*"[55]

The theme of justification is central here. Luther considers circumcision to be one of the Jews' "vain, blasphemous, invented and meaningless works."[56] However, the use of 66:2b in this context reflects a separate interpretive tradition from the one discussed above, in which this verse is understood in relation to the tenet of justification. Luther uses the text here to criticize pride; thus the verse serves his purpose because it promotes the opposite quality. As such, this use of the verse reflects the interpretive tradition in which patristic authors used it in didactic discourse regarding Christian virtues. There is, therefore, nothing inherently anti-Jewish in the fact that Luther employs the verse against pride. In fact, at least twice before, in lectures on Genesis, Luther uses the verse in a general criticism against those who are "proud" and "smug."[57] However, there is implicit anti-Jewish bias in the fact that he uses Jews as his chief example of the pride that is the opposite of the qualities that are open to God's grace.

Luther and Isaiah 66:3

Isaiah 66:3 in Luther's Lectures on Isaiah

qui immolat bovem, quasi qui interficiat virum[58]

Despite references throughout the lecture to Hebrew words that indicate Luther is working with a Hebrew text, he renders this verse with a comparative, in accordance with the Vulgate. His interpretation builds on that version: God is comparing the highest kind of sacrifice according to nature with the worst disgrace so that even common people will understand how detestable this sacrifice is. In fact, Luther takes the juxtaposition one step further; sacrificing an ox is not even equivalent with manslaughter, as bad as that would be, it is worse. Luther is not condemning sacrifice itself. He clearly does not view the Jewish cult in the same way Barnabas did. The problem is the faithless spirit in which sacrifice is performed. Luther characterizes sacrifice in the same way he characterized attempts to give God a temple, or anything else for that matter, in his commentary on 66:1: it makes God a beggar.

Luther's theology of justification by faith alone and his controversies with his theological opponents continue to be a driving force in his interpretation. He explains the text in light of his own day:

> This is what the papists are doing today. They neglect the big things and do the little things, and yet they rise up against God with their own justification. Therefore to read Mass and wear the cowl is worse than committing a murder. It is not the thing in itself, the Mass and the cowl, that God cares so much about. Rather, their justification on the basis of these works is to deny God.[59]

qui mactat pecus, i.e. ovem, quasi canem immolaret[60]

A dog is unclean and could not be offered as a legitimate sacrifice, and yet, proclaims Luther, God prefers—again, not just equates—such an abomination to legitimate sacrifice: "It is as if he said: 'I repudiate your highest righteousness more than the worst of all sins.'"[61] Luther offers no explanation as to why he interprets the text as "more than" rather than "is like". Also, he directs this criticism against the "Jews and Pharisees," but he offers no further explanation.

qui offert oblacionem[62]

In a philological aside, Luther explains the Hebrew word מִנְחָה as a sacrifice of food, such as grain and honey. He then goes on to discuss the verse as a whole:

qui offert mincha, est, ac si quis suillum sanguinem offeret[63]

Since the swine is unclean and blood is unclean, offering swine's blood is a "twofold and an extreme abomination." God prefers even this to "the highest form of religion."[64] He shifts from "Jews and Pharisees" to a clearly contemporary foe: he reads this line as a criticism of monks for not being contrite (*contritum*).

qui recordatur thuris[65]

Although Luther notes that incense is the holiest sacrifice, his comments here center on that which is compared with frankincense: עֲוֹן. He defines the Hebrew word as "idol," which he interprets as denoting vexation and toil.

quasi qui benedicat idolo[66]

Luther either knows of a tradition which interprets this verse as criticism of abhorrent cultic practices, or he recognizes with the mention of idol-worship the possibility that one could attempt to understand the text this way. He clarifies that the criticism is against the temple cult itself: "He is not speaking of sacrifice outside the temple, lest the Jews might be able to get off."[67] His mention of Jews here presumably refers to Jews in the First and/or Second Temple period when there were sacrifices. He applies the text for his own day in terms of Turks (i.e. Muslims) and papists:

> So the Turk and the papists shun idols and yet commit sacrilege. They cannot see the little sin, and they rob God of his glory. They remove a wooden image and put themselves in its place. Their heart is full of idolatry…. These idolaters are so conceited that they would rather seek their own glory than God's. They thrive on honor. They refuse to let God be the giver. They themselves want to be the givers who would honor God with their merits, religious exercises and hoods. The godly, on the other hand, understand that God is the sole dispenser and giver, and they themselves are poor.[68]

Luther's criticisms are aimed primarily at the Roman Catholic Church. Their performance of what could be a legitimate cultic act is equivalent to sacrilege because of their works-righteousness. His language again calls to mind 66:2: the papists are conceited, while the godly are humble, for they know that they are truly poor (*pauperes*).

haec omnia eligunt in viis et delecantur[69]

Luther reiterates that he is not condemning the act; similar ones were, after all, met with favor when performed by Abel and Abraham. The cultic practices are referred to here as "their own ways" because they are not brought in fear, whereas Abel and Abraham "made their sacrifices in line with the First Commandment. They did it in faith and bore witness to their faith…. Such sacrifices are the ways of God."[70]

Isaiah 66:3 in Luther's Other Writings

Luther does not often refer to Isa 66:3 outside his Isaiah commentary. When he does, he most often applies it in criticism of self-chosen worship. He is drawn to the verse because of the line: "they have chosen their own ways."

In his commentary on Genesis 17:3–6, Luther uses 66:3 to criticize choosing one's own way to know God and relying on human wisdom instead of seeking God in the signs God set before us. In his discussion of the covenant of circumcision, the reformer acknowledges it is a divinely initiated sign by which God might be known. As such, it serves as an historical example and proof for his views on what is appropriate Christian worship. Isaiah 66:3 serves as a prooftext.

The question of self-chosen as opposed to divinely appointed forms of worship is not abstract or simply historical, as he specifies Word, Baptism, and Supper as ways in which Christ manifests himself. The discussion of circumcision provides the background and reasoning, as well as proof, for contemporary function of Scripture. Luther's interpretation is motivated by his conflict with the Roman Catholic Church:

> ...the pope with his entire church, strive to divert us from these divinely appointed visible forms to their own forms: the canonization of the saints, the invocation and worship of the departed saints, and the statues set up in special places for the sake of gain, etc.[71]

Again in his sermon on John 15:16 ("You did not choose me, but I chose you...."), Luther uses Isa 66:3 to criticize human attempts at control over the relationship with God. Here Luther argues that our "friendship" with God is based on God's choice not our own; it comes, in other words, through grace not human merit. Isa 66:3 is the primary proof for his statement that "[a]ll Scripture reproves and condemns any choosing on our part before and without God's commandment." Isa 66:3 supports his claim that the prophets constantly rebuked Jews for self-instituted worship. However, Luther's exact understanding of 66:3 in this instance is difficult. He is criticizing illegitimate worship outside the temple:

> They instituted the use of the incense and sacrifice in every vale and on the mountaintops, where there was a green forest or some other attractive spot; and then they boasted that there they had found the true God, who would now have to be gracious to them. Oh how the prophets wearied themselves rebuking the people because of this abominable vice! Thus we hear Isaiah lament in chapter 66, verse 3: "These have chosen their own ways, and their soul delights in their abominations"; and in chapter 1, verse 29, we read: "For you shall be ashamed of the oaks in which you delighted, and you shall blush for the gardens which you have chosen...."[72]

If Luther had stopped here, with just this one line from Isa 66:3 as a scriptural proof, we would think he understood the line as a criticism of Israelites performing acts prohibited by cultic regulation. However, Luther comes back to the verse after his reference to Isa 1:29:

> ...and in chapter 66, verse 3, Isaiah says that he who engages in such self-chosen sacrifices and service of God reminds him of one who offers swine's blood; who slaughters an ox is like him who kills a man; he who sacrifices a lamb, like him who breaks a dog's neck."[73]

By referring to sacrificing a lamb and slaughtering an ox is he claiming that the legitimate cultic acts are also self-chosen? Elsewhere, as we have seen, he acknowledges that God established the temple cult and the problem was with misunderstanding them. Does he mention this verse here because he sees them as self-chosen *for righteousness*? Does he re-order the verse to begin with swine's blood because his point is not to criticize the temple cult? Why cite the rest of the verse then? Is his point that even what has long been understood as legitimate worship, that which is even practiced by society's most religious, may not actually be acceptable to God? While he criticizes historical Jews, Luther actually directs his censure against worship in the Roman Catholic tradition and their theology:

> We monks used to choose the things that should procure God's mercy for us. I thought, "Oh, if I enter a cloister and serve God in cowl and tonsure, he will reward and welcome me!"[74]

Isaiah 66:1–3: An Anti-Jewish Interpretation

We have seen again and again how Martin Luther uses these verses against his opponents as proof for his theological views. In his lectures, his polemic surrounding the use of 66:1–3 is often directed against his Reformation opponents, either the papacy or the radical reformers. He cites the biblical sins of Israel as an example or proof for the contemporary sins of his theological foes. This is not to say he never criticizes contemporary Jews in his lectures or that his historical criticisms do not imply present-day guilt. However, overall he does not use these verses against contemporary Jews in his lectures. His hostility against the papacy and radical reformers dominates. This is not the case in all of his writings.

In his treatise *On the Last Words of David* (1543), Luther employs 66:1–3[75] in the service of his exegesis of 2 Samuel 23:1–7, a text he uses to illustrate his view that Scripture is understood only through Christ. The treatise is motivated by Luther's desire to repudiate rabbinical exegesis, which sometimes challenged Christian translation and interpretation, especially messianic interpretation.

In reading 2 Sam 23:1–7 Luther abandons the historical exegesis we often found in his lectures; he rejects the interpretation of Jews and anyone who "insists on imitating"[76] them that the offspring to be raised up after David is Solomon, the kingdom is the people Israel, and the house is the Jerusalem temple. Instead, Luther reads this as a messianic text which speaks of Christ and thus the eternal kingdom and the Christian Church.

Isaiah 66:1, along with two other texts, serves to prove wrong the interpretation identifying the house with Solomon's temple. Interestingly, Luther proclaims the Isaiah passage to be the most forceful, while only the two other passages specifically deny that God dwells in houses:

> This house cannot be identical with the temple of Solomon, for immediately prior to this he says (1 Chron. 17:4–5): "You shall not build me a house to dwell in. For I have not dwelt in a house since I led up Israel to this day." And in 1 Kings 8:27 Solomon himself declares: "But will God indeed dwell on the earth? Behold, heaven and the highest heaven cannot contain thee; how much less this house which I have built!" And Is. 66:1 expresses this thought still more forcefully: *"Thus says the Lord: 'Heaven is my throne, and the earth is my footstool; what is the house which you would build for me, and what is the place of my rest?'"*[77]

Using Isaiah 66:2–3, Luther turns this explanation into an attack on Jews and the temple cult:

> Here God expressly repudiates the Jews' stupid zeal. They boasted that they were erecting a house for God by building the temple, that they were thereby rendering him a great service. Over this they became proud and stubborn murderers of the prophets. And yet God announces here that he scorns the temple, and that he, instead, demands *a humble and contrite spirit which stands in awe before his word*; yes, this spirit is to become the temple where he rests. God also rejects all sacrifice and temple worship, saying: *"He who slaughters an ox is like him who kills a man; he who sacrifices a lamb, like him who breaks a dog's neck; he who presents a cereal offering, like him who offers swine's blood; he who makes a memorial offering of frankincense, like him who blesses an idol."*[78]

This is not only Luther's most polemical anti-Jewish interpretation involving Isaiah 66:1–3; it is one of the harshest uses of these verses in the Christian tradition. One is reminded of the interpretation of Isa 66:1 in the *Epistula Barnabae*, if only in the intensity of the anti-Jewish writing. Unlike *Barnabae*, Luther's criticism does not deny the divinely ordained nature of temple and cult. It is Israel's lack of understanding—coupled with their pride—that is at fault:

> God did not have the temple built that they might haughtily despise his Word and, instead, give themselves to much sacrificing, thus to sanctify themselves; but he had the temple erected that his name, not he himself, might dwell there, as Scripture declares everywhere. That is, they were to hear his Word there and call upon him. Thereby he would be honored. But they wanted the reputation and honor of having such a temple be their own, and they murdered prophets because of their advocacy of God's Word.[79]

This view reinforces the idea that rabbinic translations and interpretations which challenge a messianic reading cannot be trusted. According to Luther, Jewish inability to understand what God wants is mirrored in Jews' current mistranslation and misinterpretation of Scripture.

The harshest interpretation centers around v. 2. Luther takes a positive statement about godly qualities and turns it against Jews. Instead of having humility, contrition, and fear before God's Word, Jews are boastful, proud, stubborn, and they "haughtily despise" the Word.

Luther also draws on the interpretive tradition which presents v. 2 as proof that God dwells in the human heart. However, Luther primarily identifies the temple with the Christian Church as a whole.[80]

Luther and Isaiah 66:4

Isaiah 66:4 in Luther's Lectures on Isaiah

eciam ego eligam illusiones eorum[81]

Luther once again sees here a prediction fulfilled in the New Testament: Jesus accepts sinners and Gentiles and is "a friend of tax collectors" (Luke 7:34) because Jews rejected Christ. Catholic monks are modern-day equivalents of the Jews of Jesus' time and servants are paralleled to those received by Jesus. Similarly, just as God "rejected" the temple worship which had been held in high regard, God now rejects Roman Catholic traditions of worship:

> So here the temple, sacrifice, and the whole worship are rejected in the same way the priesthood, monasticism, and every kind of hypocrisy are rejected today. Christ walks like a layman. He teaches faith alone and repudiates all self-righteousness like tow, and he chooses what the hypocrites fear. Today we see by experience that he is rejecting the highest worship associated with the Mass and the cowl.[82]

The remainder of Luther's comments on the verse are very brief and somewhat scattered:

timuerunt, ubi non est timor[83]

This line is not in the Vulgate, and Luther's comments suggest he is actually referring to the following phrase from the Vulgate: *quae timebant adducam*. Noting that what they fear is inconsequential while the essential matters of faith and the commandments go unheeded, Luther continues his attack on Roman Catholic traditions:

> But to slight the maniple [a Eucharistic vestment] or to swallow a drop of water, this is the chief sin. Therefore God says here that He will follow the indicated course of action. They pay little attention to the important things and choose the little things. "I will make their big things small, and vice versa. That is, I will provoke them. If you want to have your own way, I will have Mine."[84]

et ea, quae terrent, adducam[85]

Here Luther offers his interpretation by simply restating the line in his own words: "As they provoked and condemn me, so I will do to them."[86]

quia vocavi, et non audierunt[87]

Luther interprets this line with respect to sacrifice based on Jeremiah 7:21–23, where sacrifice is contrasted with obedience to (listening to) God. Again Luther states that sacrifice could be acceptable, or at least tolerated, under the right circumstances, namely, appropriate belief. *Audierunt* suggests the connection with Jeremiah 7:23 (*audite*).

loquutus sum, et non audierunt[88]

Luther shifts focus here, reading this line as directed towards Germany:

> It is guilty of blasphemy. For that reason the Turk will come upon them. Those who refuse to hear him now will not be heard later.[89]

He offers no further information, although clearly he is interpreting the threat of the Ottoman Empire as God's punishment.

feceruntque malum in oculis meis[90]

Luther dismisses the protest "We are doing good not evil," claiming "they" disregard God's commandments. Is he again referring to Germany? Is he back to speaking historically of Israel? Who are "they"? Luther turns to the next verse without giving any further information.

Isaiah 66:4 in Luther's Other Writings

Luther makes reference to Isa 66:4 only twice outside of his Isaiah commentary.[91] Thus, the verse plays the same minimal role here that it had played in early Christian writings. The reformer makes brief reference only to the first line of the verse, in each case using this verse as one of several prooftexts demonstrating that human values are not the same as God's.

Notes

1. Paul Althaus, *The Theology of Martin Luther* (Philadelphia: Westminster, 1966), 3.

2. According to Heinrich Bornkam, in Luther's 32 years of teaching the Bible he spent only three to four years on the New Testament. See *Luther and the Old Testament* (trans. E.W. and R.C. Gritsch; Philadelphia: Fortress, 1969), 5.

3. For a thorough study of Medieval exegesis as well as Luther's relationship to it, see the following: Beryl Smalley, *The Study of the Bible in the Middle Ages* (Notre Dame, IN: University of Notre Dame Press, 1964); Willem Kooiman, *Luther and the Bible* (Philadelphia: Muhlenberg Press, 1961); Henri de Lubac, *Medieval Exegesis* (trans. M. Sebanc and E.M. Macierowski; 2 vols.; Grand Rapids: Eerdmans 1998, 2000); Richard A. Muller, *Biblical Interpretation in the Era of the Reformation* (Grand Rapids: Eerdmans, 1996); Klaas Runia, "The Hermeneutics of the Reformers," in *CTJ* 19:2 (Nov 1984): 121–152.

4. WA 18:29. (*De servo arbitrio*)

5. For example, Alice L. Eckhardt, "The Reformation and the Jews," in *Interwoven Destinies* (ed. E. Fisher; New York: Paulist Press, 1993); Mark U. Edwards, Jr., "Towards an Understanding of Luther's Attacks on the Jews," in *Christians, Jews and Other Worlds: Patterns of Conflict and Accommodation* (ed. P. Gallagher; Lanham, MD: University Press of America, 1988); S. Bernhard Erling, "Martin Luther and the Jews in Light of his Lectures on Genesis," in *Immanuel* 18 (Fall 1984): 64–78; Eric W. Gritsch and Marc Tannenbaum, *Luther and the Jews* (New York: Lutheran Council in the USA, 1983); Heinz Kremers, ed., *Die Juden und Martin Luther - Martin Luther und die Juden* (Düsseldorf: Neukirchener Verlag, 1985); Carter Lindberg, "Luther's Attitudes Towards Judaism and Their Historical Reception" in *Tainted Greatness: Antisemitism and Cultural Heroes* (ed. N. Harrowitz; Philadelphia: Temple University Press, 1994), 15–35; Heiko Obermann, *The Roots of Anti-Semitism in the Age of the Renaissance and the Reformation* (trans. J. Porter; Philadelphia: Fortress, 1984); Olaf Roynesdal, *Martin Luther and the Jews* (Ann Arbor, MI.: University Microfilms International, 1987); E. Gordon Rupp, *Martin Luther and the Jews* (London: The Council of Christian Churches, 1972); Johannes Wallmann, "Luther on Jews and Islam," in *Creative Exegesis: Christian and Jewish Hermeneutics Through the Centuries* (ed. B. Uffenheier and H. Graf Reventlow; JSOTSupp 59; Sheffield: JSOT Press, 1988).

6. The NRSV translates "male prostitute" for כלב in Deut 23:18. The Vulgate and LXX translate "dog."

7. Cf. the index of scriptural texts in LW 55.

8. WA 31.2:567. All Latin headings are taken directly from the Weimar edition of Luther's Lectures on Isaiah. Presumably, these are the Latin phrases Luther recited in his lecture before offering his commentary. These headings do not always agree with the Vulgate, and there are frequent misspellings. Furthermore, Luther does not always recite the entire verse. Any deviation or omission from the Vulgate is an accurate reflection of Luther's lecture as published in the Weimar edition. The Vulgate here reads as follows: *haec dicit Dominus caelum sedis mea et terra scabellum pedum meorum.*

9. Cf. Jaroslav Pelikan, *Luther the Expositor: Introduction to the Reformer's Exegetical Writings* (Saint Louis: Concordia, 1959), 66, and Franz Lau's "Erstes Gebot und Ehre Gottes als Mitte von Luthers Theologie," in *Theologische Literaturzeitung* 73 (1948): 719–730.

10. LW 17:395–396.

11. WA 10.3:182, 238.

12. WA 31.2:569. The Vulgate reads *caelum sedis mea.*

13. LW 17:396.

14. LW 17:396.

15. WA 31.2:569. The Vulgate reads *quae ista domus.*

16. Cf. LW 29:176. After quoting the same question from 66:1b, Luther writes: "They, namely the Jews, would reply…."

17. LW 17:396.

18. Cf. Hilary's *De Trinitate* 1,6.

19. LW 17:397.

20. LW 17:397.

21. LW 17:397.

22. LW 17:398.

23. WA 31.2:570. The Vulgate reads the same.

24. LW 17:398.

25. Cf. his commentary on Psalm 112:4 (LW 13:405) and his *Lecture on Jonah* (LW 19:44).

26. LW 22:325.

27. LW 37:58 and LW 13:405.

28. Cf. Table 1. Luther also associates 66:1 with Isa 40:12 (LW 17:18). This is discussed below.

29. *This is My Body*, LW 37.

30. LW 37:58–59.

31. LW 51:41–42.

32. LW 51:42.

33. LW 29:175–176.

34. LW 29:176.

35. This view that Luther's harsh attacks on Jews were a product of old age or ill-health has fallen out of favor. See Mark U. Edwards, Jr., "Toward an Understanding of Luther's Attacks on the Jews," in *Christians, Jews and Other Worlds.*

36. LW 10:129.

37. LW 10:129.

38. LW 10:129.

39. Cf. Heinrich Bornkam, *Luther and the Old Testament.*

40. WA 31.2:570. The Vulgate reads the same.

41. *Requiescam.* WA 1:540; *habitaturum.* WA 43:44, 334; *wohnen.* WA 1:52; *respiciam.* WA 44:63; *ansehen.* WA 65:39; *rugen.* WA 23:518; 53:439.

42. LW 17:398.

43. WA 31.3:571. The Vulgate reads *pauperculum*.

44. LW 17:398.

45. LW 17:398.

46. WA 31.2:571. The Vulgate reads the same.

47. LW 17:399.

48. WA 31.2:571. The Vulgate reads *pauperculum et contritum spiritu et trementem*.

49. LW 17:399.

50. LW 17:399.

51. LW 25:371.

52. LW 25:377.

53. See Augustine's Sermon 8.6 and 72A.2.

54. LW 31:99–100.

55. LW 47:164.

56. LW 47:164.

57. LW 4:277 and LW 3:236.

58. WA 31.2:572. The Vulgate reads the same.

59. LW 17:400.

60. WA 1.2:572. The Vulgate reads *qui mactat pecus quasi qui excerebret canem*.

61. LW 17:400.

62. WA 31.2:572. The Vulgate reads *qui offert oblationem*.

63. WA 31.2:572. The Vulgate reads *qui offert oblationem quasi qui sanguinem suillum offerat*.

64. LW 17:400.

65. WA 31.2:573. The Vulgate reads the same.

66. WA 31.2:573. The Vulgate reads the same.

67. LW 17:401.

68. LW 17:401.

69. WA 31.2:573. The Vulgate reads *haec omnia elegerunt in viis suis et in abominationibus suis anima eorum delectata est*.

70. LW 17:401.

71. LW 3:109.

72. LW 24:259–260.

73. LW 24:260.

74. LW 24:260.

75. This is the only time Isa 66:1–3 occurs outside his lecture on Isaiah. He never uses all four verses outside the lecture.

76. Cf. LW 15:283.

77. LW 15:281.

78. LW 15:281.

79. LW 15:281.

80. Cf. LW 15:281f.

81. WA 31.2:573. The Vulgate reads *ego eligam inlusiones eorum*.

82. LW 17:402.

83. WA 31.2:574. *Timuerunt* is perhaps reading the *timebant* in the Vulgate; however, there is no equivalent to *ubi non est timor* in 66:4.

84. LW 17: 402.

85. WA 31.2:574. The Vulgate reads *et quae timebant adducam*.

86. LW 17:402.

87. WA 31.2:574. The Vulgate reads *quia vocavi et non erat*.

88. WA 31.2: 574. The Vulgate reads *locutus sum et non audierunt*.

89. LW 17:403.

90. WA 31.2:574. The Vulgate reads the same.

91. LW 51:39; 31:227.

CHAPTER 4

Isaiah 66:1–4 in the Modern Era

Biblical interpretation in the Modern Era is characterized by historical critical scholarship. While not all contemporary scholarship is such, efforts to understand the biblical text as a product of human hands and thus as historically and culturally conditioned dominate the academic study of the Bible. Such scholarship identifies the locus of meaning as being in the original historical context, and thus while historical criticism does not preclude a lens of faith, in such inquiry faith does not privilege an interpreter to discern the ancient voice in the text. Modern critical scholarship regards the exegetical methods of the early Church as superseded by historical criticism and generally pays little conscious attention to methods or interpretations of pre-modern exegesis.

However, modern biblical scholarship, which has its roots in Protestant theology departments, is ultimately influenced by Protestant theology rooted in the Reformation and Martin Luther. While Luther's methods have not been adopted, his theology of faith vs. works and of *sola scriptura* as opposed to institutional authority continues to shape the work of modern scholars. This is evident in the writings of one of the most influential figures in modern biblical scholarship, Julius Wellhausen. Although estranged from the Church, this son of a Lutheran pastor and one-time member of the theology department at the university in Griefswald holds an antagonistic view towards law and cult that betrays theological prejudice:

> It is not easy to find points of view from which to pronounce on the character of Judaism. … We are struck with the free flight of thought and the deep inwardness of feeling which are found in some passages in the Wisdom and in the Psalms; but, on the other hand, we meet with a pedantic asceticism which is far from lovely, and with pious wishes the greediness of which is ill-concealed; and these unedifying features are the dominant ones of the system. Monotheism is worked out to its furthest consequences, and at the same time is enlisted in the service of the narrowist selfishness; Israel participates in the sovereignty of the One God. The Creator of heaven and earth becomes the manager of a petty scheme of salvation; the living God descends from His throne to make way for the law. The law thrusts itself everywhere; it commands and blocks up the access to heaven; it regulates and sets limits to the understanding of divine working on earth. As far as it can, it takes the soul out of religion and spoils morality. It demands a service of God, which, though revealed, may yet with truth be

> called a self-chosen and unnatural one, the sense and use of which are apparent to
> neither the understanding nor the heart. The labour is done for the sake of the exercise;
> it does no one any good, and rejoices neither God nor man.[1]

Wellhausen contrasts "self-chosen" law with the Gospel, which he sees as protesting against the "ruling tendency of Judaism." Where Judaism is selfish and petty, Christianity is about selflessness: "[l]ove is the means, and the community of love the end."[2] Wellhausen views the Israelite cult, which he sees reflected in Jewish Torah observance, as a Canaanite perversion of pristine Yahwism; (Protestant) Christianity, on the other hand, restores true spiritual religion.

The negative assessment of law and cult which has dominated German Protestant scholarship has had direct influence on the interpretation and application of Isaiah 66:1–4. In his *Old Testament Theology*, Walther Eichrodt traces the development of the idea of God's omnipresence:

> Nevertheless, all these ways of speaking [references to Yahweh's abode or dwelling]
> were marked by a certain inadequacy, and it was possible under the influence of
> Canaanite religion for their misunderstanding in the sense of local limitation to become
> here and there an acute danger. It was therefore an increase in spiritual clarity when
> men's enlarged vision of the world and their experience of God's working as exalted
> above space and time, both of which were constantly intensified by the prophets, also
> broke the bonds of the traditional terminology and defined Yahweh's presence in every
> place in the clearest terms.[3]

He cites Isa 66:1 as evidence of the development of this belief in God, one that transcends cultic concepts. Jon Levenson has argued that Protestant theological bias continues to play out in contemporary scholarship, especially in the Biblical Theology movement, in preferences for prophets over priests and in a suspicious view of the cult.[4] As we will see, this antagonism to priests and cult has resulted in critical interpretations of Isaiah 66:1–4 that reveal the anti-cultic theology of the interpreter rather than expose the theological view of the prophet.

Problems in Jewish-Christian relations are exacerbated by the fact that many modern interpreters do not even attempt to restrain theological prejudice but instead unapologetically interpret the text with a Christian anti-Jewish bias. In some cases, such exposition appears to be in dialogue with the debates within critical scholarship while at the same time rejecting both its basic premise of the human nature of the text and its attempt to suspend presuppositions of faith. Sometimes these non-critical, faith-driven interpreters are openly hostile to critical scholarship. Thus, not all contemporary biblical interpretations seek meaning in the historical context. Usually, critical scholarship ignores non-critical interpreters. Considering that the nature of this project explores how Christians have employed the biblical text in criticism of Jewish practice and belief, as well as the fact that non-critical interpretation is prominent in Christian consciousness, I will include several contemporary confessionally-based interpreters in the survey of the recent reception of these verses.

Critical scholarship attempts to examine Isaiah 66:1–4 in its original historical context and thus to interpret the verses in terms of what the prophet likely would have meant given his religious, social, and historical setting. Generally, modern critical scholars assign this text to Third Isaiah (TI). TI is often thought to be not one prophet but rather several individuals writing anywhere from 538 to 445 B.C.E. Scholars have differed considerably with respect to the exact dating and division of the oracles as well as the identity of the TI community.[5] Opinions also vary regarding the prophetic attitude towards the temple and cult found in 66:1–4. In many cases, the former has influenced the latter. In other words, attempts to determine the historical location of TI have pre-disposed interpreters to find a cultic conflict in these verses that might serve to ground their reconstructions.

Isaiah 66:1–4 has received much attention in modern biblical scholarship both in and out of the commentaries. Several questions dominate in scholarship of the modern era addressing these verses. In Isa 66:1–2, is reference to a house to an actual or a theoretical temple? Is the prophet condemning a temple? Or is he condemning the idea of a temple? In Isa 66:3–4, is the prophet rejecting the Jerusalem cult or criticizing cultic abuses or syncretism? These questions are inevitably intertwined with other issues: the literary unity of vv. 1–4, their relationship to the rest of TI, the date of the oracle(s), the identification of the prophet's community, and the identity of the prophet's opponents. The scholarship on these verses has been surveyed several times in recent years within the context of TI studies.[6] Our particular approach and purpose here is to view both the range of interpretation for 66:1–4 as well as the concerns shaping modern exegesis in light of the history of interpretation and Christian attitudes towards the temple cult.

Isaiah 66:1–2 and Modern Interpreters

The ambiguous words in v. 1 continue to challenge interpreters in the Modern Era. The debate over vv. 1–2 has centered primarily on the question of whether or not the oracle concerns a particular house, i.e. a physical temple, or the theoretical idea of a temple and hence the very nature of worship. The following discussions concerning the identification of the temple include consideration as to whether or not the verses constitute a repudiation of it.

A Concrete Temple-building Project

Critical interpretation of Isaiah 66:1–2 grounded in historical analysis has given rise to questions regarding the setting: What, if any, temple is being referred to? What date can we assign these verses? What is the socio-religious context of the prophet? These questions are clearly interrelated and will be presented, as appropriate, within the discussion of the identification of the house in v. 1.

We will discuss the following proposals by interpreters to locate the house within the context of a specific temple-building project:

1. The house refers to a future eschatological temple.[7]
2. The house refers to a temple outside Jerusalem during or after the exile (the Samaritan temple,[8] an attempt to build a temple in Babylon,[9] or the Elephantine temple in Egypt[10]).
3. The house refers to the Jerusalem temple (the First Temple,[11] Herod's temple rebuilding project,[12] a failed attempt to rebuild the Jerusalem temple in 538 B.C.E.,[13] or the Second Temple around the time of its construction in 520–515 or shortly thereafter[14]).

Among some conservative evangelical Christians there is the belief that the Jews will rebuild the temple during the Tribulation. In his consciously anti-critical *Commentary on Isaiah*, Harry Bultema reads Isaiah through such a lens. He understands Isaiah 66:1–2 as an oracle by the eighth-century prophet Isaiah ben Amoz directed towards the "Christ rejecting Jews" who, in the end-time, "will have the illusion that they can build a house for Jehovah in which He wishes to live as in the days of old…."[15] These "unbelieving Jews" are not poor or contrite, nor do they tremble at God's Word, in contrast with the praying remnant who expect the Messiah.

Bultema directs the polemic in 66:1–2 against a specific group of Jews who will seek to restore the temple cult in the eschatological age, but his reading of the text functions more broadly as a condemnation of Judaism. Embedded in his interpretation is a fundamentally anti-cultic and anti-Jewish position; he contrasts ineffectual material worship with prayer and Jews who maintain their Judaism with those who convert to Christianity. The framework of Christian eschatology drives his biblical interpretation overall and thus his interpretation of Isa 66:1–2. Prooftexting from both the Hebrew Bible and the New Testament (especially the Book of Revelation) provides the hermeneutical foundation for his interpretation. Bultema's theology effectively overwhelms the ancient voice, and he uses the text to advance his Christian appropriation of the Hebrew Bible as well as the temple: God is now dwelling in heart of the humble and contrite follower of Christ instead of in a physical temple.[16] This interpretation is familiar from patristic writings we examined in the second chapter.

Bultema's identification of a future, end-time temple in 66:1–2 is grounded in a faulty understanding of biblical prophets as seers. Critical scholarship has shown that the focus of biblical prophecy is primarily the historical, social, and religious issues of the prophet's own day, and thus the prophetic texts must be read in terms of the prophet's own time. While Bultema's view is absent from what would be considered mainstream critical scholarship because it violates its basic tenets, it is prominent in some popular strains of Christianity and is an important example of how many Christians blatantly read the Hebrew Bible overall and Isaiah 66:1–4 in particular with a clear theological agenda that is at worst anti-Jewish and at best condescending to Judaism, considering the religion to be simply a means to Christian ends. In fact, the support of the state of Israel in some Christian circles is based on the idea that the rebuilding of the temple in Jerusalem will bring on the Rapture, or Armageddon, or other events of the "Last Days".

Unlike the view that Isa 66:1–2 refers to an eschatological temple, the view that these verses refer to a concrete temple-building project outside Jerusalem is grounded in scholarship that seeks to take seriously the historical and socio-religious context of the prophet. Bernhard Duhm argued that these verses were uttered in opposition to the construction of a schismatic Samaritan temple, which was a rival to the Jerusalem temple. He dated these verses to the building of the temple on Mt. Gerizim in the mid-fifth century in the time of Ezra, arguing that they essentially expressed the belief of pious Jews since the Deuteronomist that Yahweh designated Zion as his sole dwelling place.[17] The prophet specifically criticizes the Samaritan temple as illegitimate and sacrilegious. Duhm relies on Ezra as a framework for his reconstruction, and Isa 66:1–2 serves as the linchpin upon which Duhm argues for the chapter's setting within the 5th century conflict.

Owen Whitehouse and Karl Marti also interpret 66:1 as opposing the Samaritan temple.[18] Both caution against reading v. 1 out of context, in which case the verse might be taken as anticipation of John 4·24: "God is spirit, and those who worship him must worship in spirit and truth." Whitehouse insists that Isa 66:2–3 makes clear this passage is not about the incompatibility of a God whose true abode is in heaven with an earthly habitation. Rather, the text asserts that God's voice comes from Zion (v. 6) rather than from a schismatic temple in Samaria.[19]

John Skinner, on the other hand, adopts Duhm's view without fully relinquishing an anti-cultic reading of Isa 66:1–2 that aligns the text with John 4:24.

Skinner notes that these verses indicate that *any* temple is inadequate in face of God's majesty and therefore they stand against temple worship:

> The principle enunciated in these two verses is obviously one which, if consistently applied, would lead to the abandonment of local worship in an earthly sanctuary, and of the entire system of ceremonial religion connected with it (as in Acts vii. 48ff.).[20]

Furthermore, he writes that the view of the passage as a "protest in favour of a purely spiritual religion, without sanctuary or sacrifice—an anticipation of our Lord's great saying in John iv. 24" does "fullest justice" to the language.[21] However, Skinner hears in these verses an "implied opposition" to a concrete project that prevents him from fully adopting this Christian assessment of the prophet's intent and instead acknowledges a different historical meaning. What stops him from identifying the project with the rebuilding of the Jerusalem temple and thus rejection of it is his insistence that there is no indication of opposition to the rebuilding of this temple in the post-exilic literature,[22] and he finds it especially unlikely that either Second or Third Isaiah would have been the "solitary voice" of opposition, citing as evidence positive statements about the cult in Isaiah 44:28; 56:5, 7; 60:7; 66:6, 20.[23] Skinner concludes, therefore, that the prophet must have been referring to the Samaritan temple in 66:1.

However, while Skinner shares Duhm's view that the intent of the prophet was the criticism of a schismatic Samaritan temple, he effectively nullifies the historical meaning by describing the anti-cultic reading as best capturing the spirit of the text. While he strives to offer and to privilege an interpretation that is historically valid, he suggests the "true" meaning of the text is christocentric, projecting anti-cultic Christian theology from the New Testament back onto the words of the prophet. Although Whitehouse and Marti insist attention to the literary and historical contexts renders an anti-cultic interpretation impossible, Skinner essentially retains the anti-cultic reading as the spiritual meaning of the text. Since he offers no textual analysis for this reading, it is clear that he brings this theology to the text rather than finds it there. There is no connection between his historical and spiritual readings.

Interestingly, the interpretation of several textual issues varies among proponents of the Samaritan Temple view, and thus these varying details appear to be immaterial to conclusions about historical context. For example, the translation of אֵי־זֶה by Duhm is *where* and by Skinner *what kind*. Duhm thinks the referent of כָּל־אֵלֶּה in v. 2 is the Jerusalem community, temple, and cult; Skinner insists it is the whole of creation; Whitehouse understands it as God's true sanctuary, Zion.

The identification of the temple in 66:1–2 with a temple outside Jerusalem seems primarily to be based on 1) the assumption the text speaks against temple worship and 2) the view that the Hebrew Bible supports the Jerusalem temple and thus the author of 66:1–2, given his socio-religious context, would not condemn it. However, there is no evidence within TI to suggest the conflict concerns a rival temple. These interpreters seek to respect the historical context of the prophet, but their reconstructions are purely hypothetical.

Two other views for a temple outside Jerusalem have gained little support and are also without basis in Isaiah: Hitzig (1833) and Knobel (1872) argued vv. 1–2 refer to an attempt to build a temple in Babylon during the exile, while Haller (1915) saw in these verses a reference to the Elephantine temple.

Efforts to date and identify the social location of the author(s) of Isa 56–66 stand behind each case in which interpreters identify the house in 66:1 with a rival temple. Absence of a clear historical referent in 56–66 comparable, for example, to the mention of Cyrus in 40–55 has led to undue emphasis on 66:1–4 for the purpose of dating TI as a whole. This emphasis on the issues of dating inevitably leaves interpreters predisposed to finding a cultic conflict in these verses.

By far, the predominant view in contemporary scholarship is that Isa 66:1–2 refers to the Jerusalem temple. Most critical scholars who accept some version of the idea that Second or Third Isaiah authored 56–66 connect 66:1–2 with the reconstruction of the Second Temple or a period shortly thereafter. However, some conservative interpreters connect these verses with a Jerusalem temple of another time, such as the First Temple or the refurbishing of the Second Temple under Herod.

Like the view that Isaiah 66:1–2 refers to an eschatological temple, the idea that these verses refer to the First Temple seems to be limited to confessional circles. This is undoubtedly due to the fact that the view is grounded in a belief in a unified Isaiah authored by the 8th century prophet. Reading in 66:1–2 a reference to Solomon's temple is not a viable option if one accepts the convincing argument that only Isaiah 1–39 can be associated with the Isaiah ben Amoz.

Stanley Horton reads Isaiah 65:22–25 as an eschatological prophecy about the Millennium after the transforming work of the Messiah. However, he sees a shift in 66:1 back to concerns of the eighth century prophet's own day when worship was "empty ritual that honored the temple but not the true greatness of God."[24] Horton's classification of the cult as "empty ritual" is not grounded in textual analysis and reveals his own anti-cultic theology. His only direct interaction with the text is an explanation of the questions in 66:1; by asking where the temple is, according to Horton, the prophet is saying that the temple is not the locus of God's attention, but rather God's attention is directed is the one who is humble, etc.

Joseph A. Alexander, writing before Duhm and assuming the unity of Isaiah, discusses the options for a temple outside Jerusalem and the rebuilding of the temple after the exile as possibilities for the concrete historical situation addressed in 66:1–2. In the end he dismisses them in favor of Vitringa's view that these verses speak beyond Isaiah's lifetime by means of prophetic inspiration to the time of Herod's reconstruction of the Second Temple:

> [T]he Prophet now addresses the apostate and unbelieving Jews at the close of the old dispensation, who instead of preparing for the general extension of the church and the exchange of ceremonial for spiritual worship, were engaged in the rebuilding and costly decoration of the temple at Jerusalem. The pride and interest in this great public work, felt not only by the Herod's but by all the Jews, is clear from incidental statements from scripture (John 2:20; Matt. 24:1) as well as from the ample and direct assertions of Josephus.[25]

In other word, God will no longer dwell in temples made with hands.

His analysis of the Hebrew text supports his interpretation: he translates אֵי־זֶה as *what*. Because he thinks the question concerns quality not locality, he dismisses the possibility that the question is about a temple outside Jerusalem. Also, he defends "ye *will* build" as the simplest and best translation for תִּבְנוּ, thus lending support to the idea that this is a future building project.[26] However, Alexander's view that chapter 66 is a prediction of the replacement of the old economy with the new is not ultimately grounded in linguistic analysis; it is grounded in his belief that the ceremonies of the law had no intrinsic efficacy, functioning only as temporary signs, and his belief that God through Christ has replaced the Jewish cult with spiritual worship.[27] Thus in addition to being built on a faulty understanding of prophets as seers, his interpretation is theologically motivated. By understanding the house as Herod's temple, Alexander can appropriate the text to endorse Christian supersessionism.

More recently, Edward Young has also proposed that the prophet refers to Herod's temple in 66:1. Young, like Alexander, rejects the theory of multiple authors. His explanation of condemnation of temple worship is more complex than Alexander's contrast between spiritual and material worship: he discusses the incompatibility of God's majesty and an earthly building as well as the problem of building a temple without the spirit of true devotion. However, Young's reading in essence mirrors Alexander's christocentric orientation; he understands the prophet to be criticizing "those who built Herod's temple and continued offering the sacrifices even after the one true Sacrifice had been offered."[28]

James Smart finds in Isa 66:1–2 a condemnation of the rebuilding the Jerusalem temple after the exile. However, he understands this to refer not to the successful rebuilding in 520–515, but instead to a failed attempt to rebuild the temple in 538. He cites Ezra 1–4 as evidence of a planned rebuilding project prior to the one mentioned in Haggai and Zechariah. Smart proposes that the opposition remembered by Ezra-Nehemiah as conflict with the people of the land was actually opposition by members of the prophet's community of believers to a wrong attitude towards the temple that offends God's majesty. He offers the following translation and interpretation as capturing the spirit of 66:1:

> "What is this? A house that you would build for me? What is this? A place for me to take rest?" God has no intention of "resting" in Zion!.[29]

Smart locates these verses within the historical context of 538. This interpretation is based on his view that Isaiah 35, 40–66 should be attributed to the prophet known as Second Isaiah.

Smart insists that the prophet's opposition to the temple should not be generalized into a preaching of humility *instead of* temple worship; furthermore, he insists that Second Isaiah, as well as the author of John 4:21–24, are not opposed to institutional worship. However, whatever Smart may have in mind as institutional worship, it is not the temple cult. He thinks that the prophet equates animal sacrifice with pagan worship and repudiates it for not having been commanded by God.[30]

Ernst Sellin and Karl Elliger identified the rebuilding of the temple in 520–515 B.C.E. as the historical context and the locus of meaning for theses verses. This view has dominated modern scholarship in the last century. In *Die Einheit des Tritojesajai*, Karl Elliger insists TI would not have considered the cult to be sinful nor would he completely reject the temple itself. Arguing for the unity of TI, Elliger finds it impossible that the author of 65:11, a verse in which he reads a positive view of the temple ("But you who forsake the LORD, who forget my holy mountain…."), could here in chapter 66 be absolutely rejecting the temple and its cult. In support of his view he cites what he sees as a similar text: in the harsh cultic criticism in Isaiah 1:13, he says, that prophet interprets the cult "only" to be worthless, not sinful. Furthermore, 1 Kings 8:27ff. demonstrates that denying heaven and earth the capacity to hold Yahweh is not the equivalent of rejecting the temple. Thus the prophet rejects only the proposed rebuilding project which would allow for syncretistic people of the land to take part. Elliger argues that the text reflects a conflict between the people of the land and the returnees. Evidence for this theory lies in the conflict recorded in Ezra and Haggai.

George Knight also identifies the rebuilding project in 520–515 as the historical context for these verses and the conflict as one between the people of the land versus the returnees. However, contrary to Elliger, he identifies TI's group with the people of the land and the opponents as a party of returnees.

Furthermore, while Elliger's commitment to the unity of TI leads him to an interpretation of chapter 66 that is harmonious with 65, Knight circumvents the problem by assuming 66 cannot be from the same hand as 65.

Knight identifies TI's group as the "evangelic" group that has a different and, clearly in his view, superior concept of worship centered on the Sabbath:

> They seemed to accept the idea that God's need of a holy "place" had ended with the fall of Jerusalem, so that instead of such a building the concept of holy "time" had grown up. … It would seem that the prophet whose words we have in Isa. 66:1–2 does not believe that it is God's will that the temple should be rebuilt. For him the locus of the sacred is no longer such a building but is rather human possibility, humanity's future, mankind's destiny, broken indeed by sin yet restorable and transformable by God.[31]

Knight's own Protestant "evangelic" views are evident behind his identification of the TI group, as are his supersessionist views with regard to worship: "What God looks for is obedience, *not* ritual, *not* ecstatic worship, but a *personal acceptance* of God's call to be his suffering servant."[32] Protestant evangelical Christians place central importance on accepting Christ as one's personal savior. Knight clearly interprets 66:1–2 out of this understanding of faithfulness.

Other scholars find the prophet opposed to the temple builders because they are partaking in corrupt religious practices (Kissane, Fischer, Feldman) or building in the wrong spirit. August Pieper represents the latter position, accusing those engaged in the rebuilding to have a "worse than heathen spirit." Effectively, Pieper's criticism is theological rather than grounded in historical issues. He sees the temple cult as empty ritualism and finds this fault not only among the prophet's opponents but in Judaism overall. He uses Stephen's speech in Acts as the hermeneutical key for Isa 66:1:

> The spiritual character of Jewry as it developed after the exile, especially in Pharisaism and Sadduceeism, more and more conforms to this picture [of empty ritualism], as Stephen so plainly demonstrated to the people of his time[33]

A great number of scholars locating the verses in the context of Zerubbabel's rebuilding of the temple consider the conflict in vv. 1–2 to be one of attitude towards the temple, drawing on the qualities praised in v. 2 and contrasting them with cultic worship. According to James Muilenburg, TI is criticizing Haggai's insistence that the temple will improve the community's situation. The debate is the *importance* of the temple in relation to humility, etc.[34] This interpretation is not fundamentally anti-cultic, but it sometimes is presented along with prejudicial views of worship. While Muilenburg insists these two verses do not reject temples *per se*, nor do they proclaim a spiritual religion, he nevertheless interprets the meaning to be along those lines: "*Not* practices of cult but humility were requirements of worship."[35] [italics mine] Similarly, Grace Emmerson sees here a declaration of commitment *over* "external" rituals.[36]

Paul Hanson's view is more complex, representing the first serious attempt to ground identification of the conflict reflected in Isa 56–66 in careful socio-religious analysis.[37] He believes TI is a product of a confrontation between "disenfranchised visionaries" and the priests of the Second Temple. Isa 66:1–4 conveys the TI community's rejection of the Jerusalem temple and cult, but this rejection lies within the context of competing plans for restoration. Hanson's reconstruction of the early post-exilic period highlights the diversity of traditions of the Yahwistic faith and emphasizes the historical complexity of the Israelite religion in its socio-political context. He identifies four primary pre-exilic traditions that play a key role after the destruction of Jerusalem: 1) the prophetic tradition characterized by explaining calamity through judgment oracles, 2) the royal tradition emphasizing God's eternal promise to David, 3) the Zadokite tradition responsible for centralization of the cult and its leadership, and 4) the wisdom tradition which identified Yahweh as the source underlying order in the universe. These traditions were drawn on by competing socio-religious groups in the postexilic period. Hanson identifies TI's community as a visionary group, "an oppressed minority faithful to the prophetic tradition", that believes the priestly (Zadokite) group's attempt to rebuild the temple is illegitimate because its theology, namely that of salvation through cultic orthopraxy, is illegitimate.[38] By contrast, temple and sacrifice administered by priests who were "contrite and humble in spirit" would be well-pleasing to God. TI condemns the presiding priesthood not priesthood itself. In fact, Hanson understands the rivalry reflected in TI as one rooted in controversy between competing *priestly* groups (dominant Zadokite priestly leadership on one side and disenfranchised Levites on the other) tracing back centuries and coming to expression again in the Book of Malachi. For Hanson, this 6th century socio-religious conflict is the wellspring of apocalyptic eschatology.

A positive assessment of the role of the temple in guiding the community on the eve of the exile indicates that Hanson's view of TI's rejection of the Jerusalem temple is not grounded in anti-cultic theology:

> Individual groups could dispute over the division of religious leadership in the land, but conceptualization of divine providence was ever tied to the Temple that Solomon had built on Zion. The attacks of certain prophets on the misuse of sacrificial practices and on the false sense of security derived by some people from a high form of royal ideology do not obscure the fact that the celebration of Yahweh as king that occurred amid sacrifice and praise in the Temple united the hearts and nurtured the aspirations of most of the inhabitants of Judah.[39]

Hanson's socio-religious analysis demonstrates that criticism of the temple cult is not fundamentally anti-cultic or anti-Jewish. There are, in fact, several texts where intracommunal critique of the Jerusalem temple comes to full expression, such as in *I Enoch* and the *Temple Scroll*. For example, in the Animal Apocalypse (*I Enoch* 85–90) the old Jerusalem, including the temple, needs to be destroyed because it has been corrupted by disobedient shepherds since its inception.

Jon Levenson nevertheless believes anti-cultic theology is underlying Hanson's work. He argues that Hanson's position is "promoting sympathy with the visionaries" and thereby embodying a Protestant preference for prophecy over priesthood.[40] Furthermore, he links Hanson's view with the tendency of Old Testament theologians to dichotomize priest and prophet because Hanson identifies the visionary group (and the prophetic tradition) as standing outside the cult while identifying the hierocratic orthopraxy with those who hold the power of the cult and continue the priestly traditions of the Pentateuch.

It is worth noting that this criticism is based upon Hanson's early work, *Dawn of the Apocalyptic*. "Israelite Religion in the Early Postexilic Period" is a reworking of his ideas on the post-exilic community, and in it Hanson refines his position on the 6th century socio-religious conflict. He takes pains to emphasize that the postexilic rivalry is a priestly one. Furthermore, Hanson assesses value in each of the competing traditions he identifies, explaining that each offered Jews a way to cope with the turmoil in their midst.

Levenson offers his own interpretation of Isa 66:1–2 in which he observes what he considers to be a transformation in the priestly understanding of the temple rather than a rejection of it or a dichotomy between priestly and prophetic theology. In demonstrating parallels (culminating in "rest") between the construction of Solomon's temple and the creation account in Genesis 1, Levenson presents the temple as a "cosmic institution" actualizing the creation of the world. He finds in the biblical text the roots of the rabbinic view that "…the Temple is a visible, tangible token of the act of creation, the point of origin of the world, the 'focus' of the universe."[41] Third Isaiah does not renounce the priestly theology that equates temple and world but transforms it:

> What has broken down is 'correspondence thinking,' the notion of an archetype [the fullness of creation] and an antitype [the Jerusalem temple] standing in intrinsic and intimate relationship…. Here, the archetype eliminates the antitype."[42]

Levenson uses an intertextual approach, tracing literary themes through biblical texts, post-biblical early-Jewish texts, and rabbinic texts to "crack the code" of temple traditions.

Wim Beuken considers his interpretation to be the same as Levenson's but argued from a different point of view.[43] He develops his interpretation of 66:1–

2 in light of Jewish tradition, which he says never uses these verses to condemn the temple but often uses them as a reference for God's presence among the lowly and care for the oppressed. He gives as an example the teaching of Mekilta de-Rabbi Ishmael (Bachodesh ix), which cites Isa 66:1 in support of the claim that the meek make the divine presence stay with the people. The idea that the direction of benevolence is only from Yahweh to human beings is the basis of Beuken's interpretation; he supports it along with biblical texts that he identifies as having a similar theme (i.e. Isa 57:15; 58:7, 10; Pss 113:5–7; 117:2; 147:4–6; etc.). He develops his interpretation through intertextual connections rather than from a concrete religio-historical situation. He finds in the Isaiah passage a new way of thinking about the temple that is not opposed to the building but to the idea that God benefits from it or needs it.

The use of later Jewish tradition to argue against an interpretation of temple condemnation is interesting but problematic. While it may open the door to the possibility of a different interpretation, a Jewish interpretation is not necessarily privileged. This study has highlighted influences within the Christian interpretive tradition, but presumably the biblical interpretations of the rabbis were also subject to the influences of historical and theological struggles, and so these readings must be critically evaluated as well.

Brooks Schramm, who understands his work to be building on Levenson's and in opposition to what he sees as Hanson's "prophet vs. priest" dichotomy, offers a different view regarding the conflict reflected in Isa 56–66. Schramm identifies TI as associated with the Zadokite priesthood rather an opponent of it. The opponents of TI are Judeans (Jews who had remained in Judah during the exile) who defy the official cult and continue traditional religious practices considered syncretistic by the returnees. The conflict is essentially between the returnees and Priestly theology, on the one hand, and Judeans and their "abhorrent" cultic practices on the other.

Schramm argues that Isaiah 66:1–2 does not criticize the temple (or its leadership) but rather a way of thinking about temple, in particular that God lives in it. What he finds in these verses is not the rejection of the temple but the reinterpretation of the temple as a house of prayer. He grounds this reinterpretation in a particular socio-religious situation and attributes this position to the theology of the Babylonian *golah*.

While Schramm and Hanson have significantly different views of the postexilic conflict, it is important to note that the validity of temple worship as such is not at stake in the various reconstructions. While these scholars differ regarding the nature of the controversy and the factions involved, neither Hanson nor Schramm find in TI a rejection of the temple *per se*.

Most recently, Matthias Albani has interpreted the disagreement between the TI community and its opponents within the context of theological struggles rather than socio-religious ones. He does believe that Isa 66:1–2 rejects the temple itself. Albani, like Levenson, understands Isa 66:1–2 against the background of creation theology. However, unlike Levenson, who sees priestly creation theology intricately connected with the cult, Albani sees an either/or relationship between priestly theology and creation theology: God does not want perfect purity but fear of God and justice; God does not want a cultic, elevated priestly caste but the priesthood of all Israel.[44] According to Albani, Isaiah 66:1 conflicts with the priestly theology found, for example, in Ezekiel 40–48, and the verse is instead best understood as promoting what he sees as a counter-theological tradition: the development of the idea of the monotheistic creator God first formulated in Second Isaiah. The exclusive dwelling of Yahweh in the temple is not compatible with the belief in a universal creator-god: "the building of the temple contradicts the universal dimension of God."[45]

Albani's argument that creation theology and priestly theology are diametrically opposed is not convincing in light of the extensive work of Jon Levenson in demonstrating the intricate connection between creation theology and the cult.[46] Furthermore, Albani's position is problematic because it recalls Wellhausen's anti-cultic and anti-Jewish assessment of priestly theology as fundamentally opposed to pure Yahwism, an assessment clearly influenced by Protestant theology.[47]

Norman Snaith's interpretation of Isa 66:1 is noteworthy for its unique take on the verse: he argues that v. 1 is a *pro*-temple oracle. Like Schramm, he, too, identifies the passage as "pro-Babylonian" (a product of and sympathetic to the returnees) and thus having priestly interests. Snaith, however, perceives in Isaiah 66:1 an urgent appeal for the temple to be built in Jerusalem in the time just prior to Haggai and Zechariah: "where, then" is the house?[48]

Most recently, Jill Middlemas has also read 66:1–6 as pro-temple. Noting the important role of the temple in scholarly debates concerning the authorship and unity of TI, Middlemas examines temple-related references in the 'core nucleus' (chapters 60:1–63:6) in relation to the references in the rest of TI. Her analysis leads her to conclude that the temple is central to the message of salvation throughout TI.[49] She reads in Isa 66:1–6 a proclamation of God's presence mediated through the temple.

The Theoretical Idea of a Temple

A prominent view in modern scholarship understands Isaiah 66:1–2 not in relation to a particular temple but as rejecting *any* temple (in other words, rejecting the theoretical idea of a temple).[50] For all intents and purposes, this view is a criticism of a particular kind of worship, namely cultic. For example, Volz argues that if one approaches the passage without bias and uninfluenced by hypotheses attempting to reconstruct the community of Third Isaiah, one finds a rejection of any temple-building that stands in the same tradition as 2 Samuel 7:5f. and culminates in John 4:24. He acknowledges that Isaiah 66:1 may be related to the temple rebuilding in 520–515, but his interpretation is consciously removed from consideration of that context, because he seeks to interpret the text independently from TI debates. Volz is reacting against those like Duhm and others who would use 66:1–2 as a linchpin in their reconstructions. However, his own interpretation goes too far in that it fails to take seriously the concrete historical nature of prophetic messages. While he acknowledges a likely setting for these verses, he dismisses its role in shaping the meaning of the oracle and thereby renders it meaningless.

The interpretation of Isa 66:1–2 as general theological opposition to the idea of a physical temple rather than as polemic against a specific historical temple is prominent among scholars who de-emphasize the original historical context of the text. Brevard Childs, known for his "canonical method," is the most notable example. Like Volz, he does not deny the possible postexilic setting of TI, but he believes the historical settings are purposely suppressed by editors, and he finds theological authority only in the final form of the prophetic book. He criticizes any attempt to historicize the opponents or temple mentioned in 56–66 and considers attempts at determining literary divisions to be subjective and of little importance. The central problem Childs identifies in 66:1 is not, as he notes, conflict between a physical temple and God's majesty. Rather it is the attitude of the temple builders: "Those arrogant people who feel that God is thereby beholden to them are flatly rejected. God asserts his complete sovereignty over all creation and all its works."[51] That Childs considers this to be a universal theological problem rather than a concrete historical one is evident from his conclusion: "The enemies of God in Third Isaiah are identified with those of every age." They are to be understood "ontologically" not "chronologically."[52]

Childs distinguishes himself from traditionally conservative scholars like John Oswalt and Alec Motyer, who both maintain the fundamental unity of Isaiah and see the 8th century as the normative context for its interpretation.[53] Nevertheless, their interpretations are fundamentally the same. Like Childs, Oswalt and Moyer avoid identifying the house in v. 1 with a concrete building and interpret the text apart from a specific historical context. Oswalt, for example, finds general cultic criticism in 66:1: "The judgment pronounced here is on those who are depending on externals for their relation to God."[54] Unlike so many commentators who find cultic criticism incompatible with the immediate literary context, Oswalt considers such criticism to be prevalent in chapters 40–66, citing 57:3–13; 58:1–2; and 65:1–7 as evidence.[55] While these verses refer to pagan practices and not the biblical cult, Oswalt insists that the prevalent attitude that material worship is intrinsically valid has rendered the two systems indistinguishable. He does not see Isaiah as rejecting the medium of ritual or symbolic worship *per se*,[56] but, to borrow Childs' words, the idea that God would be "beholden" as a result of such worship: "If cult is performed to curry favor with God, to satisfy God's supposed needs, and thereby get something for ourselves from him, we should shut the doors of the temple at once and abandon the whole thing."[57] Oswalt rejects this kind of "cultic manipulation" as a source of hope for Israel's future.[58]

Charles Erdman believes chapters 40–66 are addressed to captives in Babylon, but he argues that they find "ultimate fulfillment in the redeeming works of Christ," and so for all intents and purposes his acknowledgement of the original intent is meaningless.[59] He understands Isaiah 66 to be a warning that forms and ceremonies in worship pose a risk of idolatry.[60] In contrast to temple worship, "*true* religion consists of a right relation of the soul to God."[61] [italics mine] In 66:1–2, the prophet captures the true nature of both God and worship and "anticipates the marvelous revelation of Christ in John 4:24."

Resistance to the idea that Isa 66:1–2 is polemic against a historical temple is not confined to conservative or canonical scholarship. Claus Westermann stresses the distinct literary layers of Isaiah through form criticism and identifies 66:1–2 as distinct utterance from vv. 3–4. While he does not dispute that the utterance was made after the return from exile, he considers these verses to be "as general as the normal language used in the Psalms" and thus not against an actual temple project.[62] He reads here a contrast between a new worship, grounded in God's word, as opposed to temple- or cult-oriented worship. Westermann, essentially endorsing the reading of Volz in content and method, sees this passage as denying the notion that salvation is tied to a temple.

These interpretations of Isa 66:1–2 as condemnation of the theoretical idea of a temple share a common flaw: whether by absolutizing the canonical moment or by some other suppression of the original context, these interpretations are a-historical in nature. They universalize or Christianize a message originally grounded in one particular socio-religious situation without first ascertaining how that original setting may inform its meaning. The unintended result is a reading based not on the text or its context but rather on the interpreter's own theological preferences. The anti-ritualism embedded in these interpretations calls to mind Luther's attacks on Roman Catholic worship and betrays the influence of Protestant theology. Like Luther, even though they do not see the prophet as rejecting the temple *per se*, these interpreters clearly assume a theological system of works vs. faith, project this theological disputation onto the biblical text, and effectively understand the prophet as rejecting works-righteousness, insisting God would be never be "manipulated" by cultic worship or "beholden" to anyone on account of it. The prophet's message in turn sounds very Lutheran, rejecting the very notion that salvation could be attained by any human action. Even Westermann's emphasis on God's word in place of the temple calls to mind Luther's elevation of Word above temple.

While these interpreters perhaps do not share Luther's penchant for polemical application of the biblical text, anti-Jewish or otherwise, I think their reading of Isa 66:1–2 as categorical condemnation of a temple, and accordingly of ritual, is a use of the text rooted in Luther's theological struggles. The hermeneutical key is clearly their distrust of material forms of worship. Alexander Rofé criticizes Westermann and others in a similar manner: "…in my opinion their view derives from Protestant theology which would not admit the possibility that a great prophet such as Third Isaiah would support the cult."[63]

The House of Israel

One final interpretation of Isa 66:1–2 worthy of note is that of Edwin Webster. His analysis of the text stands alone in that he does not identify the house in 66:1 as a temple, real or theoretical. Rather, Webster thinks the house in v. 1 refers to the house of Israel. His interpretation is based on the identification of a chiastic *a-b-c-c-b-a* pattern in 66:1–6:

> house/ resting place (66:1)
>
> trembles at my word (66:2)
>
> surely they themselves have chosen/ delight (66:3)
>
> surely I myself will choose/ delight (66:4)
>
> tremble at his word (66:5)
>
> city/ temple (66:6)

He uses the poetic structure to resolve the ambiguity in the text. God's attention on human qualities suggests the poet is employing a play on the words house and resting place in v. 1 similar to the play on the words temple and dynastic house in 2 Samuel 7. Citing Jeremiah 24:6 ("I will build them up") and Isaiah 11:2 ("The spirit of the Lord shall rest on him") as evidence of where the words house and resting place are used for the people Israel, he argues that this poem is concerned with the house of Israel (the covenant community): it is "an oracle … announcing to the house of Jacob that retribution is to fall on those Israelites who delight in cultic abominations and spurn the faithful."[64] Highlighting the connection between v. 1 and v. 6, where Yahweh's retribution comes from the temple ("Listen, an uproar from the city! A voice from the temple! The voice of the LORD, dealing retribution to his enemies!"), Webster deems an anti-temple reading of v. 1 to be untenable. Webster's analysis is purely rhetorical; he does not situate the poetic devices within a concrete setting.

Isaiah 66:3–4 and Modern Interpreters

The controversy in modern biblical scholarship surrounding proper understanding of Isa 66:3–4 also concerns the prophet's view of material worship. Whereas interpretation of vv. 1–2 centers on the prophet's stance with regard to the temple, interpretation of vv. 3–4 concentrates on his attitude towards sacrifice. As was the case with vv. 1–2, anti-cultic theology as well as competing reconstructions with respect to the context of Third Isaiah are driving forces behind many interpretations of vv. 3–4.

While Rofé finds the meaning of v. 3 to be "quite simple" (see below), the intense debate surrounding these verses suggests otherwise. Isaiah 66:3 juxtaposes four legitimate cultic acts with four illegitimate ones, but the MT does not specify the relationship between them. Differences of opinion concerning how to translate this verse have led to essentially two interpretations. Generally, to those reading a simile ("is like") between the legitimate and illegitimate acts (as found in the LXX, Vulgate and the first of the four pairs in the 1QIsa text) the prophet is condemning normal sacrificial worship.[65] In this case, accusations of pagan practices are metaphorical tools employed for polemical purposes. On the other hand, those who understand the connection to be copulative and read "and" or "also" insist the problem is with a syncretistic cult.[66] According to this view, the cultic criticisms reflect actual practice.

Some interpreters read v. 3 as a rejection of the sacrificial cult but not of the sacrificial system; the prophet rejects sacrifice only because it is not being performed at the temple in Jerusalem. For example, Hitzig and Knobel condemn sacrifice in Babylon as worthless and abominable, while Haller criticizes sacrifice in Egypt. Douglas Jones argues that "he that killeth an ox *is as if* he slew a man" because the temple is in ruins and therefore legitimate sacrifice cannot be offered.[67] These explanations are integrated with the authors' interpretations of vv. 1–2: in neither case is the prophet thought to be condemning cultic worship but rather only a particular manifestation of the cult. The interpretation is intricately tied to the interpreters' views regarding the historical setting of the prophet and his opponents.

Other interpreters in the modern era read v. 3 as a rejection of the entire Jerusalem sacrificial system. This view has persisted in various forms, the earliest as blatant anti-Jewish interpretation within a supersessionist framework. For example, nineteenth century biblical scholar J. Alexander insists that "the simplest" syntax for 66:3 would be to supply the verb *to be*; his resultant reading (which actually reads the first participial phrase as the subject of the second), "he that slays an ox smites a man, etc.", suggests either that the cultic participant is guilty of murder and idolatry or that there is a general presence of iniquity or moral bankruptcy rendering rituals worthless. An interpretation consistent with his translation would place the blame with specific individuals or communities rather than with sacrifice itself. Ultimately, Alexander opts instead for an interpretation consistent with his reading of v. 1 (condemnation of Herod's temple) and his Christian theology: he understands 66:3 as extending the earlier condemnation of the temple in 66:1 to a condemnation of sacrifice. With Christ's arrival sacrifice has become as hateful as idolatry.[68] Isaiah was gradually preparing the way for the end of the old, temporary dispensation. In doing so he had to navigate a narrow path, recognizing that the cult curbed Jewish idolatry yet being mindful of the errors of the "formalist," that is, one who places undue emphasis on material forms of worship while neglecting a proper spiritual stance. According to Alexander, sacrifice was divinely ordained but not intrinsically valuable; it served to contain sin and pointed towards Christ.

Similar theological assumptions concerning the general inefficacy of cultic worship are also found in contemporary scholarship. John Watts finds in 66:3 an insult directed towards the Zadokite priests. Their fault is grounded in a theological error: sacrifices are no more acceptable than the illegal acts listed. These "things that meant nothing to God" are being replaced in the new age with a more direct spirituality.[69] The division in Israel, which is beyond reconciliation, is between the faithful, on one hand, and those stubbornly insisting on ritual, on the other.

Wolfgang Lau also reads Isa 66:3 as a condemnation of normal sacrificial worship, insisting there is no evidence of syncretism in Isa 66:3. Breaking a dog's neck is simply as worthless as sacrificing a lamb. This reading of the rejection of cultic worship is harmonious with the complete rejection of the temple he perceives in v. 1. He notes that an interpretation of syncretism would not be harmonious. Just as the temple is rejected on theological grounds, so is the temple cult rejected on theological grounds. The cult does not lead to a true relationship between God and the cultic participant.[70] Walter Brueggemann similarly identifies a problem with the type of worship. Traditional acts are "recharacterized" and "reclassified" as abominations. He connects this text with Isa 1:12–15, citing the neglect of ethical mandates as the root cause of the critique. However, his ambivalence towards cultic worship itself is reflected in his statement that "the worship acts themselves *may* not be intrinsically evil."[71]

John McKenzie's reading of Isa 66:1–4 as criticism of the cult and not of syncretism is more text-based. He finds no indication of illegitimate worship as culpable; he argues that the prophet contrasts the temple and cult with the lowly not with pristine worship. He acknowledges that his interpretation would mean that these verses stand alone within TI in their hostility towards the cult, yet he offers no further explanation.[72]

While Paul Hanson also interprets Isa 66:3 as repudiation of the Jerusalem cult, his interpretation is grounded in a specific socio-religious situation, as discussed above, and is not anti-cultic. As such, his interpretation compares to that of, for example, Hitzig, Knobel, and Haller, who believe that the prophet judges the cult problematic as practiced but not in essence. According to Hanson, TI rejects the official cult for the same reason he rejected the temple: sacrifice of an ox is no better than murder because the cult is administered by an illegitimate priesthood. TI does not deem sacrifice to be categorically illegitimate; the issue is fundamentally the Zadokite leadership not material worship. The coupling of legitimate and illegitimate forms of worship does not constitute a negation of cultic worship but a harsh polemic against the Zadokites; TI metaphorically casts their worship as syncretism.[73]

Several relatively recent major translations[74] read in v. 3 "is like," "is as if," or offer another translation that suggests condemnation of the traditional cult: New Revised Standard Version (1989), New American Standard Bible (1995), English Standard Version (2001), Revidierte Elberfelde (1980) (German), Nouvelle Edition Geneve (1979) (French), New International Version (1984), New Jerusalem Bible (1985); New King James Version (1982), 21st Century King James Version (1994), Reina-Valera Actualizada (1989) (Spanish), Reina-Valera Update (1995) (Spanish), La Biblia de Las Americas (1986) (Spanish), The Message Bible (1992).

An overwhelming number of modern biblical scholars have balked at the idea of reading in Isa 66:3 a condemnation of the Jerusalem cult, in large part because reading here such anti-cultic polemic would make this text unique within the Hebrew Bible. Furthermore, elsewhere within TI there is positive assessment of the cult (56:5, 7; 60:7; etc.). This text must, therefore, be a condemnation of mixing pagan rites with the Yahwistic sacrificial cult.

James Muilenburg connects the phrases in a way that suggests the same person is performing both the legitimate and illegitimate act: "He who slaughters an ox also kills a man." Syncretism, not sacrifice, is the abomination. He understands killing a man as human sacrifice (he cites biblical references to child sacrifice). Breaking a dog's neck refers to the sacrifice of dogs which is known to have been practiced by the Carthaginians and, according to Robertson Smith, among Semites. Those who have chosen their own way are the ones practicing syncretism.[75]

One problem with a syncretistic reading of 66:3–4, as Muilenburg as well as Westermann, Whybray and Lau note, is that it separates these verses from 66:1–2, at least as they understand them. Except for Lau, these interpreters nevertheless adopt a reading that leaves the verses unrelated: they read in vv. 1–2 essentially a theological relativizing of the temple and in vv. 3–4 an accusation of syncretism. The lack of connection forces them to identify vv. 3–4 as a separate oracle.

Sasson offers a variation on the view of syncretism represented by Muilenburg. He found a close textual parallel to 66:3 in Hittite archives:

> When the army is defeated by an enemy, then the following sacrifice is prepared 'behind' the river: 'behind' the river a man, a kid, a puppy dog, and a suckling pig are cut in half.[76]

He proposes that the prophet is condemning Israel for abandoning the traditional cult in favor of pagan worship. Thus he translates the first clause in the past tense and the second in the present tense: "He who slaughtered an ox (would now) slay a man, who sacrificed a lamb (would now) break a dog's neck…."[77] The Late Bronze Age date of the Hittite texts is problematic and leads Sasson to consider a possible pre-Exilic date for 66:3–4a.

Alexander Rofé's interpretation is grounded in the terminology of 66:3 and seeks to specifically locate those participating in the syncretic cult within a social, religious, and political group. He identifies the opponents by the list in v. 3 of what he considers to have eventually become "priestly prerogatives": slaughtering an ox, sacrificing a sheep, presenting a meal offering, and offering incense. He suggests reading the first member of each pair in v. 3 as the subject and the second member as the predicate (however, he offers no explicit translation). Rofé positions the conflict within the early 5th century B.C.E. The Levitical priests of the Diaspora are accusing the "monopoly of the Jerusalemite priests" of idolatry and apostasy but also social injustice. Although both Rofé and Hanson identify the opponents with the Jerusalemite priesthood, Rofé contends his view is fundamentally different from Hanson's because he is not suggesting priestly theology is itself in question.[78] Rofé's interpretation, however, is somewhat isolated from the larger context of Third Isaiah. P.A. Smith, for example, points out that Isa 65:1–7 makes clear that the problem extended beyond the priesthood.[79] Also, Rofé offers no attempt to interpret much less integrate 66:1–2 into his reading.

Most recently Jan Koole has argued for a reference to injustice in the first two lines of 66:3 and syncretism in the second two. He agrees with scholars such as Kissane and Koenen that "killing a man" pertains to murder rather than human sacrifice. Taking his lead from Rashi, the 11th century Jewish biblical commentator, Koole finds a similar idea in the second line. Rashi explained the first phrase to mean that "he who sacrifices an ox kills its owner and steals it." The problem is murder and theft, not sacrifice. Koole suggests that a watchdog's neck has been broken in order to steal the sacrificial sheep. The last two pairs in v. 3 refer to cultic acts and therefore the presence of syncretism.[80]

Koole's reading of injustice and syncretism does not preclude a critique of cultic ritual in general that betrays a theological prejudice. He finds in v. 3 an emphasis on God's word *as opposed to* cultic practices.[81] This interpretation is integrated with his reading of 66:1–2 and obviously shaped by his faith perspective:

> The ABC of faith is this: that He casts his gracious eye on us, poor wretches. In the light of this gospel the most magnificent cathedral has only relative importance; 1 Kgs. 8:27; John 4:21ff; Acts 7:49f.[82]

In fact, many interpreters who declare the prophet is condemning syncretism frame their exegesis in a general criticism of cult that reveals theological bias. For example, Horton reads the text as communicating God's hatred of sacrifices offered by those who also are participants in the pagan cult; however, he feels compelled to add the following judgment:

> …Hebrews 10:4 points out that 'it is impossible for the blood of bulls and goats to take away sins.' The Old Testament sacrifices were temporary and God could accept them only because they were symbols that pointed ahead to the death of Christ.[83]

We find what I think is a similar if more subtle view in more mainstream critical scholarship. For example, Elizabeth Achtemeier insists v. 3 is not comparing legitimate with illegitimate cultic practices but is listing the syncretistic practices of the Zadokite priesthood. Yet she summarizes the meaning of vv. 3–4 with a negative appraisal of cultic practices in general: "As Yahweh is never bound to the temple, vv. 1–2, so here he is never coerced by ritual, and sacrifices are never automatically efficacious." That she deems cult and ritual fundamentally worthless and not simply qualified is evident from her assessment that these verses free the worshiper from "anxious ritualism."[84]

Recent translations that offer a syncretistic reading (interpreting the relationship between the pairs of acceptable and unacceptable acts as *and* as opposed to *is like*) are rare and include the following: Einheitsuebersetzung (1980) (German), JPS Tanakh (1985).[85]

Notes

1. Julius Wellhausen, "Israel" reprinted from the *Encyclopedia Britannica* in *Prolegomena to the History of Israel* (repr.; Atlanta: Scholars Press, 1994), 509.

2. Wellhausen, "Israel," 510.

3. Walther Eichrodt, *Theology of the Old Testament* (trans. J. A. Baker; 2 vols.; Philadelphia: Westminster, 1967), 2:183.

4. Jon Levenson, "The Temple and the World," *JRel* 64 (1984): 275–298; See also his *The Hebrew Bible, the Old Testament and Historical Criticism: Jews and Christians in Biblical Studies* (Louisville: Westminster John Knox, 1993), esp. chapters 1–2.

5. See Brooks Schramm's sampling of TI scholarship in *The Opponents of Third Isaiah* (Sheffield: Sheffield Academic Press, 1995), 16–20.

6. The most recent thorough surveys are Schramm, *The Opponents of Third Isaiah*; P. A. Smith, *Rhetoric and Redaction in Trito-Isaiah* (Leiden: Brill, 1995); and Jan Koole, *Isaiah* (trans. Anthony P. Runia; 3 vols.; Leuven: Peters, 1998–2001).

7. Harry Bultema, Commentary on Isaiah (transl. Cornelius Lambregste; Grand Rapids: Kregel, 1981); Homer Hailey, *A Commentary on Isaiah with Emphasis on the Messianic Hope* (Grand Rapids: Baker Book House, 1985); H. A. Ironside., *Isaiah* (rev. ed.; Neptune, NJ: Loizequx, 2000).

8. Bernhard Duhm, *Das Buch Jesaia*; T. K. Cheyne, *Introduction to the Book of Isaiah* (London: A & C Black, 1895); Owen Whitehouse, *Isaiah XL–LXVI* (New York: Oxford University Press, 1900); J. Skinner, *The Book of the Prophet Isaiah* (2 vols.; repr.; Cambridge: Cambridge University Press, 1917); A. Dillmann, *Der Prophet Jesaja* (6th ed.; ed. R. Kittel; Leipzig: S. Hirzel, 1898); Karl Marti, *Das Buch Jesaja* (Tübingen: J.C.B. Mohr, 1900); George Wade, *The Book of the Prophet Isaiah* (2nd rev. ed.; London: Methuen, 1929).

9. Ferdinand Hitzig, *Der Prophet Jesaja* (Heidelberg: C. F. Winter, 1833) and A. Knobel, *Der Prophet Jesaja* (4th ed.; Leipzig: S. Hirzel, 1878).

10. M. Haller.

11. Stanley M. Horton, *Isaiah* (Springfield, MO: Logion Press, 2000).

12. Campegius Vitringa, *Commentarius in librum prophetiarum Jesaie* (1724); Joseph Addsion Alexander, *The Later Prophecies of Isaiah* (New York: Wiley & Putnam, 1847); Edward J. Young, *The Book of Isaiah* (3 vols.; Grand Rapids: Eerdmans, 1965–72).

13. James Smart, *History and Theology in Second Isaiah* (Philadelphia: Westminster, 1965).

14. Paul D. Hanson, *Dawn of the Apocalyptic* (rev. ed.; Philadelphia: Fortress, 1979); Brooks Schramm, *The Opponents of Third Isaiah* (Sheffield: Sheffield Academic Press, 1995); R. Whybray, *Isaiah 40–66* (London: Oliphants, 1979); Hugo Gressman, *Über die in Jes. C. 56–66 vorausgesetzen zeitgeschichtlichen Verhältnisse* (Göttingen: Dieterich, 1898); Georg Fohrer, *Das Buch Jesaja* (rev. ed.; Zurich: Zwingli, 1966); Young, *The Book of Isaiah*; Hans Lubsczyk, *Das Buch Jesaja* (2 vols.; Düsseldorf: Patmos, 1970–72); Ernst Sellin, *Das rätsel der Deuterojesajanischen Buches* (Leipzig: A. Deichert, 1908); Karl Elliger, *Die Einheit des Tritojesaia*

(5th ed.; Stuttgart: Kohlhammer, 1928); Eberhard Sehmsdorf, "Studien zur Redaktionsgeschichte von Jesaja 56–66," *ZAW* 84 (1972): 517–576; Karl Pauritsch, *Die Neue Gemeinde: Gott sammelt Ausgestossene und Arme (Jesaia 56–66)* (Rome: Biblical Institute Press, 1971); Walter Brueggemann, *Isaiah* (2 vols.; Louisville: Westminster John Knox, 1998); John J. Collins, *Isaiah* (Collegeville, MN: Liturgical Press, 1986); Grace Emmerson, *Isaiah 56–66* (Sheffield: JSOT Press, 1992); Elizabeth Achtemeier, *The Community and Message of Isaiah 56– 66* (Minneapolis: Augsburg Publishing House, 1982); R. E. Clements, *God and Temple* (Oxford: Basil Blackwell, 1965); A. S. Herbert, *Isaiah 40–66* (Cambridge: Cambridge University Press, 1975); George Knight, *The New Israel: A Commentary on the Book of Isaiah 56– 66* (Grand Rapids: Eerdmans, 1985); Jan Koole, *Isaiah*; Hans-Joachim Kraus, *Das Evangelium der unbekannten Propheten Jesaja 40–66* (Neukirchen-Vluyn: Neukirchener Verlag, 1990); John Mckenzie, *Second Isaiah* (*AB* 20; Garden City: Doubleday, 1968); James Muilenburg, *The Book of Isaiah: Chapters 40–66* (IB V; Nashville: Abingdon Press, 1956); Alexander Rofé, "Isaiah 66:1–4: Judean sects in the Persian Period as Viewed by Trito-Isaiah," in *Biblical and Related Studies Presented to Samuel Iwry* (ed. A. Kort and S. Morschausen; Winona Lake: Eisenbrauns, 1985), 205–217; John Sawyer, *Isaiah* (2 vols.; Philadelphia: Westminster, 1984–86); John Scullion, *Isaiah 40–66* (Wilmington, DE: Michael Glazier, 1982); Seizo Sekine, *Die Tritojesanische Sammlung (Jes 56–66) redaktionsgeschichtlich untersucht* (Berlin: de Gruyter, 1989); Johann Fischer, *Das Buch Isaias* (Bonn: Hanstein, 1939); Edward Kissane, *The Book of Isaiah* (rev. ed.; Dublin: Browne and Nolan, 1960); P.A. Smith, *Rhetoric and Redaction in Trito-Isaiah*; John Watts, *Isaiah 34–66* (Waco: Word Books, 1987).

15. Bultema, *A Commentary on Isaiah*, 623.

16. This interpretation that God dwells in the human heart instead of the temple is also adopted by the following: H. A. Ironside, *Isaiah* (Neptune, NJ: Loizequx, 2000); John McKenna, *Second Isaiah* (Dallas: Word Books, 1994); J. A. Motyer, *Isaiah: An Introduction and Commentary* (Leicester: Inter-Varsity Press, 1999) and John Oswalt, *The Book of Isaiah, Chapters 40–66* (Grand Rapids: Eerdmans, 1998).

17. Bernard Duhm, *Das Buch Jesaia*, 481.

18. Owen Whitehouse, *Isaiah XL–LXVI* and Karl Marti, *Das Buch Jesaja*.

19. Owen Whitehouse, *Isaiah XL–LXVI*, 328.

20. Skinner, *Isaiah: Chapters XL–XLVI*, 244.

21. John Skinner, *Isaiah: Chapters XL–XLVI*, 245. One wonders if for Skinner the "fullest justice" of the language is despite the prophet's intent and divinely ordained. Such a view would clearly represent the abandonment of historical-critical scholarship.

22. He makes no mention of the disagreement over the temple rebuilding indicated in Haggai 1.

23. John Skinner, *Isaiah: Chapters XL–XLVI*, 245.

24. Stanley Horton, *Isaiah*, 463.

25. Joseph A. Alexander, *The Later Prophecies of Isaiah*, 472.

26. Joseph A. Alexander, *The Later Prophecies of Isaiah*, 470.

27. Joseph A. Alexander, *The Later Prophecies of Isaiah*, viff.

28. Edward Young, *The Book of Isaiah*, 3:519.

29. James Smart, *History and Theology in Second Isaiah*, 287.

30. James Smart, *History and Theology in Second Isaiah*, 286.

31. George Knight, *The New Israel: A Commentary on the Book of Isaiah 56–66*, 101–102.

32. George Knight, *The New Israel: A Commentary on the Book of Isaiah 56–66*, 104. Italics mine.

33. August Pieper, *Isaiah II: An Exposition of Isaiah 40–66* (Milwaukee: Northwestern Press, 1979), 683.

34. Cf. also R. N. Whybray, *Isaiah 40–66*; Collins, *Isaiah*; Walter Brueggemann, *Isaiah*; Grace Emmerson, *Isaiah 56–66*.

35. James Muilenburg, *The Book of Isaiah: Chapters 40–66*, 760.

36. Grace Emmerson, *Isaiah 56–66*, 55.

37. Paul Hanson's view regarding the conflict within the community reflected in Isa 56–66 was first put forth in *Dawn of the Apocalyptic*. In "Israelite Religion in the Early Postexilic Period," in *Ancient Israelite Religion*, he develops and refines his position. This analysis draws on both works.

38. Paul Hanson, *Dawn of the Apocalyptic*, 168–186.

39. Paul Hanson, "Israelite Religion in the Early Postexilic Period", 489.

40. See Jon Levenson, "The Temple and the World."

41. Jon Levenson, "The Temple and the World," 283.

42. Jon Levenson, "The Temple and the World," 296.

43. Wim Beuken, "Does Trito-Isaiah Reject the Temple? An Intertextual Inquiry into Isaiah 66:1–6," in *Intertextuality in Biblical Writings: Essays in Honour of Bas van Lersel* (ed. S. Draisma; Kampen: Uitgeversmaatschappij J. H. Kok, 1989), 53–66.

44. Matthias Albani, "„Wo sollte ein Haus sein, das ihr mir bauen könntet?" (Jes 66,1): Schöpfung als Tempel JHWHs?" in *Gemeinde ohne Tempel* (Tübingen: Mohr Siebeck, 1999), 48.

45. Matthias Albani, "*„Wo sollte ein Haus sein, das ihr mir bauen könntet?"* (Jes 66,1): Schöpfung als Tempel JHWHs?" 55.

46. In addition to "The Temple and the World," see, for example, Jon Levenson, *Theology of the Program of Restoration of Ezekiel 40–48* and *Creation and the Persistence of Evil*.

47. A similar blatantly anti-cultic interpretation is present in the work of several other contemporary German scholars, such as Wolgang Lau, Klaus Koenen and Seizo Sekine.

48. Norman Snaith, "Isaiah 40–66: A Study of the Teaching of the Second Isaiah and Its Consequences," in *Studies on the Second Part of the Book of Isaiah* (VTSup. XIV; Leiden: E. J. Brill, 1967), 241.

49. Jill Middlemas, "Divine Reversal and the Role of the Temple in Third-Isaiah," in *Temple and Worship in Biblical Israel* (London: T&T Clark, 2005), 178.

50. Cf. Wolfgang Lau, *Schriftgelehrte Prophetie in Jes 56–66* (Berlin: Walter de Gruyter, 1994); S. Clive Thexton, *Isaiah 40–66* (London: Epworth, 1959); Claus Westermann, *Isaiah 40–66* (trans. D. Stalker; London: SCM, 1969); Edward König, *The Exiles' Book of Consolation Contained in Isaiah XL–LXVI* (trans. J. A. Selbie; Edinburgh: T & T Clark, 1899); Brevard Childs, *Isaiah* (Louisville: Westminster John Knox, 2001); John Oswalt, *The Book of Isaiah, Chapters 40–66*; H.A. Ironside, *Isaiah*; John McKenna, *Second Isaiah*; Christopher Seitz, *The Book of Isaiah 40–66* (NIB VI; Nashville: Abingdon, 2000); Paul Volz, *Jesaia II: übersetz und erklärt* (KAT 9; Leipzig: Deichertsche, 1932); Charles Erdman, *The Book of Isaiah: An Exposition* (Westwood, NJ Revell, 1954).

51. Brevard Childs, *Isaiah*, 540.

52. Brevard Childs, *Isaiah*, 546.

53. Brevard Childs, *Isaiah*, 3.

54. John Oswalt, *The Book of Isaiah, Chapters 40–66*, 665.

55. John Oswalt, *The Book of Isaiah, Chapters 40–66*, 666, n16.

56. In fact, Oswalt argues that if a person is not willing to honor God with "costly symbolism", then God probably does not dwell in that person's heart. (667)

57. John Oswalt, *The Book of Isaiah, Chapters 40–66*, 667.

58. John Oswalt, *The Book of Isaiah, Chapters 40–66*, 666.

59. While he sees the early postexilic period as the focus of the oracle, he does not understand it to be the historical context of the author. Chapter 66 is inspired prophecy from the author of Isaiah 1.

60. Charles Erdman, *The Book of Isaiah: An Exposition*, 14, 157.

61. Charles Erdman, *The Book of Isaiah: An Exposition*, 157–158.

62. Claus Westermann, *Isaiah 40–66*, 412. Lau, *Schriftgelehrte Prophetie in Jes 56–66*, also stresses the connection between Isa 66:1 and the Psalms. He, too, refuses to read v. 1 as opposition to a concrete historical situation and understands the verse instead to be a one-of-a-kind biblical statement theologically opposing *any* temple.

63. Alexander Rofé, "Isa 66:1–4: Judean Sects in the Persian Period as Viewed by TI," 208.

64. Edwin Webster, "A Rhetorical Study of Isaiah 66," *JSOT* 34 (1986): 93–108.

65. Cf. Georg Fohrer, *Das Buch Jesaja*; Paul Hanson, *Dawn of the Apocalyptic*; Wolfgang Lau, *Schriftgelehrte Prophetie in Jes 56–66*; John Watts, *Isaiah 34–66*; Joseph A. Alexander, *The Later Prophecies of Isaiah*; Pauritsch, *Die Neue Gemeinde: Gott sammelt Ausgestossene und Arme (Jesaia 56–66)*; Sawyer, *Isaiah*; John Oswalt, *The Book of Isaiah, Chapters 40–66*; John McKenzie, *Second Isaiah*; John Scullion, *Isaiah 40–66*; George Knight, *The New Israel: A Commentary on the Book of Isaiah 56–66*; Seizo Sekine, *Die Tritojesanische Sammlung (Jes 56–66) redaktionsgeschichtlich untersuch*; Edward Young, *The Book of Isaiah*; Smart, *History and Theology in Second Isaiah*; Charles Erdman, *The Book of Isaiah: An Exposition*.

66. Cf. Paul Volz, *Jesaia II: übersetz und erklärt*; James Muilenburg, *The Book of Isaiah: Chapters 40–66*; Claus Westermann, *Isaiah 40–66*; R. N. Whybray, *Isaiah 40–66*; Brooks Schramm, *The Opponents of Third Isaiah*; Norman Snaith, "Isaiah 40–66: A Study of the Teaching of the Second Isaiah and Its Consequences;" Grace Emmerson, *Isaiah 56–66*; P.A. Smith, *Rhetoric and Redaction in Third Isaiah*; Wim Beuken, "Does Trito-Isaiah Reject the Temple? An Intertextual Inquiry into Isaiah 66:1–6;" Brevard Childs, *Isaiah*; Edward König, *The Exiles' Book of Consolation Contained in Isaiah XL–LXVI*; Karl Marti, *Das Buch Jesaja*; Elizabeth Achtemeier, *The Community and Message of Isaiah 56–66*; Jack Murad Sasson, "Isaiah LXVI 3–4a," *VT* 26 (1976):199–207; Jan Koole, *Isaiah*; Fischer, *Das Buch Isaias*; Werner Kessler, *Gott geht es um das Ganze: Jesaja 56–66 und Jesaja 24–27* (Stuttgart: Calwer, 1967).

67. Douglas Jones, *Isaiah 56–66 and Joel* (London: SCM, 1964), 117.

68. Joseph A. Alexander, *The Later Prophecies of Isaiah*, 469ff.

69. John Watts, *Isaiah 34–66*, 354.

70. Wolfgang Lau, *Schriftgelehrte Prophetie in Jes 56–66*, 173ff.

71. Walter Brueggemann, *Isaiah 40–66*, 252ff. Italics mine.

72. John McKenzie, *Second Isaiah*, 203.

73. Hanson translates v. 3 using a copulative ("Who slaughters an ox *and* kills a man," etc.), but he interprets the prophet to be equating the legitimate and illegitimate acts. See Hanson, *Dawn of the Apocalyptic*, 164, 179.

74. Based on a survey of *BibleWorks for Windows*. Version 5.0.034a. 1998/2000.

75. James Muilenburg, *The Book of Isaiah: Chapters 40–66*, 76ff.

76. Translation follows H. M. Kümmel, *Ersatzrituale fur den Hethitischen König* (Studien zu den Boghazkoey-texten, 3; 1967), 151. Quoted in Sasson, "Isaiah LXVI 3–4a", 205.

77. Jack Murad Sasson, "Isaiah LXVI 3–4a," 199–207.

78. Alexander Rofé, "Isaiah 66:1–4: Judean Sects in the Persian Period as Viewed by Trito-Isaiah," 205–217. Brooks Schramm adopts this basic view into his own understanding of the text.

79. P. A. Smith, *Rhetoric and Redaction in Third Isaiah*, 157f.

80. Jan Koole, *Isaiah*, 3:478f.

81. Jan Koole, *Isaiah*, 3:469.

82. Jan Koole, *Isaiah*, 468.

83. Stanley Horton, *Isaiah*, 464.

84. Elizabeth Achtemeier, *The Community and Message of Isaiah 56–66*, 141.

85. JPS (1917) translates 66:3 exactly as the KJV: "He that killeth an ox is as if he slew a man," etc.

Conclusion

The analysis of texts from the Patristic Era, Luther's writings, and the Modern Era has demonstrated that Christian exegesis of Isa 66:1–4 has often been theologically motivated and that the anti-cultic interpretations of these verses are a Christian imposition on the text. In illuminating the theological components effecting the interpretation of Isa 66:1–4, this book has also shed light overall on anti-cultic biblical interpretation, exposing the use of the biblical text for the purpose of polemic against Jews as grounded in eisegesis not exegesis. The results of this study call for a re-evaluation of interpretations that support anti-Jewish readings of the Hebrew Bible. After reviewing my findings regarding Isa 66:1–4 and the history of its reception, I will discuss their implications for the role of biblical interpretation in Jewish-Christian relations.

In the first chapter, my analysis of the Isa 66:1–4 revealed a text theologically aligned with the official cult during the period of the restoration in Jerusalem. The prophet proclaims the simultaneous transcendence and immanence of Yahweh and contrasts not material with spiritual worship but God's nature with human nature and God's desires with human choices. Furthermore, TI asserts Yahweh alone as the one who brings salvation and restores Israel, including the temple. The theology in Isa 66 views the temple positively as the locus of God's emanating presence. This proclamation occurs alongside a condemnation of the prophet's opponents for their theological ineptitude as well as their syncretistic practices. TI effectively casts his opponents as God's opponents; however, their identification proves difficult to ascertain, and as demonstrated in chapters two through four, Christians have time and again directed the polemic within Isa 66:1–4 against their own theological opponents, and thus theological controversy accounts in part for the misunderstanding of the text within the Christian tradition.

In chapter two we saw that issues of identity shaped the biblical interpretation of patristic authors. Often, specific interpretations arose out of particular needs of Christians to define and defend their beliefs in response to debates concerning Jewish law, Gnosticism, and philosophical ideas. The biblical text functioned similarly in christological debates. Isaiah 66:1–4 played an important role in these various interactions, meeting the needs for a biblically based 1) condemnation of Judaism, 2) defense of God's majesty, and 3) clarification of the role of Christ. The interpretation of the Bible, including Isa 66:1–4, was invariably shaped by theological necessity.

In chapter three I showed how Martin Luther carved what he received as traditional Christian interpretation of these texts in response to and to fit his own theological needs. He used Isaiah 66:1–4 in his confrontations with Roman Catholics, Enthusiasts, Jews, and Antinomians to condemn what he believed to be their common sin of works-righteousness. His anti-cultic interpretations of these verses were grounded in his theology of justification by grace through faith. Luther viewed Jews and other Christians in his own terms through an anti-cultic theological framework of works vs. faith.

Finally, in chapter four, I illustrated how critical biblical scholarship, dominated until recently by Protestant scholars, has inherited Luther's theological lens. Despite attempts at confessional objectivity, Protestant theology and its animosity towards cultic worship have influenced the reading of Isa 66:1–4 in the modern era. Furthermore, difficulties affixing a firm date to the oracles of Third Isaiah also prove problematic for interpreting these verses, predisposing historical critics to identify conflict surrounding the temple cult in order to provide a much-needed historical referent.

By revealing the function of theology in the Christian reception of Isa 66:1–4 this study has demonstrated that the interpreter's presuppositions and biases have shaped the use of the text time after time throughout the history of Christian interpretation. These findings are significant for our understanding of Isaiah 66:1–4, but they have further repercussions as well. Faulty anti-cultic interpretation of these verses has been detrimental for Jewish-Christian relations. The detailed analysis of how a passage can be and indeed has been manipulated for polemical purposes has important implications regarding the role of biblical exegetes and exegesis in church and synagogue relations and in Christian identity. I would like to discuss five areas of application for which this study offers insight for strengthening the relationship between Jews and Christians:

1.   The work of the academy and its sometimes limited importance for the Church
2.   The limited role of exegetical method for improving Jewish-Christian relations
3.   The need for Christians to be attentive to Jewish interpretations as well as Jewish self-understanding
4.   The Christian relationship with the Hebrew Bible

5. The role of controversy in biblical interpretation and in Jewish-Christian relations.

The Work of the Academy and Its Importance for the Church

There is no question that Christianity has made great strides in working to improve Jewish-Christian relations. The post-Holocaust decades have been rife with serious reflection of Christianity's contribution to anti-Semitism resulting in efforts to develop mutual respect between the two religious traditions. To this end, mainline Protestants and Roman Catholics have made fundamental changes in their theology. For example, they have officially affirmed God's continuing covenant with Jews and rejected substitution theology whereby the Church understood itself to be a replacement for the Jewish people as God's covenant community. Furthermore, although this study has focused on ways in which biblical scholarship has been problematic for Jewish-Christian relations, biblical scholarship in recent decades has also assisted in improving relations. For example, many scholars have emphasized the importance of understanding Jesus and the New Testament against the background of the Hebrew Bible and within the context of first century Judaism and thereby highlighted connections between the two religions.

There have been countless books and articles that have in various ways nurtured Jewish-Christian dialogue and mutual respect. Yet despite the progress made in this area, the laity still often reads the Hebrew Bible from a christocentric and/or supersessionist perspective. Every semester eighteen year old college students from a wide variety of denominations walk into my Introduction to the Hebrew Bible course with the hermeneutical expectation that the text is fundamentally Christian. Clearly the Church, and perhaps our culture, still teaches a supersessionist reading of the Old Testament. The very name Christians give to this portion of the Bible contributes to this problem. It is evident that the work of the academy is not being widely disseminated to ordinary Christians. Even if dialogue and respect is increasing in some settings, traditional readings continue.

One thing that might assist in solving this problem is for biblical interpreters who are part of a faith community to assume some responsibility for bridging the hermeneutical gap that divides exegetical work from the task traditionally left to theologians, namely applying the biblical text to the contemporary situation within the Church. Biblical exegetes need to ask questions of their exegesis. Historical and literary criticism should ground the interpretation of the text and hopefully thereby prevent uncritical adoption of the polemic, but the work of the biblical scholar should not end there. Exegetes must add their voices not only to academic theological discussions but also to the development of Sunday School materials, liturgy, and sermon aids, for example, in this way fostering the relationship between modern critical methods and the laity and helping to prevent teachers and preachers from resorting to traditional interpretations in education and worship because they do not have a grasp of relevant modern scholarship or they do not know how to adopt it. This might help the clergy and others within the church to turn to the work of the academy rather than be fearful of it.

Exegetical Method and Jewish-Christian Relations

In seeking to understand the text in its original historical and socio-religious setting and in insisting that what the text *means* is dependent on what the text *meant*, historical critical scholars have certainly played a role in moving biblical interpretation away from christocentric and supersessionist readings. However, method alone will not solve the problem of Christian anti-Jewish biblical interpretation. First of all, while historical criticism can support a non-supersessionist reading, we have clearly seen that it is not free from such readings. Wellhausen, the father of modern biblical scholarship, used historical criticism to assert (Protestant) Christianity's fundamental primacy over Judaism. As we saw in chapter four, Protestant anti-cultic theology has influenced the interpretation of Isaiah 66:1–4 even among practitioners of historical critical methods. The interpretations are not always explicitly anti-Jewish (in fact, it would be easier to dismiss them if they were), but because they are anti-cultic, they can be used to support readings that are.

While modern critical methods may help counter christocentric readings, they are not solutions in and of themselves. Historical criticism should be paired with careful analysis of received interpretive traditions. Exegetes should also be mindful of the theological implications of their exegesis, by which they might recognize where their own voice may be overpowering the ancient one. The isolation of historical criticism from other inquiries and its exclusive focus on ancient Israel stand in the way of its full realization as tool by which to strengthen relations between church and synagogue.

Jewish Interpretation and Self-Understanding

Biblical interpreters and theologians alike should be mindful of Jewish interpretive traditions as well as Jewish self-understanding. Jewish interpretation is not fundamentally superior to that of Christians, nor is it necessarily a better reflection of the original author's intent. In fact, as Christian readings may be influenced by the New Testament and Apocrypha, Jewish readings may be influenced by the rabbinic tradition. However, the voices of the Jewish tradition should be heard if for no other reason than to challenge Christian assumptions about the text and offer possibilities for understanding the text that Christian tradition may have obscured. Wim Beuken raised the point that Isa 66:1–4 is never interpreted as an anti-cultic text within the Jewish tradition. While this in itself does not mean the text cannot be anti-cultic, it should certainly challenge proponents of anti-cultic readings to evaluate whether or not their reading is a Christian imposition on the text, especially given the anti-cultic nature of Protestant Christian theology. Jewish interpretation is one more tool Christian scholars have at their disposal and should employ to help critically evaluate their own readings.

In addition, Jewish-Christian relations would benefit from each group striving to understand the other in their own terms (i.e., when Christians are attentive to Jewish self-understanding and vice versa). Protestant Christians often perceive Jews within the framework of faith vs. works, assuming Jews view the laws as a means to salvation and therefore condemning them for their "works-righteousness" and "legalism." Luther employed Isa 66:1–4 to criticize Jews based on such a theological framework. However, this is an assumption about Judaism based on Christian theology. Jewish theology reveals instead a view that obedience to the Torah is a proper response to what God has already done rather than the Jewish answer to the Christian question "How can I be saved?"

Christian Relationship with the Hebrew Bible

Christians have lived with a canon that includes the Hebrew Bible for almost two thousand years. Christianity's relationship with this text has been problematic with respect to Jewish-Christian relations for most of that time. Despite claims to the text in large part through the identification of Yahweh with the Father of Jesus Christ, Christianity has often struggled to make Jewish Scripture its own, especially without resorting to theologically severing the connection between the Hebrew Bible and Judaism. Instead of fully embracing its multivalent voices proclaiming both human promise and failing, and thus looking to the text as a source of understanding the common humanity as well as the common faith of Jews and Christians, Christians have most often throughout history used these scriptures to condemn Judaism. This has tragically assisted Christians in justifying the persecution of Jews.

In appropriating the Jewish Scripture as its own while identifying itself over and against Judaism, Christians have tended to associate promise and blessing in the text with Christians while associating curses and prophetic indictment with Jews. This "us vs. them" mentality has not only been problematic for Jewish-Christian relations, it has also obstructed an honest self-evaluation on the part of Christians of the implementation of their own faith. If Christians share in the biblical tradition, then they also share in the failings therein, common human failings. It is only when Christians hear the text addressed to them in its entirety, both the sounds of God's delight and the sounds of God's anger, that they hear God's word fully.

In the Hebrew Bible, prophetic criticism strikes most often *within* the community and thus when applying the text to contemporary Christian situations, the Church should look first and foremost within itself to identify where prophetic critique might resonate. Christians would do well consciously to hear the text of the Hebrew Bible in the Deuteronomistic tradition that claims the story of our ancestors is our story, too. As Moses declares to the second generation after the Exodus: "The LORD our God made a covenant with us at Horeb. Not with our ancestors, but with us, who are all of us here alive today." (Deut. 5:2–3) And again in Joshua we read the story of our ancestors is somehow our own story too:

> …I plagued Egypt with what I did in its midst; afterwards, I brought *you* out. When I brought *your ancestors* out of Egypt, *you* came to the sea; and the Egyptians pursued *your ancestors* to the Red Sea with chariots and horsemen. When *they* cried out to the LORD, he put darkness between *you* and the Egyptians, and made the sea come upon them and cover them; and *your eyes* saw what I did in Egypt. (Josh. 24:5–7) (italics mine)

We are often quick to claim the deliverance and promise as our own. If we want to do so, we must also acknowledge as our own the faithlessness and frailty, the imperfections and weakness. It is all somehow our story—or none of it is.

The Role of Controversy

Our goal in this enterprise need not be religious homogenization. We do not need to seek a Jewish-Christian theology. Jews and Christians share the Hebrew Bible, but the New Testament and Apocrypha are also foundational to Christianity while the Mishnah and Talmud are so for Jews. While there may be some theological common ground, there are also substantial differences, and we should not be afraid to confront them. Disagreement and controversy are not inherently negative. While controversy can create animosity, it can also bring into sharper focus one's own identity and relationship to others. In this way it can be useful.

There is nothing fundamentally anti-Jewish in the Protestant de-emphasis of material worship nor in questioning the adequacy of cultic worship. While I think the anti-cultic interpretation of Isa 66:1–4 is misguided and theologically driven, it is not inherently anti-Jewish. Fundamental disagreements with Jews on matters of faith does not imply anti-Judaism. Similarly, recognizing criticisms of the worship of the community within the Hebrew Bible is not equivalent with anti-Judaism. There is prophetic indictment of worship; for example, we find in the Hebrew Bible a sensitivity to abuses to the temple because of the aniconic tradition (see Jeremiah 7, Isaiah 1, 2 Samuel 7, Malachi, and Isaiah 58).

While controversy need not be avoided, I believe we must be mindful of *how* we engage in controversy, recognizing the destructive tendencies of polemical condemnation, especially prevalent if the controversy is rooted in fear and the need to eliminate the other. In such cases, controversy serves not to engender discussion and debate but to promulgate conflict and can be detrimental to society.

Concluding Remarks

Biblical interpretation is a precarious enterprise. The interpreter must struggle to overcome not only significant historical, cultural, and linguistic differences but also preconceptions about texts grounded in interpretive traditions sometimes stretching back more than two millennia. To complicate matters, we as interpreters are not always aware of the influence on our reading of interpretive traditions or even of the theological and cultural preconceptions we bring to the text. We cannot escape the culturally-conditioned lens which shapes how we read. However, as interpreters who seek to be responsible to the integrity of the biblical text, we must attempt to identify our prejudices and restrain the role of our own lens so we may hear the ancient voice in the text. Furthermore, we must read inherited interpretations suspiciously, listening for where the voice of the interpreter might have overwhelmed that of the author or redactor, which I believe has often been the case in the history of reception of Isaiah 66:1–4. Subsequent scholars will have the responsibility of weighing in as to whether my own concerns regarding Christian anti-Jewish biblical interpretation have further obscured the ancient voice or served to illuminate it.

Isaiah 66:1–4 in Transmission and Translation

Masoretic Text

Isaiah 66:1 כֹּה אָמַר יְהוָה הַשָּׁמַיִם כִּסְאִי וְהָאָרֶץ הֲדֹם
רַגְלָי אֵי־זֶה בַיִת אֲשֶׁר תִּבְנוּ־לִי וְאֵי־זֶה מָקוֹם מְנוּחָתִי:
²וְאֶת־כָּל־אֵלֶּה יָדִי עָשָׂתָה וַיִּהְיוּ כָל־אֵלֶּה נְאֻם־יְהוָה וְאֶל־זֶה
אַבִּיט אֶל־עָנִי וּנְכֵה־רוּחַ וְחָרֵד עַל־דְּבָרִי:
³שׁוֹחֵט הַשּׁוֹר מַכֵּה־אִישׁ זוֹבֵחַ הַשֶּׂה עֹרֵף כֶּלֶב מַעֲלֵה מִנְחָה
דַּם־חֲזִיר מַזְכִּיר לְבֹנָה מְבָרֵךְ אָוֶן גַּם־הֵמָּה בָּחֲרוּ בְּדַרְכֵיהֶם
וּבְשִׁקּוּצֵיהֶם נַפְשָׁם חָפֵצָה:
⁴גַּם־אֲנִי אֶבְחַר בְּתַעֲלֻלֵיהֶם וּמְגוּרֹתָם אָבִיא לָהֶם יַעַן
קָרָאתִי וְאֵין עוֹנֶה דִּבַּרְתִּי וְלֹא שָׁמֵעוּ וַיַּעֲשׂוּ הָרַע בְּעֵינַי
וּבַאֲשֶׁר לֹא־חָפַצְתִּי בָּחָרוּ:

Septuagint

Isaiah 66:1 οὕτως λέγει κύριος ὁ οὐρανός μοι θρόνος ἡ δὲ γῆ ὑποπόδιον
τῶν ποδῶν μου ποῖον οἶκον οἰκοδομήσετέ μοι ἢ ποῖος τόπος τῆς
καταπαύσεώς μου ² πάντα γὰρ ταῦτα ἐποίησεν ἡ χείρ μου καὶ ἔστιν ἐμὰ
πάντα ταῦτα λέγει κύριος καὶ ἐπὶ τίνα ἐπιβλέψω ἀλλ' ἢ ἐπὶ τὸν ταπεινὸν
καὶ ἡσύχιον καὶ τρέμοντα τοὺς λόγους μου ³ ὁ δὲ ἄνομος ὁ θύων μοι
μόσχον ὡς ὁ ἀποκτέννων κύνα ὁ δὲ ἀναφέρων σεμίδαλιν ὡς αἷμα ὕειον ὁ
διδοὺς λίβανον εἰς μνημόσυνον ὡς βλάσφημος καὶ οὗτοι ἐξελέξαντο τὰς
ὁδοὺς αὐτῶν καὶ τὰ βδελύγματα αὐτῶν ἃ ἡ ψυχὴ αὐτῶν ἠθέλησεν ⁴ κἀγὼ
ἐκλέξομαι τὰ ἐμπαίγματα αὐτῶν καὶ τὰς ἁμαρτίας ἀνταποδώσω αὐτοῖς ὅτι
ἐκάλεσα αὐτοὺς καὶ οὐχ ὑπήκουσάν μου ἐλάλησα καὶ οὐκ ἤκουσαν καὶ
ἐποίησαν τὸ πονηρὸν ἐναντίον μου καὶ ἃ οὐκ ἐβουλόμην ἐξελέξαντο

Vulgate

Isaiah 66:1 haec dicit Dominus caelum sedis mea et terra scabillum pedum meorum quae ista domus quam aedificabitis mihi et quis iste locus quietis meae [2] omnia haec manus mea fecit et facta sunt universa ista dicit Dominus ad quem autem respiciam nisi ad pauperculum et contritum spiritu et trementem sermones meos [3] qui immolat bovem quasi qui interficiat virum qui mactat pecus quasi qui excerebret canem qui offert oblationem quasi qui sanguinem suillum offerat qui recordatur turis quasi qui benedicat idolo haec omnia elegerunt in viis suis et in abominationibus suis anima eorum delectata est [4] unde et ego eligam inlusiones eorum et quae timebant adducam eis quia vocavi et non erat qui responderet locutus sum et non audierunt feceruntque malum in oculis meis et quae nolui elegerunt

Luther Bible (1545)

Isaiah 66:1 So spricht der HERR: Der Himmel ist mein Stuhl und die Erde meine Fußbank; was ist's denn für ein Haus, daß ihr mir bauen wollt, oder welches ist die Stätte, da ich ruhen soll ? [2] Meine Hand hat alles gemacht, was da ist, spricht der HERR. Ich sehe aber an den Elenden und der zerbrochenen Geistes ist und der sich fürchtet vor meinem Wort. [3] Wer einen Ochsen schlachtet, ist eben als der einen Mann erschlüge; wer ein Schaf opfert, ist als der einem Hund den Hals bräche; wer Speisopfer bringt, ist als der Saublut opfert, wer Weihrauch anzündet, ist als der das Unrecht lobt. Solches erwählen sie in ihren Wegen, und ihre Seele hat Gefallen an ihren Greueln. [4] Darum will ich auch erwählen, was ihnen wehe tut; und was sie scheuen, will ich über sie kommen lassen, darum daß ich rief, und niemand antwortete, daß ich redete, und sie hörten nicht und taten, was mir übel gefiel, und erwählten, was mir nicht gefiel.

King James Version

Isaiah 66:1 Thus saith the LORD, The heaven is my throne, and the earth is my footstool: where is the house that ye build unto me? and where is the place of my rest? [2] For all those things hath mine hand made, and all those things have been, saith the LORD: but to this man will I look, even to him that is poor and of a contrite spirit, and trembleth at my word. [3] He that killeth an ox is as if he slew a man; he that sacrificeth a lamb, as if he cut off a dog's neck; he that offereth an oblation, as if he offered swine's blood; he that burneth incense, as if he blessed an idol. Yea, they have chosen their own ways, and their soul delighteth in their abominations. 4 I also will choose their delusions, and will bring their fears upon them; because when I called, none did answer; when I spake, they did not hear: but they did evil before mine eyes, and chose that in which I delighted not.

New Jerusalem Bible

Isaiah 66:1 Thus says Yahweh: With heaven my throne and earth my footstool, what house could you build me, what place for me to rest, 2 when all these things were made by me and all belong to me?—declares Yahweh. But my eyes are drawn to the person of humbled and contrite spirit, who trembles at my word. 3 Some slaughter a bull, some kill a human being, some sacrifice a lamb, some strangle a dog, some present an offering of pig's blood, some burn memorial incense, a revolting blessing; all these people have chosen their own ways and take delight in their disgusting practices. 4 I too take delight in making fools of them, I shall bring what they most fear down on them because I have called and no one would answer, I spoke and no one listened. They have done what I regard as evil, have chosen what displeases me.

Tanakh: The New JPS Translation

Isaiah 66:1 Thus said the LORD: The heaven is My throne And the earth is My footstool: Where could you build a house for Me, What place could serve as My abode? 2 All this was made by My hand, And thus it all came into being— declares the LORD. Yet to such a one I look: To the poor and brokenhearted, Who is concerned about My word. 3 As for those who slaughter oxen and slay humans, Who sacrifice sheep and immolate dogs, Who present as oblation the blood of swine, Who offer incense and worship false gods—Just as they have chosen their ways And take pleasure in their abominations, 4 So will I choose to mock them, To bring on them the very thing they dread. For I called and none responded, I spoke and none paid heed. They did what I deem evil And chose what I do not want.

New Revised Standard Version

Isaiah 66:1 Thus says the LORD: Heaven is my throne and the earth is my footstool; what is the house that you would build for me, and what is my resting place? 2 All these things my hand has made, and so all these things are mine, says the LORD. But this is the one to whom I will look, to the humble and contrite in spirit, who trembles at my word. 3 Whoever slaughters an ox is like one who kills a human being; whoever sacrifices a lamb, like one who breaks a dog's neck; whoever presents a grain offering, like one who offers swine's blood; whoever makes a memorial offering of frankincense, like one who blesses an idol. These have chosen their own ways, and in their abominations they take delight; 4 I also will choose to mock them, and bring upon them what they fear; because, when I called, no one answered, when I spoke, they did not listen; but they did what was evil in my sight, and chose what did not please me.

Bibliography

Classical Works

Ambrose, Bishop of Milan. *De Spiritu Sanctu.* Corpus scriptorum ecclesiasticorum latinorum 79. Vindobonae: Hoelder-Pichler-Tempsky, 1964.

———. *Epistulae et acta.* Corpus scriptorum ecclesiasticorum latinorum 82. 4 vols. Vindobonae: Hoelder-Pichler-Tempsky, 1968–1996.

———. *Qua continentur libri.* Corpus scriptorum ecclesiasticorum latinorum 32.1. Vindobonae: Tempsky, 1867.

The Ante-Nicene Fathers. Edited by Alexander Roberts and James Donaldson. 1885–1887. 10 vols. Repr. Peabody, MA.: Hendrickson, 1994.

Athenagoras. *Legatio and De Resurrectione.* Oxford Early Christian Texts. Edited and translated by William R. Schoedel. Oxford: Clarendon, 1972.

Augustine, *Enrationes in psalmos 101–150.* Edited by Franco Gori. Corpus scriptorum ecclesiasticorum latinorum 95. Vienna: Verlag der österreichischen Akademie der Wissenschaften, 2001.

Barnabae, Epistula. Edited by Karl Bihlmeyer. Die Apostolischer Väter. Tübingen: J.C.B. Mohr, 1956.

Biblia Hebraica Stuttgartensia. Edited by K. Elliger and W. Rudolph. Stuttgart: Deutsche Bibelgesellschaft, 1983.

Biblia Sacra iuxta Latinam Vulgatam versionem ad codicum fidem. Rome: Typis polyglottis Vaticanis, 1926

Clement of Alexandria. *Protrepticus.* Edited by M. Marcovich. *Supplements to Vigiliae Christianae* 39. New York: Brill, 1995.

———. *Works.* Edited by Otto van Staehlin. Griechischen Christlichen Schriftsteller 12. Berlin: Akademie-Verlag, 1960.

Corpus Christianorum: Series graeca. Turnhout, 1977–.

Corpus Christianorum: Series latina. Turnhout, 1953–.

D. Martin Luthers Werke. Deutsche Bibel (Weimar, 1906–).

D. Martin Luthers Werke. Kritische Gesamtausgabe (Weimar, 1883–).

Deferrari, Roy J. *Saint Ambrose: Theological and Dogmatic Works.* Fathers of the Church 44. Washington: Catholic University of America Press, 1977.

DeSimone, Russell J. *The Treatise of Novatian, the Roman Presbyter: On the Trinity. A Study of the Text and the Doctrine.* Studia ephemeridis "Augustinianum" 4.

Rome: Institutum Patristicum Augustinianum, 1970.

Didache. Edited by Karl Bihlmeyer. Die Apostolischer Väter. Tübingen: J.C.B. Mohr, 1956.

Epiphanius Constantiensis. *Panarion.* Edited by K. Holl. Griechischen Christlichen Schriftsteller 25, 31, 37. Leipzig : J. C. Hinrichs, 1915–33.

Eusebius of Caesarea. *Historia Ecclesiastica.* 2 Vols. Edited by Kirsopp Lake and J.E.L. Oulton. Loeb Classical Library. Cambridge, MA: Harvard University Press, 1972.

———. *Works.* Griechischen Christlichen Schriftsteller der ersten drei Jahrhunderte. Berlin: Akademie Verlag, 1999.

Gregory of Nyssa. *Opera.* Edited by Werner Jaeger. 10 vols. Leiden: Brill, 1960.

Hilary of Poiters. *De Trinitate.* Translated by E.P. Meijerling. Philosophia Patrum, 6. Leiden: E.J. Brill, 1982.

———. *De Trinitate.* Translated by Stephen McKenna. Fathers of the Church 25. Washington: Catholic University of America Press, 1968

Hilary of Poiters: Conflicts of Conscience and Law in the Fourth Century Church. Translated by Lionel R. Wickham. Liverpool University Press, 1997.

Hill, Edmund, ed. and trans. *The Works of Saint Augustine: A Translation for the 21ˢᵗ Century.* Brooklyn: New City Press, 1990–.

Irenaeus. *Proof of the Apostolic Preaching.* Translated by Joseph P. Smith. Ancient Christian Writers 16. Westminster, MD: Newman Press, 1952.

Justin Martyr. *Apologiae pro Christianis.* Edited by Miroslav Marcovich. Patristische Texte und Studien 38. New York: Gruyter, 1994.

———. *Dialogus cum Tryphone.* Edited by Miroslav Marcovich. Patristische Texts und Studien 47. New York: Gruyter, 1997.

Luther's Works (Saint Louis: Concordia Publishing House, 1955–).

Midrash Rabbah. Edited by H. Freedman and M. Simon. 10 vols. London: Socino Press, 1939.

Nicene and Post-Nicene Fathers. First Series. Edited by Philip Schaff. Repr. Peabody, MA: Hendrickson, 1994.

Nicene and Post-Nicene Fathers. Second Series. Edited Philip Schaff and Henry Wace. Repr. Peabody, MA: Hendrickson, 1994.

Novatian. *De Trinitate.* Translated by R. De Simone. Fathers of the Church 67. Washington: Catholic University of America Press in association with Consortium Press, 1974.

Origen. *Homiliae in Genesim.* Translated by Robert Heine. Fathers of the Church 71. Washington, D.C.: Catholic University of America Press, 1982.

———. *Works.* 12 vols. Griechischen Christlichen Schriftsteller. Leipzig: J.C. Hinrichs, 1899–1955.

Patrologia graeca. Edited by J.-P. Migne. 162 vols. Paris, 1857–1886.

Patrologia latina. Edited by J.-P. Migne. 217 vols. Paris, 1844–1864.

Robinson, James M., ed. *The Nag Hammadi Library in English.* Rev. ed. New York: E.J. Brill, 1966.

Rule of the Community and Related Documents. The Dead Sea Scrolls: Hebrew, Aramaic and Greek Texts with English Translations. Vol. 1. Ed. James H. Charlesworth. Louisville: Westminster/John Knox, 1994.

Savage, John J. Saint *Ambrose: Hexameron, Paradise and Abel.* Fathers of the Church 42. New York: Fathers of the Church 1961.

Septuaginta. Ed. Alfred Ralfs. 9th edition. Stuttgart: Deutsche Bibelstiftung, 1979.

Smith, Richard, ed. *The Nag Hammadi Library in English.* New York: E.J. Brill, 1996.

Sources chrétiennes. Paris: Cerf, 1943–.

Tertullian. *Adversus Iudaeos.* Edited by H. Traenkle. Wiesbaden: Franz Steiner Verlag, 1964.

———. *Adversus Marcion.* Edited and translated by Ernest Evans. Oxford Early Christian Texts. Oxford: Clarendon, 1972.

———. *Adversus Praxeam.* Edited by A. Kroyman. Corpus scriptorium ecclesiasticorum latinorum 2. Turnholti Brepols, 1954.

Theodoret of Cyrus. *Interpretatio in Psalmos.* Translated by Robert C. Hill. Fathers of Church 102. Washington: The Catholic University of America Press, 2001.

Thesaurus linguae graeca: Canon of Greek Authors and Works. Edited by L. Berkowitz and K.A. Squitier. 3d. ed. Oxford, 1990.

Wagner, Monica, trans. *Ascetical Works.* Fathers of the Church 9. Washington: Catholic University Press of America, 1970.

Windisch, Hans. *Der Barnabasbrief.* Die Apostolischen Vaeter III. Tübingen: J.C.B. Mohr (Paul Siebeck), 1920.

Yarnold, E. *Cyril of Jerusalem.* The Early Church Fathers. NY: Routledge, 2000.

Zandee, Jan. *The Teaching of Sylvanus (Nag Hammadi Codex VII, 4): Text, Translation, and Commentary.* Nag Hammadi and Manichaean Studies 30. The Coptic Gnostic Library. New York City: E.J. Brill, 1996.

Modern Works

Achtemeier, Elizabeth. *The Community and Message of Isaiah 56–66.* Minneapolis: Augsburg Publishing House, 1982.

Albani, Matthias. "„Wo sollte ein Haus sein, das ihr mir bauen könntet?" (Jes 66,1): Schöpfung als Tempel JHWHs?" Pages 37–56 in *Gemeinde ohne Tempel.* Tübingen: Mohr Siebeck, 1999.

Albl, Martin C. *"And Scripture Cannot Be Broken": The Form and Function of the Early Christian Testimonia Collections.* Leiden: Brill, 1999.

Alexander, Joseph Addison. *The Later Prophecies of Isaiah.* New York: Wiley & Putnam, 1847.

Alexander, Philip S. "'The Parting of the Way' from the Perspective of Rabbinic Judaism." Pages 1–25 in *Jews and Christians: The Parting of Ways: A.D. 70 to 135.* Edited by James D.G. Dunn. Grand Rapids: Eerdmans, 1999.

Alon, Gedaliah. *The Jews in Their Land in the Talmudic Age (70–640 C.E.).* Translated by Gershon Levi. 2 Vols. Jerusalem: The Magnes Press, The Hebrew University, 1980, 1984.

Althaus, Paul. *The Theology of Martin Luther.* Philadelphia: Westminster Press, 1966.

Anderson, Robert T. "The Use of Hebrew Scripture in Stephen's Speech." Pages 205–216 in *Uncovering Ancient Stones.* Edited by Lewis M. Hopfe. Winona Lake, IN: Eisenbrauns, 1994.

Backus, Irena. "The Fathers in Calvinist Orthodoxy: Patristic Scholarship." Pages 839–863 in *The Reception of the Church Fathers in the West.* Vol. 2. Edited by Irena Backus. Leiden: E.J. Brill, 1997.

Baltzer, Klaus. "The Meaning of the Temple in the Lukan Writings." *Harvard Theological Review* 58 (July 1965): 263–277.

Bammel, C.P. "Law and Temple in Origen." Pages 464–476 in *Templum Amicitiae.* Journal for the Study of the New Testament Supplement Series 48. Sheffield: JSOT Press, 1991.

Barnard, Leslie W. "Saint Stephen and Early Alexandrian Christianity." *New Testament Studies* 7 (1960): 32–45.

———. *Justin Martyr: His Life and Thought.* Cambridge: Cambridge University Press, 1967.

———. *Studies in the Apostolic Fathers and Their Background.* Oxford: Basil Blackwell, 1966.

Barrett, Charles K. "Attitudes to the Temple in the Acts of the Apostles." Pages 345–367 in *Templum Amicitiae.* Journal for the Study of the New Testament Supplement Series 48. Sheffield: JSOT Press, 1991.

Baumgerten, Albert I. "Marcel Simon's *Versus Israel* as a Contribution to Jewish History." *Harvard Theological Review* 92 (O 1999): 465–478.

Beuken, Wim. "Does Trito-Isaiah Reject the Temple? An Intertextual Inquiry into Isaiah 66:1–6." Pages 53–66 in *Intertextuality in Biblical Writings: Essays in Honour of Bas van Lersel.* Edited by S. Draisma. Kampen: Uitgeversmaatschappij J. H. Kok, 1989.

BibleWorks for Windows. Version 5.0.034a. 1998/2000.

Biblia patristica: index des citations et allusions bibliques dans la littérature patristique, 7 vols. Ed. Jean Allenbach et al. Paris: Editions du Centre national de la recherché scientifique, 1975–.

Bornkamm, Heinrich. *Luther and the Old Testament.* Translated by Eric W. and Ruth C. Gritsch. Philadelphia: Fortress, 1969.

Brueggemann, Walter. *Isaiah.* 2 vols. Louisville: Westminster John Knox, 1998.

Bultema, Harry. *Commentary on Isaiah.* Translated by Cornelius Lambregste. Grand Rapids: Kregel, 1981.

Burgess, Joseph A. "Lutheran Interpretation of Scripture." Pages 110–143 in *The Bible in the Churches.* Edited by Kenneth Hagan. Milwaukee: Marquette University Press, 1998.

Carleton Paget, J. "Clement of Alexandria and the Jews." *Scottish Journal of Theology* 51, no. 1 (1998): 86–97.

———. "The Christian Exegesis of the Old Testament in the Alexandrian Tradition." Pages 478–542 in *Hebrew Bible/Old Testament: The History of Its Interpretation*. Vol. I/1. Edited by Magne Saebo. Göttingen: Vandenhoeck & Ruprecht, 1996.

———. *The Epistle of Barnabas: Outlook and Background*. Tübingen: J.C.B. Mohr, 1994.

Charlesworth, James H. *The Old Testament Pseudepigrapha*. Vol. 1. New York: Doubleday, 1983.

Cheyne, T. K. *Introduction to the Book of Isaiah*. London: A & C Black, 1895.

Childs, Brevard. *Isaiah*. Louisville: Westminster John Knox, 2001.

Clarke, G.W., translator and annotator. *The Letters of St. Cyprian of Carthage*. 4 vols. Ancient Christian Writers 43, 44, 46, 47. New York: Newman Press, 1984–1989.

Clements, R. E. *God and Temple*. Oxford: Basil Blackwell, 1965.

Coggins, R.J. "The Samaritans and Acts." *New Testament Studies* 28 (1982): 423–434.

Collins, John J. *Isaiah*. Collegeville, MN: Liturgical Press, 1986.

Conzelmann, Hans. *Acts of the Apostles*. Translated by James Limburg *et al*. Hermeneia. Philadelphia: Fortress, 1987.

Daniélou, Jean. *A History of Early Christian Doctrine before the Council of Nicea*. Translated by John A. Baker. 3 vols. Philadelphia: Westminster Press, 1967–1977.

Davies, Graham I. "The Presence of God in the Second Temple and Rabbinic Doctrine." Pages 32–36 in *Templum Amicitiae*. Journal for the Study of the New Testament Supplement Series 48. Sheffield: JSOT Press, 1991.

De Lange, Nicholas R.M. *Origen and the Jews: Studies in Jewish-Christian Relations in Third-Century Palestine*. New York: Cambridge University Press, 1976.

De Lubac, Henri. *Medieval Exegesis*. Translated by Marc Sebanc (vol. 1) and E.M. Macierowski (vol. 2). Grand Rapids: Eerdmans, 1998, 2000.

Delitzsch, Franz. *Jesaja*. Repr. Giessen: Brunnen Verlag, 1984.

Dillmann, August. *Der Prophet Jesaja*. Edited by Rudolf Kittel. 6th ed. Leipzig: S. Hirzel, 1898.

Duhm, Bernhard. *Das Buch Jesaia*. 5th ed. Göttingen: Vandenhoeck & Ruprecht, 1968.

Dunn, James D.G. *The Acts of the Apostles*. Petersborough: Epworth: 1996.

———. *The Partings of the Ways: Between Christianity and Judaism and their Significance for the Character of Christianity*. 2d ed. London: SCM, 2006.

———. "The Question of Anti-Semitism in the New Testament." Pages 177–211 in *Jews and Christians: The Parting of Ways: A.D. 70 to 135*. Edited by James D.G. Dunn. Grand Rapids: Eerdmans, 1999.

Eckardt, Alice L. "The Reformation and the Jews." Pages 111–133 in *Interwoven Destinies*. Edited by Eugene J. Fisher. New York: Paulist Press, 1993.

Edwards, Mark U. Jr. "Towards an Understanding of Luther's Attacks on the Jews." Pages 1–19 in *Christians, Jews and Other Worlds: Patterns of Conflict and*

Accommodation. Edited by Philip F. Gallagher. Lanham, MD: University Press of America, 1988.

Eichrodt, Walther. *Theology of the Old Testament*. Translated by J. A. Baker. 2 vols. Philadelphia: Westminster, 1967.

Elliger, Karl. *Die Einheit des Tritojesaia*. 5th ed. Stuttgart: Kohlhammer, 1928.

Emmerson, Grace. *Isaiah 56–66*. Sheffield: JSOT Press, 1992.

Erdman, Charles. *The Book of Isaiah: An Exposition*. Westwood: Revell, 1954.

Erling, S. Bernhard. "Martin Luther and the Jews in Light of his Lectures on Genesis." *Immanuel* 18 (Fall 1984): 64–78.

Evans, Craig A., Robert L. Webb and Richard A. Wiebe, eds. *Nag Hammadi Texts and the Bible: A Synopsis and Index*. New Testament Tools and Studies 18. New York: E.J. Brill, 1993.

Fischer, Johann. *Das Buch Isaias*. Bonn: Hanstein, 1939.

Fitzmyer, Joseph A. *The Acts of the Apostles: A New Translation with Introduction and Commentary*. The Anchor Bible 31. New York: Doubleday, 1998.

Fohrer, Georg. *Das Buch Jesaja*. Rev. ed. Zurich: Zwingli, 1966.

Forde, Gerhard. "Law and Gospel in Luther's Hermeneutic." *Interpretation* 37:3 (July 1983): 240–252.

Forell, George Wolfgang. "The Reformation and the Modern World." *Word and World* Supplement Series 2 (Sept. 1994): 13–22.

Goldingay, John. *Isaiah*. New International Bible Commentary. Peabody, MA: Hendrickson, 2001.

Goodenough, Erwin R. *The Theology of Justin Martyr*. Amsterdam: Philo Press, 1968.

Gressman, Hugo. *Über die in Jes. C. 56–66 vorausgesetzen zeitgeschichtlichen Verhältnisse*. Göttingen: Dieterich, 1898.

Gritsch, Eric W. "Luther and the Jews: Toward a Judgment of History." *Stepping-stones to Further Jewish-Lutheran Relationships*. Edited by Harold H. Ditmanson. Minneapolis: Augsburg, 1990.

Gritsch, Eric W. "The Cultural Context of Luther's Interpretation." *Interpretation* 37:3 (July 1983): 266–276.

Haenchen, Ernst. *The Acts of the Apostles: A Commentary*. Philadelphia: Westminster, 1971.

Hagen, Kenneth. "The History of Scripture in the Church." *The Bible in the Churches*. Edited by Kenneth Hagan. Milwaukee: Marquette University Press, 1998.

Hailey, Homer. *A Commentary on Isaiah with Emphasis on the Messianic Hope*. Grand Rapids: Baker Book House, 1985.

Hanson, Paul. *Dawn of the Apocalyptic*. Rev. ed. Philadelphia: Fortress, 1979.

———. "Israelite Religion in the Early Postexilic Period." Pages 485–508 in *Ancient Israelite Religion*. Edited by Patrick D. Miller, Paul D. Hanson and S. Dean McBride. Philadelphia: Fortress, 1987.

Haran, Menachem. "The Divine Presence in the Israelite Cult and the Cultic Institution." *Biblica*. 50.2 (1969): 251–267.

Harrington, Daniel J. *The Gospel of Matthew.* Sacra Pagina Series, 1. Collegeville, MN: Liturgical Press, 1991.

Harris, Rendel. *Testimonies.* 2 vols. Cambridge: Cambridge University Press, 1916–1920.

Headley, John M. *Luther's View of Church History.* New Haven: Yale University Press, 1963.

Hendrix, Scott H. "Luther Against the Backdrop of the History of Biblical Interpretation." *Interpretation* 37:3 (July 1983): 229–239.

Herbert, A. S. *Isaiah 40–66.* Cambridge: Cambridge University Press, 1975.

Holladay, Carl R. "Acts." *The HarperCollins Bible Commentary.* Edited by James L. Mays. San Francisco: HarperSanFrancisco, 2000.

Holleric, Michael. *Eusebius of Caesarea's Commentary on Isaiah.* Clarendon Press: Oxford, 1999.

Holz, Barry, W., ed. *Back to the Sources: Reading the Classic Jewish Texts.* New York: Summit Books, 1984.

Horbury, William. "Jewish-Christian Relations in Barnabas and Justin Martyr." Pages 315–345 in *Jews and Christians: The Parting of Ways: A.D. 70 to 135.* Edited by James D.G. Dunn. Grand Rapids: Eerdmans, 1999.

Horton, Stanley M. *Isaiah.* Springfield, MO: Logion Press, 2000.

Hvalvik, Reidar. *The Struggle for Scripture and Covenant: The Purpose of the Epistle of Barnabas and Jewish-Christian Competition in the Second Century.* Tübingen: J.C.B. Mohr (Paul Siebeck), 1996.

Ironside, H. A. *Isaiah.* Rev. ed. Neptune, NJ: Loizequx, 2000.

Johnson, Luke Timothy. *The Acts of the Apostles.* Collegeville, MN: Liturgical Press, 1992.

Jones, Douglas. *Isaiah 56–66 and Joel.* London: SCM, 1964.

Juel, Donald. *Messianic Exegesis: Christological Interpretation of the Old Testament in Early Christianity.* Philadelphia: Fortress, 1987.

Katz, Steven T. "Issues in the Separation of Judaism and Christianity after 70 C.E.: A Reconsideration." *Journal of Biblical Literature* 103/1 (1984): 43–76.

Kedar, Benjamin. "The Latin Translations." Pages 299–338 in *Mikra: Text, Translation, Reading and Interpretation of the Hebrew Bible in Ancient Judaism and Early Christianity.* Edited by M.J. Mulder and H. Sysling. Philadelphia: Fortress, 1988.

Kessler, Werner. *Gott geht es um das Ganze: Jesaja 56–66 und Jesaja 24–27.* Stuttgart: Calwer, 1967.

Kilgallen, John. "The Function of Stephen's Speech (Acts 7,2–53)." *Biblica* 70:2 (1989) 173–193.

————. *The Stephen Speech: A Literary and Redactional Study of Acts 7,2–53.* Rome: E. Pontificio Instituto Biblico, 1976.

Kissane, Edward. *The Book of Isaiah.* Rev. ed. Dublin: Browne and Nolan, 1960.

Klijn, A. F. "Stephen's Speech—Acts VII. 2–53." *New Testament Studies* 4 (1957–58): 25–31.

Knight, George. *The New Israel: A Commentary on the Book of Isaiah 56–66.* Grand

Rapids: Eerdmans, 1985.

Koenen, Klaus. *Ethik und Eschatologie im tritojesajabuch.* Wissenschaftliche Monographien zum Alten und Neuen Testament 62. Neukirchen-Vluy: Neukirchener, 1990.

König, Edward. *The Exiles' Book of Consolation Contained in Isaiah XL–LXVI.* Translated by J. A. Selbie. Edinburgh: T & T Clark, 1899.

Kooiman, Willem J. *Luther and the Bible.* Philadelphia: Muhlenberg, 1961.

Koole, Jan. *Isaiah.* Translated by Anthony P. Runia. 3 vols. Leuven: Peters, 1998–2001.

Kraft, Robert A. "Barnabas' Isaiah Text and the 'Testimony Book' Hypothesis." *Journal of Biblical Literature* 79 (1960): 336–350.

Kraus, Hans-Joachim. *Das Evangelium der unbekannten Propheten Jesaja 40–66.* Neukirchen-Vluyn: Neukirchener Verlag, 1990.

Kremers, Heinz, ed. *Die Juden und Martin Luther—Martin Luther und die Juden.* Duesseldorf: Neukircherner Verlag, 1985.

Kugel, James L. and Rowan A. Greer. *Early Biblical Interpretation.* Philadelphia: Westminster, 1986.

Kugel, James L. *In Potiphar's House: The Interpretive Life of Biblical Texts.* Cambridge: Harvard University Press, 1990.

Larsson, Edvin. "Temple Criticism and the Jewish Heritage: Some Reflections on Acts 6–7." *New Testament Studies* 39 (1993): 379–395.

Lau, Franz. "Erstes Gebot und Ehre Gottes als Mitte von Luthers Theologie." *Theologische Literaturzeitung* 73 (1948): 719–730.

Lau, Wolfgang. *Schriftgelehrte Prophetie in Jes 56–66.* Berlin: Walter de Gruyter, 1994.

Leupold, Herbert Carl. *Expositions in Isaiah.* Grand Rapids: Baker Books, 1971.

Levenson, Jon D. "From Temple to Synagogue." Pages 143–166 in *Traditions in Transformation.* Edited by Baruch Halpern and Jon D. Levenson. Winona Lake, IN: Eisenbrauns, 1981.

———. *Sinai and Zion: An Entry into the Jewish Bible.* Minneapolis: Winston, 1985.

———. "The Temple and the World." *Journal of Religion* 64 (July 1984): 275–298.

———. *The Hebrew Bible, the Old Testament, and Historical Criticism.* Louisville: Westminster/John Knox, 1993.

Levine, Baruch. "An Essay on Prophetic Attitudes Toward Temple and Cult in Biblical Israel." Pages 202–225 in *Minhah le-Nahum: Biblical and Other Studies Presented to Hanum M. Sarna in Honour of his 70th Birthday.* Edited by Marc Brettler and Michael Fishbane. JSOT Supplement 154. Sheffield: JSOT Press, 1993.

Lindars, Barnabas. *New Testament Apologetic: The Doctrinal Significance of the Old Testament Quotations.* Philadelphia: Westminster, 1961.

Lohse, Bernhard. *Martin Luther: An Introduction to his Life and Work.* Philadelphia: Fortress, 1986.

———. *Martin Luther's Theology: Its Historical and Systematic Development.* Minneapolis: Fortress, 1999.

Lowry, S. "The Confutation of Judaism in the Epistle of Barnabas." *Early Christianity and Judaism.* Studies in Early Christianity, 6. Edited by Everett Ferguson. New York: Garland, 1993.

Lubsczyk, Hans. *Das Buch Jesaja.* 2 vols. Düsseldorf: Patmos, 1970–72.

Luz, Ulrich. "Wirkungsgeschichtliche Exegese," *Berliner Theologische Zeitschrift* 2. Jarhgang Heft 1. (1985): 18–32.

Luz, Ulrich. *Matthew 1–7: A Commentary.* Translated by Wilhelm C. Linss. Edinburgh: T&T Clark, 1989.

Marti, Karl. *Das Buch Jesaja.* Tübingen: J.C.B. Mohr, 1900.

McDonald, Lee Martin. "Anti-Judaism in the Early Church Fathers." *Anti-Semitism and Early Christianity: Issues of Polemic and Faith.* Edited by Craig A. Evans and Donald A. Hagner. Minneapolis: Fortress, 1993.

McKenna, John. *Second Isaiah.* Dallas: Word Books, 1994.

Mckenzie, John. *Second Isaiah. Anchor Bible* 20. Garden City, NY: Doubleday, 1968.

Meijerling, E.P. "The Fathers in Calvinist Orthodoxy: Systematic Theology." Pages 867–887 in *The Reception of the Church Fathers in the West.* Vol. 2. Edited by Irena Backus. Leiden: E.J. Brill, 1997.

Meredith, Anthony. *Gregory of Nyssa.* London and New York: Rutledge, 1999.

Middlemas, Jill. "Divine Reversal and the Role of the Temple in Trito-Isaiah." Pages 164–187 in *Temple and Worship in Biblical Israel.* Edited by John Day. London: T&T Clark, 2005.

Miscall, Peter D. *Isaiah.* Sheffield: JSOT Press, 1996.

Motyer, J. A. *Isaiah: An Introduction and Commentary.* Leicester: Inter-Varsity Press, 1999.

Muilenburg, James. *The Book of Isaiah: Chapters 40–66.* Interpreter's Bible V. Nashville: Abingdon Press, 1956.

Muller, Richard A. *Biblical Interpretation in the Era of the Reformation.* Grand Rapids: Eerdmans, 1996.

Munck, Johannes. *The Acts of the Apostles.* The Anchor Bible 31. Garden City, NY: Doubleday, 1967.

Newland, G.M. *Hilary of Poiters: A Study in Theological Method.* Bern: Peter Lang, 1978.

Niederwimmer, Kurt. *The Didache: a Commentary.* Hermeneia. Minneapolis: Fortress, 1998.

Oberman, Heiko, ed. *Luther and the Dawn of the Modern Era.* Leiden: E.J. Brill, 1974.

———, ed. *The Reformation: Roots and Ramifications.* Grand Rapids: Eerdmans, 1994.

———, ed. *The Roots of Anti-Semitism in the Age of the Renaissance and the Reformation.* Philadelphia: Fortress, 1984.

———. *Luther: Man between God and the Devil.* Translated by E. Walliser-Scharzbart. New Haven: Yale University Press, 1989.

Odeberg, Hugo. *Trito-Isaiah (Isaiah 56–66): A Literary and Linguistic Analysis.* Uppsala: A. B. Lundequistska, 1931.

Osborn, Eric Francis. "From Justin to Origen: The Pattern of Apologetic." *The Early Church and Greco-Roman Thought*. Edited by Everett Ferguson. Studies in Christianity, 8. New York City: Garland, 1993.

Osborn, Eric Francis. *Justin Martyr*. Beitraege zur historischen Theologie 47. Tübingen: J.C.B. Mohr (Paul Siebeck), 1973.

Oswalt, John. *The Book of Isaiah, Chapters 40–66*. Grand Rapids: Eerdmans, 1998.

Oxford Dictionary of the Christian Church. Edited by F.L. Cross. 3d ed. London: Oxford University Press, 1997.

Pauritsch, Karl. *Die Neue Gemeinde: Gott sammelt Ausgestossene und Arme (Jesaia 56–66)*. Analecta Biblica 47. Rome: Biblical Institute Press, 1971.

Pelikan, Jaroslav. *Luther the Expositor*. Luther's Works Companion Volume. St. Louis: Concordia, 1959.

———. *The Reformation and the Bible, The Bible and the Reformation*. New Haven: Yale University Press, 1996.

Perrot, Charles. "The Reading of the Bible in the Ancient Synagogue." Pages 137–159 in *Mikra*. Philadelphia: Fortress, 1988.

Pieper, August. *Isaiah II: An Exposition of Isaiah 40–66*. Repr. Milwaukee: Northwestern Press, 1979.

Prigent, Pierre. *Justin et L'Ancien Testament*. Paris: J. Gabalda, 1964.

———. *Les Testimonia dans le christianisme primitif: l'Epitre de Barnabe I–XVI et ses sources*. Paris: J. Gabalda, 1961.

Quasten, Johannes. *Patrology*. 3 vols. Westminster, MD: Newman Press, 1950–1986.

Remus, Harold. "Justin Martyr's Argument with Judaism." Pages 59–80 in *Anti-Judaism in Early Christianity*. Edited by Stephen G. Wilson. 2 vols. Waterloo: Wilfrid Laurier University Press, 1986.

Rofé, Alexander. "Isaiah 66:1–4: Judean sects in the Persian Period as Viewed by Trito-Isaiah." Pages 205–217 in *Biblical and Related Studies Presented to Samuel Iwry*. Edited by A. Kort and S. Morschausen. Winona Lake: Eisenbrauns, 1985.

Roth, Wolfgang. *Isaiah*. John Knox Preaching Guides. Edited by John H. Hayes. Atlanta: John Knox, 1988.

Ruether, Rosemary Radford. "The *Adversus Judaeos* Tradition in the Church Fathers: The Exegesis of Christian Anti-Judaism." *Essential Papers on Judaism and Christianity in Conflict: From Late Antiquity to the Reformation*. Edited by Jeremy Cohen. New York: New York University Press, 1991.

Runia, Klaas. "The Hermeneutics of the Reformers." *Calvin Theological Journal* 19:2 (Nov 1984): 121–152.

Sanders, Jack T. *The Jews in Luke-Acts*. Philadelphia: Fortress, 1987.

Sasson, Jack Murad. "Isaiah LXVI 3–4a." *Vetus Testamentum* 26 (1976):199–207.

Sawyer, John. *Isaiah*. 2 vols. Philadelphia: Westminster, 1984–86.

Scherrer, Steven. *A Commentary on the Book of Isaiah: Isaiah as Sacred Scripture*. Maryknoll, N.Y.: St. Jerome Publications, 1993.

Schramm, Brooks. *The Opponents of Third Isaiah*. Sheffield: Sheffield Academic

Press, 1995.

Schulze, Manfred. "Martin Luther and the Church Fathers." Pages 573–626 in *The Reception of the Church Fathers in the West*. Vol. 2. Edited by Irena Backus. Leiden: E.J. Brill, 1997.

Scullion, John. *Isaiah 40–66*. Wilmington, DE: Michael Glazier, 1982.

Sehmsdorf, Eberhard. "Studien zur Redaktionsgeschichte von Jesaja 56–66." *Zeitschrift für die alttestamentliche Wissenschaft* 84 (1972): 517–576.

Seitz, Christopher. *The Book of Isaiah 40–66. New Interpreter's Bible* VI. Nashville: Abingdon, 2000.

Sekine, Seizo. *Die Tritojesanische Sammlung (Jes 56–66) redaktionsgeschichtlich untersucht*. Berlin: de Gruyter, 1989.

Sellin, Ernst. *Das Rätsel der deuterojesajanischen Buches*. Leipzig: A. Deichert, 1908.

Shotwell, Willis A. *The Biblical Exegesis of Justin Martyr*. London: S.P.C.K., 1965.

Shukster, Martin B. and Peter Richardson. "Barnabas, Nerva, and the Yavnean Rabbis," *Journal for Theological Studies* 34 (1983) 32–55.

———. "Temple and *Bet Ha-midrash* in the Epistle of Barnabas." Pages 17–31 in *Anti-Judaism in Early Christianity*. Edited by Stephen G. Wilson. 2 vols. Waterloo: Wilfrid Laurier University Press, 1986.

Simon, Marcel. "Saint Stephen and the Jerusalem Temple." *Journal of Ecclesiastical History* 2 (July–Oct 1951): 127–142.

———. *Versus Israel: A Study of the Relations between Christians and Jews in the Roman Empire (135–425)*. Translated by H. Keating. New York: Oxford University Press, 1986.

Skarsuane, Oskar. "The Development of Scriptural Interpretation in the Second and Third Centuries—except Clement and Origen." Pages 373–442 in *Hebrew Bible/Old Testament: The History of Its Interpretation*. Vol. I/1. Edited by Magne Saebo. Göttingen: Vandenhoeck & Ruprecht, 1996.

———. *Proof from Prophecy: A Study in Justin Martyr's Proof Text Tradition*. Supplements to Novum Testamentum, 56. Leiden: E.J. Brill, 1987.

Skinner, J. *The Book of the Prophet Isaiah*. 2 vols. Repr. Cambridge: Cambridge University Press, 1917.

Smalley, Beryl. *The Study of the Bible in the Middle Ages*. Notre Dame, IN: University of Notre Dame Press, 1964.

Smart, James. *History and Theology in Second Isaiah*. Philadelphia: Westminster, 1965.

Smith, P. A. *Rhetoric and Redaction in Trito-Isaiah*. Leiden: Brill, 1995.

Smolinsky, Heribert. "The Bible and Its Exegesis in the Controversies about Reform and Reformation." Pages 115–130 in *Creative Exegesis: Christian and Jewish Hermeneutics Through the Centuries*. Edited by Benjamin Uffenheier and Henning Graf Reventlow. JSOT Supplement Series 59. Sheffield: JSOT Press, 1988.

Snaith, Norman. "Isaiah 40–66: A Study of the Teaching of the Second Isaiah and its Consequences." *Studies on the Second Part of the Book of Isaiah*. Vetus Testamentum Supplement XIV. Leiden: E. J. Brill, 1967.

Steck, Otto Hannes. *Studien zum Tritojesaja.* Berlin: de Gruyter, 1991.

Steinmetz, David. *Luther in Context.* Grand Rapids: Baker Books, 1995.

Stendahl, Krister. *The School of St. Matthew and its use of the Old Testament.* Uppsala: C.W.K. Gleerup, 1954.

Stylianopoulos, Theodore. *Justin Martyr and the Mosaic Law.* SBL Dissertation Series 20. Missoula, MT: Society of Biblical Literature and Scholars Press, 1975.

Sweet, J.P.M. "A House Not Made with Hands." *Templum Amicitiae.* Journal for the Study of the New Testament Supplement Series 48. Sheffield: JSOT Press, 1991.

Sylva, Dennis D. "The Meaning and Function of Acts 7:46–50." *Journal of Biblical Literature* 106/2 (1987): 261–275.

Thexton, S. Clive. *Isaiah 40–66.* London: Epworth, 1959.

Thornton. T. C. G. "Stephen's Use of Isaiah LXVI.1." *Journal of Theological Studies* 25 (1974): 432–435.

Van den Hoek, Annewies. *Clement of Alexandria and his use of Philo in the Stromateis.* Leiden: E.J. Brill, 1998.

———. "How Alexandrian was Clement of Alexandria: Reflections on Clement and his Alexandrian Background." *Heythrop-Journal* 31 (Ap 1990): 179–194.

Van Ort, Johannes. "John Calvin and the Church Fathers." *The Reception of the Church Fathers in the West.* Vol. 2. Edited by Irena Backus. Leiden: E.J. Brill, 1997.

Volz, Paul. *Jesaia II: übersetz und erklärt.* Kommentar zum Alten Testament 9. Leipzig: Deichertsche, 1932.

Wade, George. *The Book of the Prophet Isaiah.* 2d rev. ed. London: Methuen, 1929.

Wallmann, Johannes. "Luther on Jews and Islam." *Creative Exegesis: Christian and Jewish Hermeneutics Through the Centuries.* Edited by Benjamin Uffenheier and Henning Graf Reventlow. JSOT Supplement Series 59. Sheffield: JSOT Press, 1988.

Watts, John. *Isaiah 34–66.* Waco: Word Books, 1987.

Webster, Edwin C. "A Rhetorical Study of Isaiah 66." *Journal for the Study of the Old Testament* 34 (1986): 93–108.

Weinert, Francis D. "Luke, Stephen, and the Temple in Luke-Acts." *Biblical Theological Bulletin* 17 (July 1987): 88–90.

Wellhausen, Julius. *Prolegomena to the History of Israel.* Reprint. Atlanta: Scholars Press, 1994.

Westermann, Claus. *Isaiah 40–66.* Translated by D. Stalker. London: SCM, 1969.

Whitehouse, Owen. *Isaiah XL–LXVI.* New York: Oxford University Press, 1900.

Whybray, R. N. *Isaiah 40–66.* London: Oliphants, 1979.

Wiens, Delbert. *Stephen's Sermon and the Structure of Luke-Acts.* N. Richland Hills, TX: Bibal, 1995.

Williams, A. Lukyn. *Adversus Judaeos: A Bird's-eye View of Christian Apologiae Until the Renaissance.* London: Cambridge University Press, 1935.

Willimon, William H. *Acts.* Interpretation. Atlanta: John Knox, 1988.

Wilson, Stephen G. "Marcion and the Jews." Pages 45–58 in *Anti-Judaism in Early Christianity.* Vol. 2. Edited by Stephen G. Wilson. Waterloo: Wilfrid Laurier University Press, 1986.

Young, Edward J. *The Book of Isaiah.* 3 vols. Grand Rapids: Eerdmans, 1965–72.

Young, Frances M. "Temple Cult and Law in Early Christianity." *New Testament Studies* 19 (1973): 325–338.

Index of Biblical Passages

Index of Ancient Texts

Studies in Biblical Literature

This series invites manuscripts from scholars in any area of biblical literature. Both established and innovative methodologies, covering general and particular areas in biblical study, are welcome. The series seeks to make available studies that will make a significant contribution to the ongoing biblical discourse. Scholars who have interests in gender and sociocultural hermeneutics are particularly encouraged to consider this series.

For further information about the series and for the submission of manuscripts, contact:

> Dr. Hemchand Gossai
> Georgia Southern University
> Department of Literature and Philosophy
> P.O. Box Office 8023
> Statesboro, GA 30460-8023

To order other books in this series, please contact our Customer Service Department:

> (800) 770-LANG (within the U.S.)
> (212) 647-7706 (outside the U.S.)
> (212) 647-7707 FAX

or browse online by series at:

WWW.PETERLANG.COM